Luxor

to

Aswan

Vanessa Betts

Credits

Footprint credits
Editor: Felicity Laughton
Maps: Kevin Feeney

Managing Director: Andy Riddle
Content Director: Patrick Dawson
Publisher: Alan Murphy
Publishing Managers: Felicity Laughton, Jo Williams, Nicola Gibbs
Marketing and Partnerships Director: Liz Harper
Marketing Executive: Liz Eyles
Trade Product Manager: Diane McEntee
Accounts Managers: Paul Bew, Tania Ross
Advertising: Renu Sibal, Elizabeth Taylor

Photography credits
Front cover: Dreamstime
Back cover: Dreamstime

Printed in Great Britain by CPI Antony Rowe, Chippenham, Wiltshire

Every effort has been made to ensure that the facts in this guidebook are accurate. However, travellers should still obtain advice from consulates, airlines, etc about travel and visa requirements before travelling. The authors and publishers cannot accept responsibility for any loss, injury or inconvenience however caused.

Publishing information
Footprint *Focus Luxor to Aswan*
1st edition
© Footprint Handbooks Ltd
May 2012

ISBN: 978 1 908206 68 8
CIP DATA: A catalogue record for this book is available from the British Library

® Footprint Handbooks and the Footprint mark are a registered trademark of Footprint Handbooks Ltd

Published by Footprint
6 Riverside Court
Lower Bristol Road
Bath BA2 3DZ, UK
T +44 (0)1225 469141
F +44 (0)1225 469461
www.footprintbooks.com

Distributed in the USA by Globe Pequot Press, Guilford, Connecticut

All rights reserved. No part of this publication may be reproduced, stored in a retrieval system, or transmitted, in any form or by any means, electronic, mechanical, photocopying, recording, or otherwise without the prior permission of Footprint Handbooks Ltd.
The content of Footprint *Focus Luxor to Aswan* has been taken directly from Footprint's *Egypt Handbook*, which was researched and written by Vanessa Betts.

Contents

5 Introduction
  4 *Map: Luxor to Aswan*

6 Planning your trip
  6 Getting to Luxor and Aswan
  7 Transport in Luxor and Aswan
  11 Where to stay in Luxor and Aswan
  12 Food and drink in Luxor and Aswan
  15 Festivals in Luxor and Aswan
  16 Shopping in Luxor and Aswan
  18 Local customs and laws in Luxor and Aswan
  22 Essentials A-Z

29 Luxor and around
  30 *Map: Luxor overview*
  31 Luxor and the east bank
  36 *Map: Luxor*
  40 *Map: Karnak*
  46 *Map: Sharia Khalid Ibn El-Walid*
  47 Luxor and the east bank listings
  60 West bank and Theban Necropolis
  62 *Map: West Bank*
  65 *Map: Valley of the Kings*
  81 *Map: Valley of the Queens*
  87 West bank and Theban Necropolis listings
  92 Sohag to Dendara
  100 Sohag to Dendara listings

103 South of Luxor
  105 South of Luxor to Aswan
  113 South of Luxor to Aswan listings
  117 Aswan
  120 *Map: Aswan*
  122 *Map: Aswan centre*
  125 *Map: Around Aswan*
  132 Aswan listings
  140 Lower Nubia
  141 *Map: Lake Nasser Temples*
  153 Lower Nubia listings

157 Footnotes
  158 Basic Egyptian Arabic for travellers
  161 Glossary
  164 Index

Luxor to Aswan Contents • 3

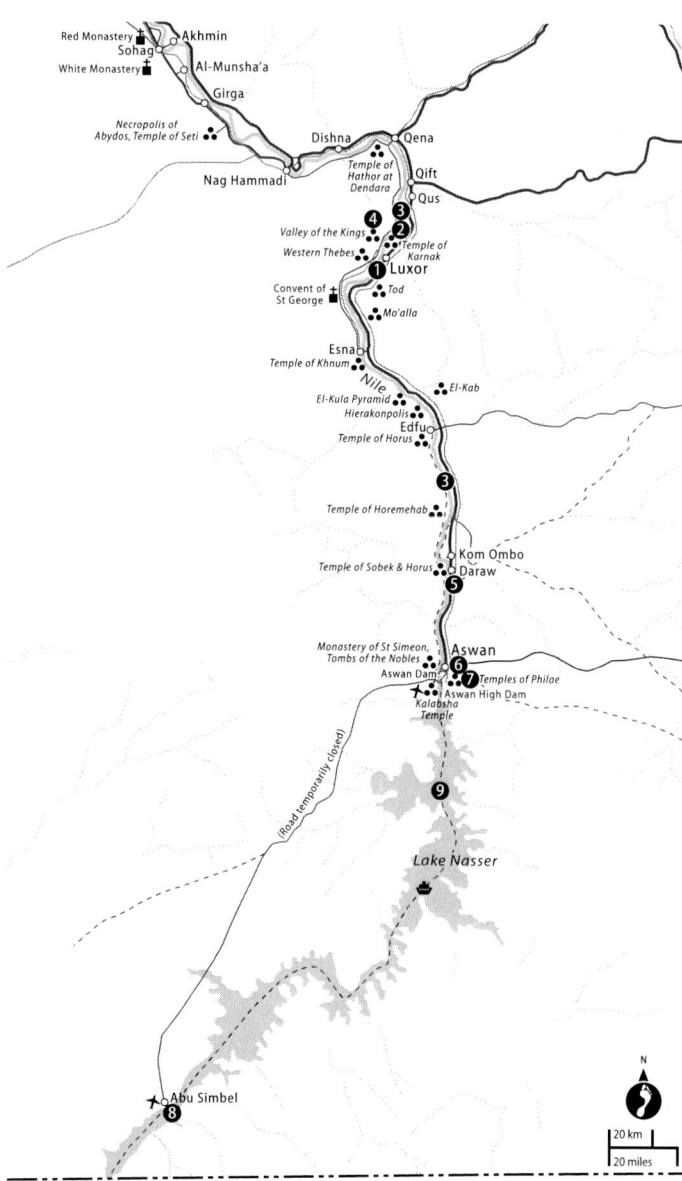

4 • Luxor to Aswan

Second only to the Pyramids as Egypt's most visited attraction, the ancient capital of Thebes (1567-1085 BC) is among the world's oldest tourist destinations. A city built upon cities of millennia past, the area has been inhabited for at least 6000 years. With an overwhelming number of well-preserved sandstone temples and elaborate tombs, many deem Luxor the world's greatest open-air museum.

Across the river is the west bank, spotted with tombs and magnificent mortuary temples, where the Valley of the Kings yields a taste of the profound and vital journey to the next life. Nearby, the intimate and little-visited Tombs of the Nobles reveal in glorious technicolour how everyday life was lived over 3000 years ago. It's wise to be selective and to intersperse tomb- and temple-hopping with a sunset *felucca* ride, a meander through the colourful tourist *souk*, or an exploration of the west bank villages. Luxor also serves as a convenient base for day trips to the temples of Dendara and Abydos to the north, and the temples of Esna and Edfu to the south.

The Nile Valley between Aswan and Luxor is home to some of the world's most stunning monuments; but in this region it is the Nile itself that is the luminary and the central vein. The area is best explored by boat – from the deck of a cruiser or more intimately in a *felucca* or *dahabiya* – with the Nile so close you can feel it mumbling and sighing, still as glass in the morning and raging like a rough sea by midday. Placed at strategic and commercial centres near the river, the striking Graeco-Roman monuments of Edfu and Kom Ombo are among the most colourful and complete pharaonic structures in the country.

The further south you venture, the more apparent the melding of Africa and Arabia. Although Aswan, the provincial capital, has become as commercial as Luxor, endless time can be lost wandering around nearby islands, walking in Nubian villages and reclining on *feluccas* watching birds soar overhead. Close by, the island temple of Philae is a spiritual place, especially after dark. After the Pyramids and the Sphinx, Abu Simbel, adorned with four enormous colossi of Ramses II, is the defining image of Egypt.

Planning your trip

Getting to Luxor and Aswan

It is possible to fly direct to Egypt from Europe, the Middle East, the USA and most adjacent African countries.

Airfares vary according to season. They peak from June to September and around other holiday times (Christmas and New Year). The cheapest times to travel are during November and January. As a rule, the earlier you buy a ticket, the cheaper it will be. It's worth checking in with a few travel agents to see if any special promotions are available and sometimes tour companies offer cheaper fares as they buy them in big numbers. Return tickets are usually a lot cheaper than buying two one-way tickets or opting for an open-ended return, unless you fly with a charter airline. Round-the-World tickets don't include Cairo on their standard itineraries and you will have to go through a company that will custom-build trips.

From Europe From London, **BMI**, www.flybmi.com, **British Airways**, www.ba.com, and **EgyptAir**, www.egyptair.com, offer daily flights to Cairo International airport. Flight time is about five hours and ticket prices range from £350 in the off-season to £450 during peak tourist season. You can save a bit of money if you fly indirect via a European capital (see below), usually in Eastern Europe, Germany or Greece. There are also consistent charter flights to Hurghada, Luxor and (especially) Sharm El-Sheikh, some of which leave from regional airports. Have a look at www.thomsonfly.com, www.firstchoice.co.uk, www.jet2.com and www.flythomascook.com, as there are some great deals (as low as £50 one way if you get lucky).

There are no direct flights from Ireland and most people fly via London. **Air France**, www.airfrance.com, offers direct flights to Cairo via Paris. From Germany, **Lufthansa**, www.lufthansa.com, via Frankfurt, and **TUIfly**, www.TUIfly.com, are a good budget choice from Berlin, Munich and Cologne. **KLM**, www.klm.com, flies to Cairo from Amsterdam. **Austrian Airlines**, www.aua.com, **Czech Airlines**, www.czechairlines.com, **Malev**, www.malev.hu, and **Olympic Airways**, www.olympic-airways.com, have services too, often at competitive prices.

From North America From New York EgyptAir offers an 11-hour daily direct flight to Cairo, ticket prices range from US$1000 in the off-season up to US$1500 during peak travel times. Most European carriers offer flights from major North American cities to Cairo via their European hubs. **British Airways** and **KLM** serve the bigger cities on the west coast. From Canada, there are direct flights with **EgyptAir** from Montreal two or three times a week, taking about 11 hours. Some European airlines also have connecting services from Montreal and Toronto that do not necessitate overnight stays in Europe.

From Australia and New Zealand There are no direct flights from Australia or New Zealand, but many Asian and European airlines offer services to Cairo via their hub cities. Tickets can be expensive, so it may be worth opting for a Round-the-World ticket, which could be comparable in price or even cheaper than a round-trip flight. From Australia to

Don't miss ...

1 **Luxor Temple**, page 34.
2 **Karnak**, page 40.
3 **A felucca trip up the Nile**, pages 56 and 115.
4 **Valley of the Kings**, page 65.
5 **Daraw Camel Market**, page 113.
6 **Aswan**, page 117.
7 **Philae temples**, page 126.
8 **Abu Simbel**, page 147.
9 **Lake Nasser cruising**, page 154.

Numbers refer to map on page 4.

Egypt tickets range from about AUS$1750 during the off-season to AUS$2500 in the peak season. **Qantas**, www.qantas.com, **Austrian Airlines**, www.aua.com, and **Alitalia**, www.alitalia.com, in addition to a few Asian carriers, offer competitive prices.

Airport information Departure tax is included in the price of airline tickets. Confirm airline flights at least 48 hours in advance. Most airports require that travellers arrive at least two hours before international departure times. Have all currency exchange receipts easily available, though it is unlikely you will be asked for them. Before passing into the departure lounge it is necessary to fill in an embarkation card. Only a limited amount of currency can be reconverted before you leave, which is a tedious process and not possible at Luxor airport. Sometimes suitable foreign currency is not available. It is better to budget with care, have no excess cash and save all the trouble.

Baggage allowance General airline restrictions apply with regard to luggage weight allowances before a surcharge is added; normally 30 kg for first class and 20 kg for business and economy class. If you are travelling with a charter flight or budget airline, you might have to pay for even one item of luggage to go in the hold. Carry laptops in your hand luggage, and check the airline's website to see what the restrictions are on hand luggage as this varies between different carriers.

Transport in Luxor and Aswan

From camel to plane to *felucca*, Egypt is equipped with numerous transport options. Congestion and chaos can be a bit anxiety-inducing on long road ventures, but with a bit of courage and flexibility, you can access most areas without too much effort. As for timetables and infrastructure, the country seems to run on magic. There are few regulations and little consistency, but somehow, people always seem to get where they want to go.

Restricted areas Potentially risky are Egyptian border areas near Libya and Sudan, as well as off-road bits of Sinai, where landmines (usually marked by barbed wire) may exist.

Air

The national airline is **EgyptAir**, www.egyptair.com, who have rebranded and became the first Middle Eastern member of Star Alliance in July 2008. In the past, foreigners paid a different (and much more expensive) price for internal flights than Egyptian residents or nationals, but now there is one ticket price for all and flying has become an affordable option for many travellers. In peak seasons, demand can be high and booking ahead is essential. You can buy E-tickets on the EgyptAir website, though it doesn't always accept the final payment. In this case, you'll have to go to an EgyptAir office or travel agent.

There are daily flights from Cairo to Luxor, Aswan and Abu Simbel.

Rail

Rail networks are limited, but travel by train can be delightful, especially to a few key destinations along the Nile. First class is most comfortable in that it tends to be the quietest with air conditioning and a waiter service, but second-class air-conditioned is very similar and almost half the price. Third class never has air conditioning and can be quite cramped and dirty, and a foreigner travelling on main routes would not be sold a ticket anyway. There are daily sleeper trains to Luxor and Aswan, which are pricey but mean you can actually lie horizontally. A 33% discount is given to those with an ISIC student card on all trains, except the sleeper cars to Aswan and Luxor. Carriages are non-smoking but people tend to collect and smoke in the corridor by the toilets. Long-distance trains generally have food and beverages available.

For detailed train information, contact the **Cairo information office**, T02-2575 3555, or check their useful website, www.egyptrail.gov.eg. Approximate journey times from Cairo by train: Aswan 12 hours; Luxor nine hours.

Restricted travel Though there are a dozen daily trains travelling south from Cairo to Middle and Upper Egypt, foreigners are technically only permitted to ride on one, which is guarded by policemen. For train travel once in Upper Egypt, the tickets visitors can purchase are still restricted, but it's sometimes possible to board the train and pay the conductor once in motion. It's highly unlikely you will be kicked off.

River

Nile cruises, feluccas and dahabiyas Heading up the Nile on a cruise boat, *felucca* or *dahabiya* is one of the quintessential Egyptian experiences. Cruise boats travel from Luxor or Esna to Aswan, while *dahabiyas* go between Esna and Aswan, and on Lake Nasser. *Feluccas* go downstream from Aswan to finish at Kom Ombo (one night) or Edfu (two nights), though the actual distance covered depends on the wind. River trips are a great way to get around Egypt and see some wonderful sights along the way. For more detailed descriptions of trips see page 54 (cruise boats), page 57 (*dahabiyas*) and page 115 (*feluccas*).

Road

Bicycle and motorcycle Bicycle hire is available in any town where there are tourists, but the mechanical fitness of the machines is often dubious. Take a bike for a test ride first to check the brakes and tyres are OK. It is feasible to cycle long-distance through Egypt but the heat is punishing, and in between towns and cities along the Nile Valley, cyclists find they are accompanied by their own personal police convoy. In urban areas, traffic conditions

Hazardous journeys

Bear in mind that Egypt currently tops the statistic charts for the highest mortality rate due to motor accidents in the world. You are taking your life in your hands on many road journeys and this is particularly true at night, when driving without headlights is the norm and buses seem to career wildly into the unknown blackness. Long-distance service taxis are the most dangerous, at any time of day, and should be taken only when there are no other options. Drivers push all limits to get there as fast as they can, so as to be able to start filling up with passengers again and complete as many return journeys as possible per day.

---

make cycling a very dangerous sport. Motorcycles can also be hired, though it's less common. The problems regarding cycles apply also to motorcycles – only more so.

Bus Buses, the main mode and cheapest means of transport, link nearly all towns in Egypt. Air-conditioned coaches ply the major routes and keep to a timetable. It's advisable to book tickets 24 hours in advance, though this is not possible in some oasis towns or from Aswan. **Upper Egypt**, **East Delta** and **West Delta** are the three main operators covering the whole country and are cheapest, usually with air conditioning and assigned seats. **Superjet** and **GoBus** also offer buses to/from most towns to Cairo, with newer and more luxurious buses that are about 30% more expensive. The downside is they play videos half the night. There are usually night buses that can save you losing a day on long journeys, and drivers always make a couple of tea-and-toilet stops at roadside coffee shops. Inner-city buses are usually dirty and crowded, and there's a jostle when the bus arrives. In the larger cities, buses often fail to come to complete stops so prepare to run and jump if you do not get on from a route's hub point. Using buses to travel from one city to another is a good way to get around but sorting out the routes of most inner-city buses makes taking the tram, subway, or a cheap taxi, a better option.

Note Buses in Middle and Upper Egypt, if carrying more than four foreigners, are a bit wary. It is essential, therefore, if travelling by bus, that you purchase your ticket in advance (where possible) to ensure a seat. Because of these restrictions, travel by train offers the most flexibility and reliability in the region. It's also generally faster, more consistent and comfortable.

Car hire Vehicles drive on the right in Egypt. An international driving licence is required. Petrol (super) is E£2-3 per litre. Road signs are in Arabic, with most offering the English transliteration. Road conditions vary from new dual carriageways to rural tracks only one-vehicle wide to far flung roads that are a rough, unsurfaced *piste*. Problems include encroaching sand, roads that end with no warning and lunatic drivers. Driving at night is especially hazardous as people only put their headlights on to flash at oncoming vehicles. Likewise, driving in the major cities can be nightmarish with no margin for error and constant undertaking. If you are going to give driving a shot, make sure that you are well insured as the road accident rate is one of the highest in the world.

Car hire cost varies greatly relative to the quality of the vehicle and the location of the rental agency. The minimum is about US$40 per day, and a large deposit is generally

With friends like the tourist police

Those travelling around Egypt in private cars will often find themselves in the bear hug of the police authorities – mainly the tourist police. This is especially the case in Middle Egypt and Upper Egypt outside of the tourist bubbles of Luxor and Aswan. You may also come upon the free escort service when travelling between the Red Sea coast and the Nile Valley, or when exploring the Western Desert and central Sinai. Individual or small groups of foreigners find their transport under close official guard that can be uncomfortable, despite the good intentions. Officers may suggest they ride in the car with you, and if you refuse or there's not enough room, a police vehicle may follow you.

There is little that can be done to gain liberty. The Egyptian government is determined in the wake of the 1997 massacre at Luxor and bomb blasts in the Sinai that no further tourist lives will be lost to terrorist attacks. Police chiefs know that any publicized tourist deaths by Islamists in their district will mean instant transfer to an isolated village in the deep south! The best way to handle the problem is to create as profound a cordon sanitaire around your vehicle as possible; keep well out of sight line of the weapons of your watchdogs and keep as great a distance between your own car and that of your escort so as to avoid a collision. Approach the game with a sense of humour.

required. Some companies place restrictions on areas that can be visited. Be aware that there are many police check points for cars in Egypt and they often request to see your papers, so have them on hand or be prepared for a hefty fine on the spot. The problems of driving your own or a hired car are twofold – other drivers and pedestrians.

The main car hire firms are Avis, www.avis.com and Hertz, www.hertz.com. See listings in each individual town transport section. Approximate **journey times** from Cairo by road: Aswan 16 hours; Luxor 10 hours.

Hitchhiking This is only really a consideration in outlying places not well-served by public transport. Rides are often available on lorries and in small open trucks but payment is often expected. Hitchhiking has a measure of risk attached to it and is not normally recommended, but in out-of-the-way places it is often the only way to travel. Solo women travellers are strongly advised not to hitchhike.

Taxi and service taxi Private vehicles, often Toyota Hiaces (called microbuses or service taxis, pronounced *servees*), cover the same routes as buses and usually cost less. They and the large stationwagon-like long-distance service taxis (Peugeots), sometimes following routes not covered by buses run on the 'leave when full' principle, which can involve some waiting around. For more space or a quicker departure the unoccupied seats can be purchased. However, the drivers can be some of the most reckless in the country (particularly in the nippier Toyotas) and it is probably only worth taking them if you've missed the bus and are stuck somewhere. Inner-city taxis are smaller, rarely have a working meter, and can also be shared. In urban centres taxis are unquestionably the easiest way to get around, and extraordinarily cheap.

Note Until very recently service taxis in Upper Egypt would not accept foreigners when travelling between towns so they could avoid the confines of the convoys. Though the convoys (with the exception of Aswan to Abu Simbel) no longer function, some drivers remember the problems of the past and are reluctant to take foreigners. Be calmly persistent and you should get on in the end.

Where to stay in Luxor and Aswan

Hotels

As tourism is one of Egypt's major industries, accommodation is widely available at the main sites and in all the major cities. With prices to suit all pockets, this varies from de luxe international hotels to just floor or roof space for your sleeping bag. Most quality hotel chains are represented and offer top-class facilities in their rooms and business centres. There are also many cheap hotels with basic and spartan rooms ranging from the clean to the decidedly grimy. Mid-range accommodation is a bit more limited, though the occasional gem exists. There is a pronounced seasonality to demand for accommodation and in the spring, autumn and winter holiday months the main tourist areas can be very busy and the choicest hotels fully booked. Advanced reservations are recommended, especially for luxury hotels. Finding cheap accommodation is easy throughout the country, even in high season. Make sure you ask to see the room first.

Prices for the top-class hotels are on a par with prices in Europe while mid-range hotels are generally cheaper in comparison. Note that while price is a reasonable reflection of the type of hotel and service you can expect, some hotels are expensive but very ordinary while others are wonderful and quite cheap. International hotels have an uncomfortable habit of changing owner and name. Be prepared for this and if confused ask for what it was called before.

In almost every case, the advertised room price (that charged to the individual traveller) is higher than that paid by the package tourist. Bargaining is common, especially when tourism is scarce. The categories used in this book are graded as accurately as possible by cost converted to American dollars. Our hotel price range is based on a double room in high season and includes any relevant taxes and service. We try to note when a meal is included. Please be aware that prices for hotels are constantly shifting, sometimes significantly, depending on the season and the political climate. As we have quoted high season prices, expect to find costs equal to, or less than, the prices indicated. When in doubt, always ask as prices can literally be sliced in half in the hot summer months. At hotels of three-stars and higher, credit cards are almost always accepted.

Note Tax and a service charge will be added to your accommodation bill, apart from in budget hotels or unless it is clearly stated as inclusive.

Youth hostels

Information from **Egyptian Youth Hostels Association** ⓘ *1 El-Ibrahimy St, Garden City, Cairo, T02-2796 1448, www.iyhf.org*. There are 17 hostels (in Egypt's main historic and tourist towns) that are open year round. Overnight fees range from US$1.5-9 and often include breakfast. Visitors may stay more than three consecutive nights if there's space. Although cheap meals are available, all the big hostels have a members' kitchen where guests can prepare meals for themselves (use of the kitchen is free). Rules generally include no alcohol or gambling, single-sex dormitories, and lights out between

2300-0600. Booking is recommended during peak travel times. They can be a good way to meet Egyptians, but are generally a couple of kilometres out of the centre of town and are horribly busy during student holidays.

Camping

There are only a few official campsites with good facilities and guards. Beware of veering too far off road in regions that are desolate as landmines are still widely scattered around some regions, especially near El-Alamein, Sinai and along the Red Sea coast.

Food and drink in Luxor and Aswan

Forget the stories of sheep's eyes and enjoy the selection of filling, spicy and slightly unusual meals. Less adventurous, Western-style food (other than pork) can be found in many restaurants, and high-end hotels have fantastic international cuisine (but for the price you would pay at home). Basic street-stall food can be delicious, but if you are wary or they look a bit grungy, a multitude of cheap restaurants also serve local favourites often brought out *mezze*-style with a basket of bread so you can enjoy tasting a bit of everything. Do bear in mind the suggestions in the Health section on food best avoided in uncertain conditions, see page 23.

Food

Egyptian food is basically a mixture of Mediterranean cuisines, containing elements of Lebanese, Turkish, and Greek cooking, with few authentic local dishes.

Breakfast is usually *fuul*, fava beans simmered slowly overnight, the national dish and a cheap meal at most stalls. These are served in a thick spicy sauce, sometimes with an egg, and usually in a sandwich. When it's fresh and when it's been done well, it is a mouth-watering savoury delight. Some of the best *fuul* comes from the colourful carts on wheels, which station themselves in the same places every day so hungry customers can gather round. The *fuul* is ladled out of a vast pot, hidden in the depths of the cart and heated from below, before being mashed with spices, oil, lemon, salt and pepper. Tourists rarely stop and sample a plate, but the vendors will be pleased and surprised if you do, while other customers will be highly entertained. It's probably best to avoid the chopped salad that comes with the dish, but the *ai'ish* (bread) is certainly safe enough. Equally cheap and popular is *taamiyya*, deep fried balls of ground fava beans spiced with coriander and garlic, again often served in a sandwich garnished with *tahina* (sesame seed dip) and *torshi* (brightly coloured pickled vegetables such as turnips, carrots, and limes). These constitute Egyptian fast food with the addition of *shawarma*, sliced lamb kebab sandwiches, and *fatir*, which is sold in special *fatatri* cafés, where the thin dough pancake is made to order with either sweet or savoury fillings.

Bread is the staple of the Egyptian diet, its Arabic name *ai'ish* means life. The local *ai'ish baladi*, a brown flat loaf similar to pita, tastes good fresh and should only be eaten on the day of purchase. The white flour *ai'ish shami* is less common.

Lunch is the main meal of the day, eaten anytime between 1300 and 1700. Carbohydrates, usually rice and bread, form the bulk of the meal accompanied by fresh seasonal vegetables and either meat or fish. *Mezzas*, a selection of small salads, are served at the beginning of the meal and include *tahina*, *babaghanoug* (*tahina* with mashed

Price codes

Where to stay

| €€€€ | over €150 | €€€ | €65-150 |
| €€ | €30-65 | € | under €30 |

Price for a double room in high season. During the low season it's often possible to bargain the room rate down.

Restaurants

| €€€ | over US$20 | €€ | US$5-20 | € | under US$5 |

Prices for a two-course meal for one person, excluding drinks or service charge.

---

aubergines), olives, local white fetta-style cheese, *warra einab* or stuffed vine leaves, and *kobeiba*, deep fried bulgar wheat stuffed with meat and nuts. Like most Middle Eastern countries, *kebab*, lamb pieces grilled over charcoal on a skewer, and *kofta*, minced lamb, are common main dishes. Chicken and pigeon are also widely available, the latter considered a local delicacy when stuffed with rice and nuts. Fish is commonly eaten in coastal regions and often superb. Try the sea bass or red snapper but watch the bones in the latter. Lobster and shrimp are relatively cheap.

Egyptian **main dishes** include *molokhia*, finely chopped mallow leaves, prepared with garlic, spices and either rabbit or chicken, and a good deal more tasty than its glutinous texture suggests; *fatta*, layers of bread, rice, chunks of lamb or beef, yogurt, raisins and nuts, drenched in a vinegar garlic broth; *koshari*, a poor man's feast that will fill a belly for at least four hours, is composed of macaroni, rice and brown lentils covered with fried onions and a spicy tomato sauce; and *mahshi*, vegetables, typically black or white aubergines, tomatoes, green peppers, cabbage leaves or courgettes, stuffed with rice, herbs and vegetables.

Fruits, like vegetables, are seasonal although there is a wide variety available all year round. Produce is picked when it's ripe and so generally fruit and vegetables are absolutely delicious. Winter offers dates of various colours ranging from yellow to black, citrus fruits, small sweet bananas, pears, apples, and even strawberries. Summer brings plums, peaches, figs, pomegranates, guava, mangoes, grapes, melons and a brief season, for a few weeks in May, of apricots.

Traditional Egyptian **desserts** are sweet, sticky, fattening, and delicious. The best of all is *Om Ali*, or Mother of Ali, a warm pudding of bread or pastry covered with milk, coconut, raisins, and nuts. Also try the oriental pastries including *atayef*, deep fried nut-stuffed pancakes; *baklava*, honey-drenched filo pastry layered with nuts; *basbousa*, a syrupy semolina cake often filled with cream and garnished with pistachio nuts and *konafa*, shredded batter cooked with butter and stuffed with nuts. Cold rice pudding is on offer at most *koshari* restaurants, and is much better than it sounds.

Vegetarianism is not a concept with which Egyptians are familiar. While vegetable dishes are plentiful, and the majority of Egyptians only rarely eat any large quantity of meat, it is difficult to avoid tiny pieces of meat or meat stock in vegetable courses. Even

Fuul for all

Fuul has been an important dish for Egyptians since banqueting scenes were painted on the pharaonic tombs. It is nutritious and cheap and is the staple diet for low-income and strong-stomached locals. In Cairo a meal from one of the 25,000 (illegal) street vendors will start the day. At E£1 per sandwich it fills an empty hole and provides protein and carbohydrates.

Fuul is also considered 'in' by the Cairo smart set, who frequent luxury outlets such as Akher Saa, El-Tabei and El-Omda to buy it with onions, pickles, lemon and fresh bread – to eat in or take away.

The *fuul* bean is grown in most agricultural areas of Egypt, as an accompaniment to a major crop – the best is said to come from Minya. Nevertheless, imports are still necessary to supply consumption demands.

Variants on *fuul* dishes include: *fuul bil zeit el harr* – with oil; *fuul bil samna* – with ghee (clarified butter); *bisara* – with oil, onion, garlic and coriander. *Fuul* is also the main ingredient in *ta'ameya* and *felafel*.

the wonderful lentil soup, like most Egyptian soups a meal on its own, often has the addition of a chicken stock cube. Fortunately, basic staples such as *koshari*, *fuul* and *taamiyya* are omnipresent in any town and true life-savers for vegetarians. In the smaller oases, a diet of rice, salad and potatoes or courgettes stewed in tomato sauce is tasty though repetitive.

Drink

Tea (*shai*) is the essential Egyptian drink, taken strong without milk but with spoonfuls of sugar. Tea is also prepared with mint, *shai bil na'ana*, and said to be good for the digestion. Instant **coffee**, just called 'Nescafé', is available. If you want it with milk, ask for *laban* and if you want sugar separately request *sucre burra*. The thick Turkish coffee known as *ahwa*, which is usually laced with cardamom or occasionally cinnamon, should be ordered either *saada*, with no sugar; *arriha*, with a little sugar; *mazbut*, medium; or *ziyada*, with extra sugar. Leave the thick mud of coffee grains in the bottom half of the cup. The *mazbut* is the most popular.

Other hot drinks include a cinnamon tea, *irfa*, reportedly good for colds; and the less common *sahleb*, a milk drink with powdered arrowroot, coconut, and chopped nuts.

Cold drinks include the usual soft drink options of Coca-Cola, Pepsi, 7-Up, and Fanta. Of more interest are the traditional *ersoos* (liquorice juice); *asir limon*, tangy and delicious but highly sweetened lemon juice; *karkade*, made from the dried petals of the red hibiscus, drunk both hot and cold; and *tamarhindi*, from the tamarind. Freshly squeezed juice stands are located throughout all cities, and mean you can drink seasonal pomegranate, mango, or orange juice for just E£2-3 a glass.

Bottled water is sold widely. Check that the seal is intact and that the bottle has not been refilled. Be prepared for shortage or restriction of water in more rural areas. Tap water in the urban centres is generally safe to drink, but so chlorinated it's intolerable for a lot of travellers. It's better to opt for bottled water which is cheap and easily available.

Although Egypt is a Muslim country, **alcohol** is available in bars and some restaurants. While five-star hotels are beginning to import beer in barrels, the local

'Stella' beer is the most popular sold, with the better-quality 'Stella Export', in half litre bottles. There are a few local wines, the reds and rosés are very drinkable and the whites less so. Most commonly found are Omar Khayyam, Obelisque, Cape Bay and Sherazad (who do a good rosé). The local spirits are bottled to resemble international brands, and include an ouzo called *zibib*, a rum 'Zattos', and a 'Big Ben' gin. Beware of local liqueurs that don labels and names resembling Western brands such as 'Jhony Wakker' and the like, they have been known to contain alcohol so strong that they can cause blindness if drunk to excess.

Festivals in Luxor and Aswan

The Islamic year (*Hejra/Hijra/Hegira*) is based on 12 lunar months that are 29 or 30 days long depending on the sighting of the new moon. The lengths of the months vary therefore from year to year and from country to country depending on its position and the time at sunset. Each year is also 10 or 11 days shorter than the Gregorian calendar. The Islamic holidays are based on this Hejarian calendar and determining their position is possible only to within a few days.

The important festivals that are also public holidays (with many variations in spelling) are *Ras El-Am*, the Islamic New Year; *Eïd Al-Fitr* (also called *Aïd Es Seghir*), the celebration at the end of Ramadan; *Eïd Al-Adha* (also called *Aïd El-Kebir*), the celebration of Abraham's willingness to sacrifice his son and coinciding with the culmination of the *Hajj* in Mecca; *Mouloud* (also called Moulid An-Nabi), the birthday of the Prophet Mohammed.

The day of rest for Muslims is Friday. Observance of Friday as a religious day is general in the public sector, though privately owned shops may open for limited hours. The main exception is tourism where all systems remain operative. Holy days and feast days are taken seriously throughout the country.

Ramadan, the ninth month of the Muslim calendar, is a month of fasting for Muslims. The faithful abstain from eating between dawn and sunset for about one month until an official end is declared to the fast and when *Eïd Al-Fitr*, a three-day celebration, begins. During the fast, especially if the weather is hot or there are political problems affecting the Arab world, people can be depressed or irritable. The pace of activity in official offices slows down markedly, most closing by 1400. You may want to stay out of the area during Ramadan and particularly the *Eïd Al-Fitr*, but for the patient and curious traveller, it can be a fascinating time. As the sun sets during the holy month and everyone rushes homeward to break fast, it offers a rare and delightful occasion to wander through barren city streets. *Iftar* (breaking the fast) in the company of local people is an interesting experience, and anyone is welcome to join a communal meal at one of the mercy tables that encroach on to the street each sunset. The country's poor are looked after by the mosques and the wealthy, who provide set meals every day for whoever is in need; this can involve feeding hundreds of people. Although you shouldn't expect true culinary delights, you might get dates, bird's tongue (a kind of pasta) soup, hearty stews and traditional sweets. For the rushed or impatient traveller, note that travel facilities immediately before and after Ramadan are often very congested since families like to be together especially for the *Eïd Al-Fitr*.

Islamic festivals
These are approximate dates for 2012:
4 Feb Prophet's Birthday.
20 Jul Beginning of Ramadan.
19 Aug End of Ramadan
(Eid El-Fitr).
26 Oct Eid El-Adha.
15 Nov Islamic New Year.

Coptic celebrations
These are approximate dates for 2012:
20 Jan Epiphany.
7 Apr Annunciation.
15 Apr Easter.

Cultural and sporting events
22 Feb Sun Festival of Ramses II, Abu Simbel.
Apr Sham El-Nessim (Sniffing of the Breeze, or the first day of spring) is celebrated with family picnics.
Oct Pharaoh's Rally, 3100-km motor vehicle race across the desert, Cairo.
22 Oct Sun Festival of Ramses II, Abu Simbel.

Public holidays
1 Jan New Year's Day.
7 Jan Coptic Christmas.
15 Mar El Fayoum National Day.
25 Apr Liberation of Sinai.
1 May Labour Day.
18 Jun Evacuation Day –
the day the British left Egypt in 1954.
23 Jul Anniversary of 1952 Revolution.
26 Jul Alexandria National Day.
6 Oct Armed Forces' Day –
parades and military displays.
13 Oct Suez Day.
23 Dec Victory Day.

Shopping in Luxor and Aswan

There are department stores and malls in Cairo and Alexandria but the most interesting shopping is in the bazaars and *souks*. The process can take time and patience, but bargains abound. For a truly off-the-beaten-track shopping experience, visit one of the many fruit and vegetable *souks* scattered throughout the country. You'll find chickens milling about, people singing songs about their wares and dead cows hanging from storefront windows. Prices are clearly marked in Arabic numerals, usually indicating the cost of a kilogram. Bargaining is not appropriate in this context but learn the numerals so that nobody takes advantage of you.

What to buy
Egypt is well known for its **cotton and textiles**. Higher-end stores in luxury hotels and shopping malls sell linen and new clothes. **Jewellery**, in particular, gold, silver and some precious stones, are cheap in Egypt. Sold by weight, with a bit of money tacked on for craftsmanship, you can have pieces made to order. Particularly popular are cartouches bearing your name or the name of a friend.

Papyrus can be found, albeit of varying quality, everywhere. Ensure when you are shopping around for papyrus that it is real, not the increasingly common imitation banana leaf. Real papyrus is not chemically treated, a process which causes the picture to disintegrate after three or four years. You can tell chemically treated papyrus by its

The art of bargaining

Haggling is a normal business practice in Egypt. Modern economists might feel that bargaining is a way of covering up high-price salesmanship within a commercial system that is designed to exploit the lack of legal protection for the consumer. But even so, haggling over prices is the norm and is run as an art form, with great skills involved. Bargaining can be fun to watch between a clever buyer and an experienced seller but it is less entertaining when a less-than-artful buyer such as a foreign traveller considers what he/she has paid later! There is great potential for the tourist to be heavily ripped off. Most dealers recognize the wealth and gullibility of travellers and start their offers at an exorbitant price. The dealer then appears to drop his price by a fair margin but remains at a final level well above the real local price of the goods.

To protect yourself in this situation be relaxed in your approach. Talk at length to the dealer and take as much time as you can afford to inspect the goods and feeling out the last price the seller will accept. Do not belittle or mock the dealer – take the matter very seriously but do not show commitment to any particular item you are bargaining for by being prepared to walk away empty-handed. Never feel that you are getting the better of the dealer or feel sorry for him. He will not sell without making a profit. Also it is better to try several shops if you are buying an expensive item such as a carpet or jewellery. This will give a sense of the price range. Walking away – regretfully of course – from the dealer normally brings the price down rapidly but not always. Do not change money in the same shop where you make your purchases, since this will be expensive.

homogenous surface and pliability. Thick and unmalleable, real papyrus can't be rolled or folded. Authentic papyrus also has variants of colour as the stalks have lighter and darker patches, which you can see in the meshwork when you hold it up to the light. Rest assured that the papyrus sellers you will trip over at every major tourist site are not selling the real thing, though if you just want to pick up some cheap presents then they have their uses.

You'll find **perfume** stalls as well as an abundance of fragrant and incredibly colourful stalls selling **herbs and spices** displayed in large burlap sacks. They sell everything from dried hibiscus to thyme, cumin to saffron, which is priced higher per kilo than gold, but still comparatively cheap.

Other things of interest you will find in larger *souks* and bazaars: kitsch souvenirs galore, *sheesha* pipes, musical instruments (drums in particular) copper and brass ware, wooden boxes inlaid with intricate designs and backgammon and chess sets.

Bargaining

Haggling is expected in the *souks*. Most shop owners site the start price at two to three times the amount they hope to make. Start lower than you would expect to pay, be polite and good humoured, enjoy the experience and if the final price doesn't suit, walk away. There are plenty more shops. Once you have gained confidence, try it on the taxi drivers and when negotiating a room. The bargaining exchange can be a great way to meet people and practise your Arabic.

Interestingly, a barter exchange system still exists in some rural weekly markets, where goods such as seeds, eggs or beans can be exchanged for a haircut or access to education. This is unlikely to be something you will get involved with as a traveller, however.

Local customs and laws in Luxor and Aswan

Though Egypt is among the more liberal and 'Westernized' of the Arab countries, it is still an Islamic country where religion is deeply embedded in daily life. While Islam is similar to Judaism and Christianity in its philosophical content and the three revealed religions are accepted together as the religions of the book (Ahl Al-Kitab), it is wise for travellers to recognize that Islamic practices in this traditional society are a sensitive area. Public observance of religious ritual and taboo are important, just as is the protection of privacy for women and the family. Islam of an extremist kind is on the wane in Egypt but bare-faced arrogance by visitors will engender a very negative response even among normally welcoming Egyptians who generally have no tendencies towards fundamentalist views.

Islam has a specific code of practices and taboos but most will not affect the visitor unless he or she gains entry to local families or organizations at a social level. In any case a few considerations are worthy of note by all non-Muslims when in company with Muslim friends or when visiting particularly conservative areas. (1) Dress modestly. Women in particular should see the dress code, below, for further explanation. (2) If visiting during the holy month of Ramadan where Muslims fast from sunrise to sunset, dress particularly conservatively and avoid eating, drinking and smoking in public places. (3) If offering a gift to a Muslim friend, be aware that pork and alcohol are forbidden. If you choose to offer other meat, ensure it is *hallal*, killed in accordance with Muslim ritual. (4) If dining in a traditional Bedouin setting or context, do not use your left hand for eating since it is ritually unclean. (If knives and forks are provided, then both hands can be used.) Do not accept or ask for alcohol unless your host clearly intends to imbibe. Keep your feet tucked under your body away from food.

Class discrepancies and the *khawagga* (foreigner)

Compared with other developing countries, there are particularly great discrepancies among Egyptians with regard to their experience, openness, education and worldliness. Some are extremely sophisticated, knowledgeable and well travelled while others (widely known as *fellaheen* – peasants) are markedly conservative and parochial. Class is often a delineating factor, as is education and the urban/rural divide. For the traveller, maintaining awareness of social context is essential for positive and culturally sensitive interchanges with locals.

Another evident discrepancy is the cost of services for Egyptians and foreigners. If you have not yet stumbled upon the word *khawagga* (foreigner), you soon will, as it holds similar implications to the word gringo in many Latin American countries. Taxi fares, entries to many attractions, even the price of luxury accommodation all cost foreigners more. Bear in mind that the average Egyptian makes about US$1500 per head per year; the average foreign tourist lives on approximately US$32,000.

Courtesy

Politeness is always appreciated. You will notice a great deal of hand shaking, kissing, clapping on backs on arrival and departure from a group. There is no need to follow this to the extreme but handshakes, smiles and thank yous go a long way. Shows of affection and physical contact are widely accepted among members of the same sex. Be more conservative in greeting and appreciating people of the opposite sex. Do not show the bottom of your feet or rest them on tables or chairs as this gesture is regarded as extremely rude in Egypt. Be patient and friendly but firm when bargaining for items and avoid displays of anger. However, when it comes to getting onto public transport, forget it all – the description 'like a Cairo bus' needs no explanation.

Dress code

Daily dress for most Egyptians is governed by considerations of climate and weather. Other than labourers in the open, the universal reaction is to cover up against heat or cold. For males other than the lowest of manual workers, full dress is normal. Men breaching this code will either be young and regarded as being of low social status or very rich and Westernized. When visiting mosques, *madresas* or other shrines/tombs/religious libraries, Muslim men wear full and normally magnificently washed and ironed traditional formal wear. In the office, men will be traditionally dressed or in Western suits and shirt sleeves. The higher the grade of office, the more likely the Western suit. At home people relax in a loose *gallabiyya*. Arab males will be less constrained on the beach where swimming trunks are the norm.

For women the dress code is more important and extreme. Quite apart from dress being a tell-tale sign of social status among the ladies of Cairo or Alexandria or of tribal/regional origin, decorum and religious sentiment dictates full covering of body, arms and legs. The veil is increasingly common for women, a reflection of growing Islamic revivalist views. There are still many women who do not don the veil, including those with modern attitudes towards female emancipation, professional women trained abroad and the religious minorities – Copts in particular. Jewellery is another major symbol in women's dress, especially heavy gold necklaces.

The role of dress within Islamic and social codes is clearly a crucial matter. While some latitude in dress is given to foreigners, good guests are expected to conform to the broad lines of the practice of the house. Thus, except on the beach or 'at home' in the hotel (assuming it is a tourist rather than local establishment), modesty in dress pays off. This means jeans or slacks for men rather than shorts together with a shirt or T-shirt. For women, modesty is slightly more demanding. In public wear comfortable clothes that at least cover the greater part of the legs and arms. If the opportunity arises to visit a mosque or *madresa*, then a *gallabiyya* and/or slippers are often available for hire at the door. Most women do not swim in public and if they do, they tend to dive in fully clad. If you choose to swim outside a touristy area, wear shorts and an opaque T-shirt. Offend against the dress code – and most Western tourists in this area do to a greater or lesser extent – and you risk antagonism and alienation from the local people who are increasingly conservative in their Islamic beliefs and observances.

Avoiding hassle

Here are some general hints to minimize the pestering that will certainly occur on some level as a woman travelling in Egypt. Try to walk with confidence and at least pretend that you know where you're going. Dress modestly – the less bare flesh the better (especially avoid revealing your shoulders, cleavage and legs). In conservative areas, don't reveal your legs at all and consider tying long hair up. Always carry a thin shawl or scarf to wrap around you in case you suddenly feel over-exposed. When swimming pretty much anywhere outside of the Red Sea resorts, wear leggings and a opaque T-shirt rather than a bathing suit. Ignore rude and suggestive comments and most importantly, avoid looking onlookers in the eye. In general, try not to react in a way that may aggravate a situation – it's best not to react at all.

When riding public transport, if possible sit next to women and avoid late-night transport if alone. If seeking advice or directions outside of hotels and other touristy places try to ask a woman or an older businessman-type. If you feel exceptionally uncomfortable, deliberate embarrassment of the man in question can be a powerful weapon – shout *haram* ('it's forbidden'). You may want to don a wedding band to dissuade potential suitors. If you're travelling with a man, you can avoid a lot of interrogations and confusion by saying that you're married. Absolutely avoid going into the desert or solitary places alone with a man you don't know.

Note that men and women in Egypt relate to one another differently from men and women in many Western countries. The Western concept of 'friendship' can be misunderstood. Opt to be conservative in the way you interact and engage with Egyptian men, as a mere smile can be misinterpreted as an expression of more than platonic interest. Most importantly, trust your instincts, be smart and keep a sense of humour. The rewards of travelling alone as a female in Egypt far outweigh any of the hassle. If you cloak yourself in baggy clothes and try to look as androgynous as possible, you'll be able to go wherever you want and be treated as a man would be, with the added bonus of everyone looking out for you just because you are a 'woman on your own'. Remember, the consequences for serious violations against foreigners in Egypt are so dire that the incidence of rape and other forms of extreme harassment and violation is significantly less than in most other countries.

Mosque etiquette
Do not enter mosques during a service and take photographs only after asking or when clearly permissible. Visitors to mosques and other religious buildings will be expected to remove their shoes. Men should never enter the area designated solely for women, but foreign women are tolerated in the main prayer halls of most mosques unless it is actually a time of prayer. If you are wandering somewhere you aren't supposed to be, someone will point it out to you soon enough.

Photography
Photographs of police, soldiers, docks, bridges, military areas, airports, radio stations and other public utilities are prohibited. Photography is also prohibited in tombs where much damage can be done with a flash bulb. Photography is unrestricted in all open, outdoor historic areas but some sites make an extra charge for cameras. Flashes are not permitted for delicate relics such as the icons in St Catherine's Monastery. Many museums have now banned photography completely to avoid any accidental use of flash. This includes the Egyptian Museum. Taking photographs of any person without permission is unwise, of women is taboo, and tourist attractions like water sellers, camels/camel drivers, etc, may require *baksheesh* (a tip). Even the goat herder will expect an offering for providing the goats. Always check that use of a video camera is permitted at tourist sites and be prepared to pay a heavy fee (E£100+) for permission.

Essentials A-Z

Accident and emergencies
Ambulance T123. **Fire** T125. **Police** T122 (from any city). **Tourist Police** T126.

Report any incident that involves you or your possessions. An insurance claim of any size will require the backing of a police report. If involvement with the police is more serious, for instance as a result of a driving accident, remain calm and contact the nearest consular office without delay. Some embassies advise leaving the scene of an accident immediately and heading straight to your embassy.

Electricity
The current in Egypt is 220V, 50Hz. Sockets are for 2-pin round plugs, so bring an appropriate adapter. If you have US-made appliances that use 110V it's a good idea to bring a converter. Power cuts do not happen that frequently, but in remote hotels be aware that generators are usually switched off at night and for a few hours during the day.

Embassies and consulates
For embassies and consulates of Egypt abroad, see www.embassiesabroad.com.

Health
The local population in Egypt is exposed to a range of health risks not usually encountered in the Western world and, although the risks to travellers are fairly remote, they cannot be ignored. Obviously 5-star travel is going to carry less risk than backpacking on a minimal budget. The healthcare in the region is varied. Your embassy or consulate can advise you where the recommended clinics are.

Ideally, you should see your GP or travel clinic at least 6 weeks before your departure for general advice on travel risks, malaria and vaccinations. Make sure you have adequate travel insurance.

Vaccinations
Vaccinations are not required unless you are travelling from a country where yellow fever or cholera frequently occurs. You are advised to be up to date with **polio, tetanus, diphtheria, typhoid** and **hepatitis A**. **Rabies** is not generally a risk in Egypt but it has been reported in a few rural areas off the tourist trail.

Health risks
It is a very rare event indeed for travellers, but if you are unlucky (or careless) enough to be bitten by a **venomous snake, spider, scorpion** or sea creature, try to identify the creature, without putting yourself in further danger. Immobilize the limb with a bandage or a splint and take the victim to a hospital or a doctor without delay. Do not walk in snake territory in bare feet or sandals – wear proper shoes or boots. Spiders and scorpions may be found in the more basic hotels. If stung, rest and take plenty of fluids and call a doctor. The best precaution is to keep beds away from the walls and always look inside your shoes and under the toilet seat. Certain sea fish when trodden upon inject venom into bathers' feet. This can be exceptionally painful. Wear plastic shoes if such creatures are reported. The pain can be relieved by immersing the foot in hot water (as hot as you can bear) for as long as the pain persists or citric acid juices in fruits such as lemon is reported as useful.

Dengue fever is a viral disease spead by mosquitos that tend to bite during the day. The symptoms are fever and often intense joint pains, also some people develop a rash. It should all be over in 7 to 10 unpleasant days. Unfortunately there is no vaccine against this. Employ all the anti-mosquito measures that you can.

The standard advice to prevent **diarrhoea** or intestinal upset is to be careful with water and ice for drinking. If you have any doubts then boil it or filter and treat it. Food can also transmit disease. Be wary of salads, re-heated foods or food that has been left out in the sun having been cooked earlier in the day. There is a simple adage that says 'wash it, peel it, boil it or forget it'. Also be wary of unpasteurized dairy products. The key treatment with all diarrhoeas is rehydration. Try to keep hydrated by taking the right mixture of salt and water. This is available as Oral Rehydration Salts (ORS) in ready-made sachets or can be made up by adding a teaspoon of sugar and a half teaspoon of salt to a litre of clean water. Drink at least 1 large cup of this drink for each loose stool. You can also use flat carbonated drinks as an alternative.

Pre-travel **hepatitis A** vaccine is advised. There is also a vaccine for **hepatitis B**, which is spread through blood and unprotected sexual intercourse. Unfortunately there is no vaccine for **hepatitis C**, the prevalence of which is unusually high in Egypt.

Malaria is not widespread in Egypt. Minimal risk exists in the El-Fayoum area only. Risk is highest from Jun-Oct. Check with your doctor before you go about which prophylactic (if any) you should take if travelling in this region. Use insect repellent frequently.

Protect yourself adequately against the **sun**. Wear a hat and stay out of the sun, if possible, between late morning and early afternoon. Apply a high-factor sunscreen (greater than SPF15) and also make sure it screens against UVB. A further danger in tropical climates is heat exhaustion or more seriously heatstroke. This can be avoided by good hydration.

Money

Currency → *E£1 = US$0.17, €0.12 or GB£0.10.* You will see prices throughout this guide listed in either **US dollars**, **euro** or **Egyptian pounds** depending on how they're quoted in different parts of the country and for different activities. Due to recent fluctuations in the value of the US dollar, many upmarket hotels and tourist centres in Egypt (such as Hurghada and Sharm El-Sheikh) now quote their prices in euro rather than dollars. However, Egyptian pounds are used for the vast majority of everyday transactions and hotels are generally happy to accept the equivalent value in local currency.

The Egyptian pound is divided into 100 piastres (pt). Notes are in denominations of E£5, E£10, E£20, E£50, E£100, E£200, while the old 25 and 50 piastres notes and E£1 notes are being phased out. Newer E£1 coins are in circulation, and other denominations (which are almost not worth carrying) are 10, 25, and 50 piastres. It's a good idea to always have lots of pound coins to hand so you don't get short changed the odd extra pound or 2 when taking a taxi.

Regulations and money exchange

Visitors can enter and leave Egypt with a maximum of E£10,000. There are no restrictions on the import of foreign currency provided it is declared on an official customs form. Export of foreign currency may not exceed the amount imported. Generally, it's cheaper to exchange foreign currency in Egypt than in your home country. It's always wise to change enough money at home for at least the first 24 hrs of you trip, just in case. The bank counters on arrival at Cairo airport are open 24 hrs. A small amount of foreign cash, preferably US$, although sterling and euro are widely accepted, is useful for an emergency.

Banks

There is at least one of the national banks in every town plus a few foreign banks (such as HSBC and Citibank) in the big cities and Barclays have recently started operating in all major towns. Banking hours are 0830-1400 Sun-Thu (0930-1330 during Ramadan); some banks have evening hours. Changing money in banks can be a bit time-consuming, though commission is not usually charged. **ATMs** are widely available (but not in all the oases) but require a surcharge of between US$3-5, and often have a daily withdrawal limit of around E£2500-4000. They are also known to munch on the occasional card, so beware. Still, using an international credit or debit card is the easiest and quickest way to access your money and means you receive trade exchange rates which are slightly better than rates given by banks. Maestro, MasterCard, Plus/Visa and Cirrus are all widely accepted.

Credit cards

Access/MasterCard, American Express, Diners Club and Visa are accepted in all major hotels, larger restaurants and shops, and tend to offer excellent exchange rates. Outside of the tourist industry, Egypt is still a cash economy.

Traveller's cheques

Traveller's cheques are honoured in most banks and bureaux de change. US$ are the easiest to exchange particularly if they are well-known brands like Visa, Thomas Cook or American Express. There is always a transaction charge so a balance needs to be struck between using high-value cheques and paying one charge and carrying extra cash or using lower-value cheques and paying more charges. Egypt supposedly has a fixed exchange rate – wherever the transaction is carried out.

Cost of travelling

Depending on the standards of comfort and cleanliness you are prepared to accept for accommodation, food and travel, it is still possible to survive on as little as US$10-15 per person per day. However, prices for everything in Egypt are rising all the time with inflation soaring (basic foods have increased by 50%, gasoline 90%); tourists should be aware that hotel prices and transport costs continue to rise, and that the ticket prices for monuments are put up every Oct/Nov. Accommodation runs from about US$8-15 for a basic double in a liveable hotel to well over US$200 for 5-star luxury comfort. Basic street food can fill you up for less than US$1, or you can opt for a more Western-style meal, still affordable at US$6-10 a plate. Transport varies according to mode, but distances between the major cities can be covered for around US$15-20. The Cairo metro is less than US$0.25 and local buses are around the same. Renting a car is a significantly more expensive option at around US$60 per day.

There are costs often not accounted for in other parts of the world that you will inevitably encounter in Egypt. Most sit-down restaurants include a 12% tax (after the service charge, which is 10%) on the bill and it is common practice to tip an additional 10%. Another kind of tipping, known as *baksheesh*, occurs when you are offered a small service, whether or not you ask for it. If someone washes the windows of your car or looks after your shoes in a mosque, they will expect a modest offering. Carry around a stash of E£1 coins and take it in your stride, it's part of the culture.

Opening hours

Banks Sat-Thu 0830-1400.
Government offices 0900-1400 every day, closed Fri and national holidays.
Museums Daily 0900-1600 but generally close for Fri noon prayers, around 1200-1400.
Shops Normal opening hours are summer 0900-1230 and 1600-2000, winter 0900-1900, often closed on Fri or Sun. Shops in tourist areas seem to stay open much longer.

Safety

The level of petty crime in Egypt is no greater than elsewhere. It is very unlikely that you will be robbed but take sensible precautions. Put your valuables in a hotel deposit box or keep them on your person rather than leave them lying around your room. Avoid carrying excess money or wearing obviously valuable jewellery when sightseeing. External pockets on bags and clothing should never be used for carrying valuables, pickpockets do operate in some crowded tourist spots. It is wise to stick to the main thoroughfares when walking around at night.

Trading in antiquities is illegal and will lead to confiscation and/or imprisonment. Should you need to buy currency on the black market do so only when it is private and safe. Be careful as Egypt, like most countries, has tight laws against currency smuggling and illegal dealing.

Keep clear of all political activities. Particularly in light of the recent events where foreign journalists have been targeted. By all means keep an interest in local politics but do not become embroiled as a partisan. The *mokharbarat* (secret services) are singularly unforgiving and unbridled in their action against political interference.

Following the war on Iraq, there was a fairly widespread anti-American and anti-Anglo sentiment, but for the most part the disillusion is not mis-targeted. Egyptians seem to separate their disdain for foreign governments from individual travellers. Nonetheless, with such a volatile political climate, it's wise to check with your national authorities before departure for Egypt. If coming from the UK, for travel advice, check the Foreign and Commonwealth Office at www.fco.gov.uk; from the US, check the Dept of State at www.travel.state.gov.

9/11, the war on Iraq and the attacks on foreigners in the Sinai in 2004-2006 brought about a new set of challenges for the tourist industry and reinforced the government's attempts at ensuring safety for foreign visitors. Part of the system required most Western tourists travelling in private cars, hired taxis and tourist buses to travel in police-escorted convoys when journeying between towns in certain regions. This still applies in Upper Egypt, where scheduled convoys travel between Aswan and Abu Simbel. In 2010, restrictions were eased in other areas of Upper Egypt and now tourists are permitted on public transport. However, not all drivers are aware of the change in the rules and it can be a headache getting a ride in certain areas (such as Luxor to Dendara and Abydos, and along the east coast). Independent travellers are better off using trains where possible. If you want to drive through, inquire with the tourist authority. See box, page 10.

Confidence tricksters

The most common 'threat' to tourists is found where people are on the move, at airports, railway and bus stations, offering extremely favourable currency exchange rates, selling tours or 'antiques', and spinning hard-luck stories. Confidence tricksters are, by definition, extremely convincing and persuasive. Be warned – if the offer seems too good to be true, it probably is.

Time

GMT + 2 hrs.

Tipping

Tipping, or *baksheesh*, a word you will fast learn, is a way of life – everyone except high officials expects a reward for services actually rendered or imagined. Many people connected with tourism get no or very low wages and rely on tips to survive. The advice here is to be a frequent but small tipper. The principle of 'little and often' seems to work well. Usually 12% is added to hotel and restaurant bills but an extra tip of about 10% is normal and expected. In hotels and at monuments tips will be expected for the most minimal service. Rather than make a fuss, have some small bills handy. Tips may be the person's only income.

Alms-giving is a personal duty in Muslim countries. It is unlikely that beggars will be too persistent. Have a few small bills ready and offer what you can. You will be unable to help everyone and your donation may be passed on to the syndicate organizer.

Tourist information

Depending on where you are in Egypt the provision of tourist information is variable, as is the usefulness of information provided. The offices in bigger cities tend to be quite well equipped and at least have an English speaker on duty. They're worth a visit if you are nearby. The particularly helpful tourist offices are noted in the relevant chapter sections. When the tourist offices fall short, hotels, pensions and other travellers are often even better resources to access reliable travel information.

Egyptian state tourist offices abroad

Austria, Elisabeth Strasse, 4/Steige 5/1, Opernringhof, 1010 Vienna, T43-1-587 6633, aegyptnet@netway.at.
Belgium, 179 Av Louise 1050, Brussels, T32-2647 3858, touregypt@skynet.be.
Canada, 1253 McGill College Av, Suite 250, Quebec, Montreal, T1-514-861 4420.
France, 90 Champs Elysées, Paris, T33-1-4562 9442/3, Egypt.Ot@Wanadoo.Fr
Germany, 64A Kaiser Strasse, Frankfurt, T49-69-252319.
Italy, 19 Via Bissolati, 00187 Rome, T39-6-482 7985.
Spain, Torre de Madrid, planta 5, Oficina 3, Plaza de España, 28008 Madrid, T34-1-559 2121.
Sweden, Dorottningatan 99, Atan 65, 11136 Stockholm, T46-8-102584, egypt.Ti.Swed@alfa.telenordia.se
Switzerland, 9 rue des Alpes, Geneva, T022-732 9132.

UK, Egyptian House, 170 Piccadilly, London W1V 9DD, T020-7493 5283.
USA, 630 5th Av, Suite 1706, New York 10111, T1-212-332 2570, egyptourst@ad.com.

Egypt on the web

www.bibalex.gov.eg Detailed information and up-to-date news on the new Alexandria Library, and has a calendar of events.
www.touregypt.net A comprehensive site put together by the Ministry of Tourism. Detailed listings include online shopping from Khan El-Khalili, maps of most cities, walking routes of national parks, hotel and tour guide index and general information on life in Egypt.
www.weekly.ahram.org.eg Online version of the weekly English-language sister paper to the national daily *Al-Ahram*, extensive archive with search engine.

Visas and immigration

Passports are required by all and should be valid for at least 6 months beyond the period of your intended stay in Egypt. Visas are required by all except nationals of the following countries: Bahrain, Jordan, Kuwait, Libya, Oman, Saudi Arabia and the UAE. Cost varies between different embassies in different countries but payment must be in cash or by postal order, cheques are not accepted. It can take up to 6 weeks for some embassies to process a postal application, or they can be issued in 1 day if you turn up in person. They are valid for 3 months from date of arrival and for 6 months from date of issue and cannot be post-dated. Visas issued from embassies are either single-entry or multiple entry (which allows you to re-enter Egypt twice). Most Western tourists find it easiest to buy a renewable 30-day tourist visa (US$15 or equivalent in euro or sterling) on arrival at all international airports – but this is not possible when you are entering via an overland border crossing or a port.

Visa extensions can be obtained in 1 day (turn up early) at the Mogamma, Midan Tahrir, Cairo; Sharia Khaled Ibn El-Walid in Luxor; and 28 Sharia Talaat Harb in Alexandria. Some governorate capital cities, such as Ismailia and El-Tor, also have passport offices with extension facilities and these can be quite efficient places to renew (check the information under the appropriate section in the text). You will need your passport, 2 new photographs, cash to pay for renewal (cost varies depending what sort of visa, single- or multiple-entry, you require) and possibly bank receipts to prove you have exchanged or withdrawn enough hard currency to warrant your travels. Overstaying by 15 days does not matter, but after 2 weeks, be prepared for an E£153 fine and some hassle.

Weights and measures
Metric.

Luxor & around

Contents

31 Luxor and the east bank
- 31 Arriving in Luxor and the east bank
- 32 Background
- 34 Visiting Luxor and the east bank
- 47 Listings

60 West bank and Theban Necropolis
- 60 Arriving in west bank and Theban Necropolis
- 65 Valley of the Kings
- 73 Tomb of Ay
- 73 Howard Carter's House
- 73 Deir El-Bahri
- 76 Tombs of the Nobles
- 81 Valley of the Queens
- 82 Private tombs
- 85 Other temples and sites
- 87 Listings

92 Sohag to Dendara
- 92 Sohag
- 93 Abydos
- 97 Qena
- 100 Listings

Footprint features

- 32 24 hours in Luxor
- 35 The hassle, haggle and hustle
- 39 Mummification
- 55 Luxor with kids
- 57 Dahabiya trips
- 61 The singing colossus of Memnon
- 64 Theban Death Rites and the Book of the Dead
- 66 Books of the afterlife
- 71 The curse of Tutankhamen
- 72 The 'lost' tomb
- 74 Howard Carter
- 83 Ramses The Great (1304-1237)
- 94 The Nile ran red
- 95 Brick-making in Egypt

At a glance

⊖ **Getting around** *Calèches* and microbuses will get you to Karnak. Bikes are great for the west bank.

⊙ **Time required** Possible in 2 days, but better to spend at least 4.

❄ **Weather** Winter is perfect climatically. May-Sep is hot but still busy with tour groups.

✘ **When not to go** European school holidays are always crowded, Christmas in particular.

• 29

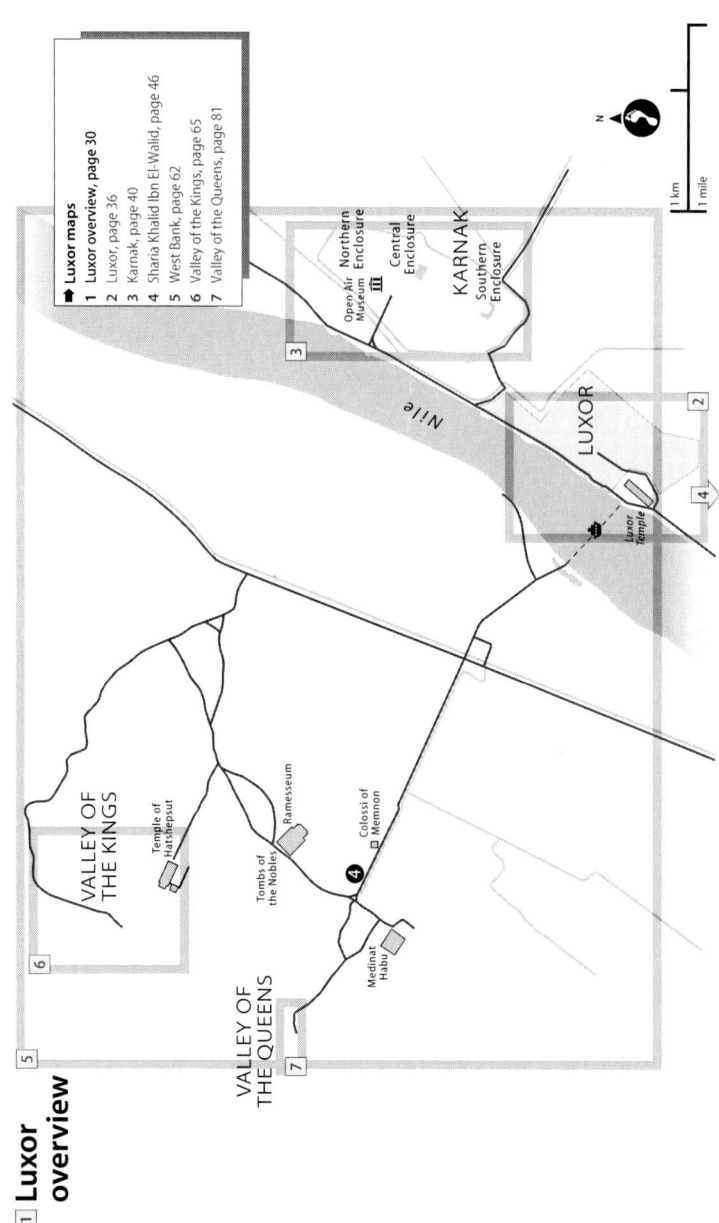

Luxor and the east bank

There is a reason Luxor is deemed the world's biggest open-air museum: it brims over with extraordinary sights. In brief, on the east bank, the Luxor Temple (see page 34), and Karnak Temple complex (see page 40) are the two essential stops. Large tour parties on day trips from Hurghada tend to arrive at Karnak Temple at 1100-1230 and 1600-1730, and these times are definitely best avoided. Karnak at dawn, being first through the gate, is the best way to do it. Visit Luxor Temple at night – it's beautifully lit and easily accessible as it's right in the middle of town.

Arriving in Luxor and the east bank → *Population: 45,000.*

Getting there
Luxor is 676 km south of Cairo, 65 km south of Qena and 223 km north of Aswan. The airport is 7 km east of the town centre. Visas are on sale just before passport control. From the airport, a taxi to the town centre should cost E£30-40. The airport is not well connected by public transport so taxis are unquestionably the easiest way to go. The new bus terminal is also a fair trek out, and taxis from here demand E£30 for a ride into the centre or there are microbuses into town for E£1. Arrival at the train station is easier as it's in the middle of Luxor and it's possible to walk to most budget hotels, or if you're hauling a lot of luggage you can take a *calèche* (horse-drawn carriage) or taxi anywhere in town for E£10.

Getting around
Luxor is small enough to be explored on foot (depending on how you tolerate the heat), large enough to feel like there's always something happening and full enough to need a week to really see it; but with so much to see, a visit can be overwhelming. But besides the ubiquitous hassle that can make even the most rugged traveller weary, Luxor is a comfortable place, easy to get around and impossible to get lost in with the Nile as a marker. Most of the main hotels, shops, tour offices, museums and temples are adjacent to the river on the eastern side. Most budget hotels are scattered around Sharia Mohamed Farid and Sharia Televizion, south of Sharia Al-Mahatta. Karnak temple is about 2 km north of town. Access to the west bank is provided by public ferries and private hire motorboats or *feluccas* along the Corniche. There is also a bridge, 7 km from town that gives access to west bank-bound vehicles. ➤➤ *See Transport, page 58.*

Information
The main **Egyptian Tourist Authority (ETA) office** ⓘ *T095-237 3294, open daily 0800-2000, English-speaking staff tend to turn up around 1000*, is directly opposite the train station. It is good for checking bus and train times and current official prices for everything including *calèches* and taxis, and for checking the Sound and Light schedule at Karnak. There are further offices in the train station, T095-237 0259, and the airport, T095-237 2306, which work the same hours. The **Tourist Police** ⓘ *T095-237 0750*, are next to the railway station.

Warning Bear in mind that as tourism sustains the bulk of the city's economy, the hustle and hassle in Luxor is among the most intense in the country. Expect to be bombarded by

24 hours in Luxor

At first light, take a *calèche* to **Karnak** and spend a couple of hours in Egypt's best-preserved and most impressive temple. Then, if you haven't booked a tour already, catch the ferry across the river and book a taxi for a half day at the west bank sights. Start with either **Medinat Habu** or the **Ramesseum**, followed by **Deir El-Bahri** and three of the **Nobles' Tombs**. Try to be in the **Valley of Kings** at lunchtime when it's least busy, then enjoy some hearty local food at one of the small restaurants near Medinat Habu or by the riverbank.

In the afternoon, visit the cool interiors of the **Luxor Museum** and follow it with an hour on a *felucca* for sunset. Have an aperitif at the **Windsor Hotel**, before dinner and a meander through the *souk*. Visit **Luxor Temple** at night (before 2200), beautifully lit, before a nightcap of *karkade* and *sheesha* in a coffee shop.

---

horse-drawn carriages, *felucca* captains, souvenir peddlers and hotel touts. And expect to be ripped off at least once. Hotel touts congregate to meet all tourist trains coming in, making arrival at the station quite stressful. It is even worse on arrival at the bus station, where young guys who meet the incoming buses are quite aggressive in their activities. It is best to know exactly where you're going before arriving. You may be told your hotel of choice has closed, is full, or the price has changed. These tales are unlikely to be true, as the accommodation situation doesn't really change that much in Luxor. If a driver tries to take you to his brother's hotel instead, adamantly insist to be dropped where you want to go and don't pay until you get there. Try to inform yourself about fair prices and the games people play, and remember that everyone is just trying to make a living. With a bit of patience and a sense of humour, you'll come to find that behind the frenzy lie a warm, welcoming people.

Best time to visit

Tourist season extends from October to March, peaking around Christmas and the New Year, when the weather is sunny and sublime. Most monuments and museums are open 0600-1800 in winter, 0500-1900 in summer, take note that offices will stop selling tickets 45 minutes or one hour before closing times. In the thick of summer, it's best to visit tombs and temples in the early morning hours, although the heat of the mid-afternoon, if you can bear it, does wonders to drive away the hordes of tourists and touts.

Background

On the site of the present-day town of Luxor stood the ancient city that the Greeks called **Thebes** and which was described in Homer's *Iliad* as the "city of a hundred gates". Later the Arabs described it as '*el-Uqsur*' or 'city of palaces' from which it gets its current name.

The town and the surrounding limestone hills had been settled for many centuries but during the Old Kingdom (2616-2181 BC) it was little more than a small provincial town called Waset. It first assumed importance under Menutuhotep II who reunited Egypt and made it his capital, but it was during the 18th-20th Dynasty of the New Kingdom (1567-1085 BC) that Thebes really reached its zenith. Except for the brief reign of Akhenaten (1379-1362 BC), it was the capital of an Egyptian Empire that stretched from

Palestine to Nubia for nearly 500 years, and at its peak the population reached almost one million. Besides being the site of the largest and greatest concentration of monuments in the world it was, for the ancient Egyptians, the prototype for all future cities.

When the capital later shifted elsewhere it remained a vibrant city and the focus for the worship of Amun ('the Supreme Creator'). Although there is no obvious connection with the Greek city of Thebes the name was subsequently given to the city by the Greeks. It was a shadow of its former self during the Ptolemaic (323-30 BC) and Roman (30 BC-AD 640) periods but, unlike ancient Memphis to the south of Cairo, it was never abandoned and it became an important Christian settlement. In the Luxor region a number of temples became Coptic monasteries. For example, at both Deir El-Medina and Deir El-Bahri Egyptian monuments were taken over and converted for Christian use.

After the Muslim conquest in AD 640, the town continued to decline and it was not until the beginning of the 19th century, during Napoleon's expedition to Egypt, that its historical importance began to be recognized. The display of some of its treasures in Paris's Louvre museum sparked off considerable interest from the world's archaeologists – who continue to make important discoveries even today. Since 1869, when Thomas Cook took his first party of travellers to Egypt for the opening of the Suez Canal, Luxor has become the foremost tourist destination in Upper Egypt. Today, although it has become an important administrative town, the economic livelihood of Luxor is (as the sudden collapse in business during the 1990-91 Gulf war and as the mass exodus of thousands of tourists in November 1997 demonstrated) almost totally dependent on the tourist industry.

Modern-day Luxor is undergoing a transformation, as the current governor has initiated a series of radical schemes in an effort to expose more of the ancient past and to make the most of the monuments. Some of these initiatives are regretted by locals and tourists alike, as the organic nature of the city is being altered and many homes lost as the layers of buildings are stripped back. Not only has Sharia Al-Mahatta been widened to allow a view of Luxor Temple on arrival at the station, but the gritty old *souk* has been sanitized and is now strictly a tourist bazaar. A tunnel is being constructed beneath the Corniche between the Mummification Museum and Luxor Museum, in order to allow the road to be pedestrianised and become a waterside promenade. The village of Old Gurna on the west bank used to delight the eye on the approach to Thebes, with its colourful *hajj* paintings on buildings clustering below the ridge. Now the vast majority of houses have been demolished, only a few remain (which are being kept as a model of how life was in Old Gurna), to enable proper excavation of the Tombs of the Nobles and protect them from water drainage from the village. Further long-term plans, which will take 10-15 years to complete, include the relocation of all the cruise boats to a new mooring beyond the bridge 7 km to the south (not many people will complain about this one), to protect Luxor Temple from pollution. Already in full swing is an ambitious scheme to reconnect Luxor and Karnak temples via the Avenue of the Sphinxes, which involves demolishing every building and home that stands in the way. What will happen to any mosques that have grown up over the ancient passage is still being debated. Probably every person you meet in Luxor will have a tale to tell about their parents, uncle or daughter-in-law being re-homed as a consequence and the inadequate compensation they have been paid.

Visiting Luxor and the east bank

Luxor Temple

ⓘ *The temple, in the centre of town on the Corniche, is open daily 0600-2030 in winter, 0600-2130 in summer, E£50, students E£25, cameras free. Allow a couple of hours. It is particularly striking at night; a ticket permits re-entry, but only on the same day. Entrance is from Sharia Karnak (not from the Corniche, as was previously the case).*

Like the much larger Karnak Temple, Luxor Temple is dedicated to the three Theban gods Amun, Mut and Khonsu. **Amun** is usually depicted as a man wearing ram's horns or a tall Ostrich-feathered Atef crown. His wife **Mut** was considered to be the mistress of heaven and **Khonsu** was their son who was believed to travel through the sky at night assisting the scribe god.

Because it is smaller, quite compact and fewer pharaohs were involved in its construction, Luxor Temple is simpler and more coherent than Karnak Temple. Although the 18th Dynasty pharaoh Amenhotep III (1417-1379 BC) began the temple, his son Amenhotep IV, better known as Akhenaten, concentrated instead on building a shrine to Aten adjacent to the site. However, Tutankhamen (1361-1352 BC) and Horemheb (1348-1320 BC) later resumed the work and decorated the peristyle court and colonnade. Ramses II (1304-1237 BC) completed most of the building by adding a second colonnade and pylon as well as a multitude of colossi. The Temple subsequently became covered with sand and silt which helped preserve it, although salt encrustation has caused some damage. Because the ground level has risen 6 m since its construction the temple now stands at the bottom of a gentle depression. The avenue of sphinxes lining the approach, a 30th Dynasty (380-343 BC)

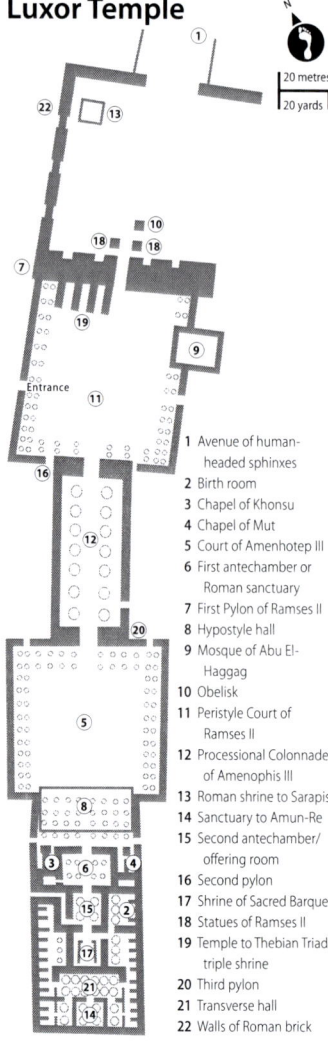

Luxor Temple

1 Avenue of human-headed sphinxes
2 Birth room
3 Chapel of Khonsu
4 Chapel of Mut
5 Court of Amenhotep III
6 First antechamber or Roman sanctuary
7 First Pylon of Ramses II
8 Hypostyle hall
9 Mosque of Abu El-Haggag
10 Obelisk
11 Peristyle Court of Ramses II
12 Processional Colonnade of Amenophis III
13 Roman shrine to Sarapis
14 Sanctuary to Amun-Re
15 Second antechamber/offering room
16 Second pylon
17 Shrine of Sacred Barque
18 Statues of Ramses II
19 Temple to Thebian Triad/triple shrine
20 Third pylon
21 Transverse hall
22 Walls of Roman brick

The hassle, haggle and hustle

Luxor is as synonymous with 'hassle' as it is with the 'Valley of the Kings'. Many visitors get frustrated and depressed by the constant pesterings of *felucca* men and *calèche* drivers, the harsh battles when bargaining in the *souk*, the need to be mistrustful of friendly overtures and of the locals' conspiracy in the overcharging of all foreigners. But before getting too irate, it's as well to remember the other side.

The effects of terrorist attacks in Egypt, 9/11 and the war in Iraq have meant the number of tourists in Luxor has fluctuated wildly in recent years. In a town where most people's bread is connected to tourism, the impact has been dire. As a result, everyone does everything they can to get as much as they can. Sometimes it means budget hotels cut their rates in half just to earn a few pounds, or guides offer the same tour to one hard haggler for 100 pounds less than to another. This is how people get by. Especially when the season is slumping, every tourist counts. Most tour guides and *felucca* captains will make a chunk of money in a day and not see another chunk for a long spell. When bargaining for a cheaper deal, bear in mind that less is not always best and the quality of your experience may suffer if you take advantage of this situation. Be fair and realistic and try to maintain a sensitivity to the people on your back. They are used to seeing the vast majority of Western tourists paying to stay in five-star hotels, eat international cuisine (in restaurants locals would not be allowed into), and have two-week holidays with their children every year. It's not surprising that they try to take advantage.

---

addition, once stretched all the way to the Karnak Temple complex. Though at first glance they all appear identical, actually each face (that of Amenhotep III) is subtly different, some a little plump and others very serious, but all with the mysterious secret smile of the sphinx. Excavation and demolition work is underway to uncover this avenue, buried under the modern city for countless centuries, and it's estimated it will take until 2030 to reconnect the two temples and realign any ruinous sphinxes which lie in fields and backyards.

In front of the gigantic First Pylon are the three remaining colossi of Ramses II and to the left stands a single obelisk towering 25 m high. A 22.8-m-high second obelisk was given to France by Mohammed Ali Pasha in 1819 and re-erected in the Place de la Concorde in Paris, where it still stands. The **First Pylon** gives a powerful and immediate impression of how awe-inspiring the temple must have looked in its prime. Its reliefs depict Ramses' supposed victory at the Battle of Kadesh, with later embellishments by Nubian and Ethiopian kings.

Passing through the pylon, the **Peristyle Court** is set at a slight angle to the rest of the temple to encompass earlier shrines built by Tuthmosis III (1504-1450 BC), on the right, dedicated to the Theban triad. The double row of columns surrounding the court are shaped into the classic representation of papyrus reeds bound together to form a bud at the top. The east end of the court has not been fully excavated because it is the site of the **Mosque of Abu El-Haggag**, which can be entered from the other side. At the south end of the court, the portal flanking the entrance to the colonnade supports two black granite statues bearing the name of Ramses II, but the feathers of Tutankhamen.

Luxor

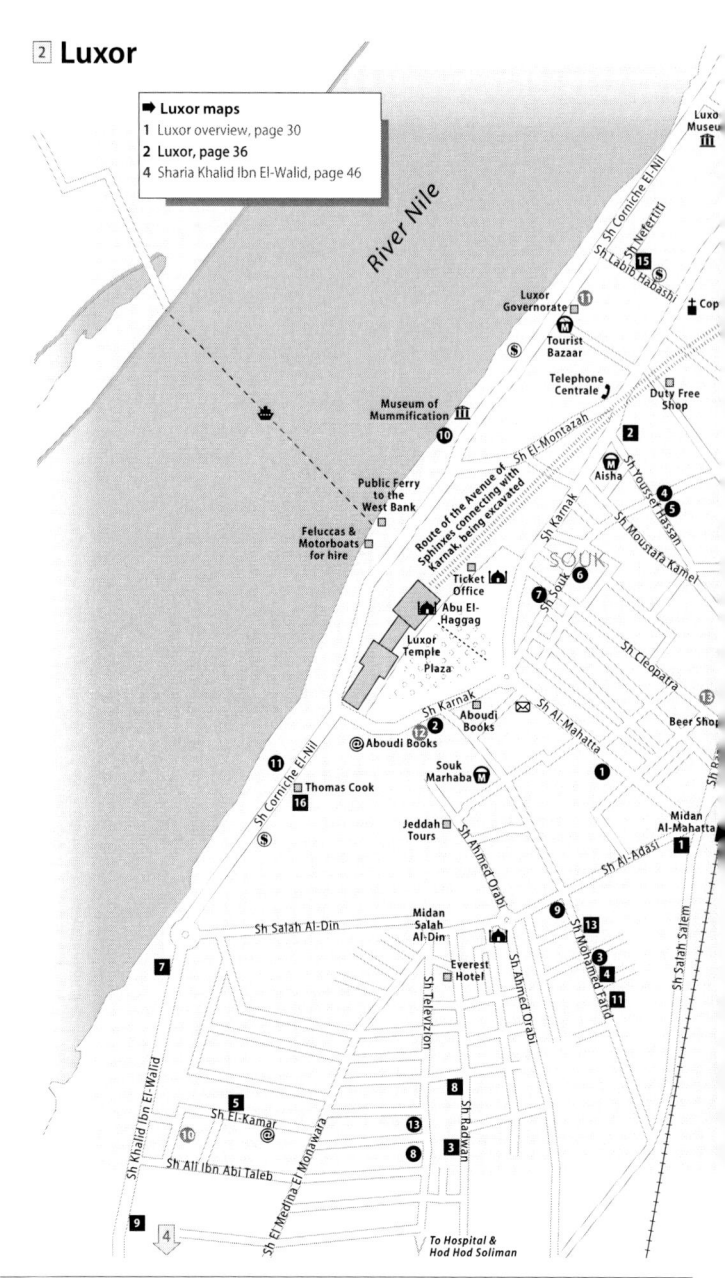

➡ **Luxor maps**
1 Luxor overview, page 30
2 Luxor, page 36
4 Sharia Khalid Ibn El-Walid, page 46

River Nile

Luxor Museum

Sh Corniche El-Nil
Sh Nefertiti
Sh Labib Habashi
Luxor Governorate
Cop
Tourist Bazaar
Telephone Centrale
Duty Free Shop
Museum of Mummification
Sh El-Montazah
Aisha
Sh Youssef Hasan
Public Ferry to the West Bank
Route of the Avenue of Sphinxes connecting with Karnak, being excavated
Sh Karnak
Sh Moustafa Kamel
Feluccas & Motorboats for hire
Ticket Office
SOUK
Abu El-Haggag
Sh Souk
Luxor Temple Plaza
Sh Cleopatra
Sh Karnak
Aboudi Books
Sh Al-Mahatta
Beer Shop
Aboudi Books
Sh Corniche El-Nil
Souk Marhaba
Thomas Cook
Jeddah Tours
Sh Ahmed Orabi
Sh Al-Adasi
Midan Al-Mahatta
Midan Salah Al-Din
Sh Salah Al-Din
Everest Hotel
Sh Televizion
Sh Ahmed Orabi
Sh Mohamed Farid
Sh Salah Salem
Sh El-Kamar
Sh Radwan
Sh Khalid Ibn El-Walid
Sh Ali Ibn Abi Taleb
Sh El Medina El Monawara
To Hospital & Hod Hod Soliman

36 • Luxor & around Luxor & the east bank

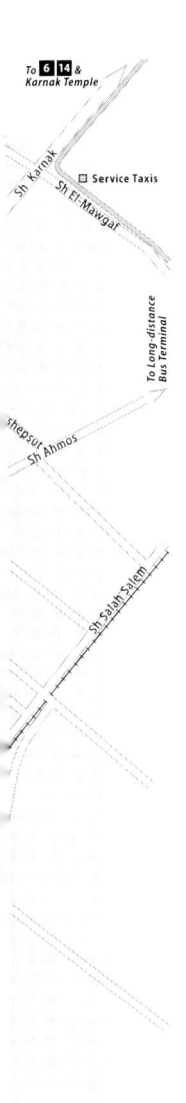

The daunting **Colonnade** of 14 columns with papyrus capitals leads to the older part of the temple. The walls are detailed with the procession of the **Opet Festival**, following an anticlockwise direction, decorated by Tutankhamen and Horemheb. Beyond it is the **Court of Amenhotep III**, a second sweeping peristyle court with double rows of columns flanking three of the sides. None of the original roof remains, and the floor and 22 massive columns have had to be relaid because the rising water table was undermining the foundations. It leads to the **Hypostyle Hall** with 32 papyrus columns that were taken over by Ramses IV and Ramses VII, who took no part in their erection but still added their cartouches. Look out for the chamber that was converted into a Coptic church during the fourth century. The pharaonic reliefs were plastered over and early Christian paintings covered the whitewash, their colour and detail just recently exposed by a restoration project. In other areas the stucco is crumbling away to reveal the original reliefs.

Beyond is a smaller second vestibule, the **Offerings Chamber**, with its four columns still in place. Further on, in the **Sanctuary of the Sacred Barque**, the doors were made of acacia and inlaid with gold. Alexander the Great (332-323 BC) rebuilt the shrine in accordance with Amenhotep III's original plans, and left reliefs of himself on the outer wall. Also look out for the depiction of a virile Amun, whose erect phallus has been weathered over the centuries by the touch of women who want to conceive. The east passage leads to the **Birth Room** built because of Amenhotep's claim that he was the son of the god Amun, who is depicted as entering the queen's chamber disguised as Tuthmosis IV and breathing the child into her nostrils. The furthest hall has 12 poorly maintained papyrus-bud columns and

---

Where to stay
Anglo **1**
Boomerang **4**
Domina Inn Emilio **2**
Fontana **3**
Happy Land **5**
Iberotel Luxor **7**
Little Garden **8**
Luxor Hilton Resort & Spa **6**
New Pola **9**
Nubian Oasis **12**
Oasis **13**
Philippe **15**
Rezeiky Camp **14**
Seven Heaven **11**
Sofitel Winter Palace **16**

Restaurants
Abu Ashraf **1**
Abu El-Hassan El-Shazly **9**
Ali Baba **2**
El Zaeem **5**
Jamboree **6**
Kebabgy **11**
Lotus **7**
Metropolitan **10**
Mish Mish **8**
Quick **13**
Sofra **3**

Bars & clubs
Esquire **10**
Mercure **11**
Saint Mina Hotel **13**
Sinbad **12**

Luxor & around Luxor & the east bank • 37

leads on to the small **Sanctuary of Amenhotep III** where the combined god Amun-Min is represented.

Mosque of Abu Haggag

This mosque, built atop the ruins of Luxor Temple, contains the tomb of Abu Haggag, the patron saint of Luxor who died in 1243. Although another mosque with the same name has been built nearby, this one is still preferred by locals. After a fire in 2009, the mosque has been renovated and many of the pharaonic elements that were incorporated into the building have been re-exposed. Stucco that had been covering columns carved with hieroglyphs was removed revealing, among others, the cartouche of Ramses II. While most of the present-day mosque is 19th-century, the northern minaret is very much older. As well as the small grave of Abu Haggag, there are shrines containing the remains of his uncles and family. The atmospheric mosque is worth a visit: the prayer hall is beautiful and there are views down to the temple; generous *baksheesh* will be expected by the mosque attendants.

Luxor Museum

ⓘ *The museum is on the Corniche halfway between Luxor and Karnak temples, daily 0900-1400 and 1600-2100 (last tickets 1230 and 2030) winter, 0900-1500 and 1700-2100 summer, Ramadan 1300-1600. Entrance E£80, students E£40, no cameras/video permitted.*
The exhibits in this modern museum, ranging from pharaonic treasures to the Mamluk period, are tastefully displayed after a relatively recent reorganization and the opening of a new wing. A seven-minute documentary is shown in the small cinema behind the ticket booth, which helps put the artefacts in context, and it is worth looking at the statues in the small garden at the front before entering the museum proper.

On entering, visitors are greeted by a statue of Amun, taking the facial features of King Tutankhamun. Close by is a splendid gilded head of Hathor (the cow-goddess) and a huge sloe-eyed head of Amenhotep III in pink granite. Down the steps to the right are the New Kingdom statues that were found in a cache at Luxor Temple in 1989, probably the most important items in the museum. Twenty-four statues were unearthed, though not all can be seen here; of particular note is the red quartzite statue of Amenhotep III, preserved in complete perfection down to his sandalled feet, and a smooth grey granite Hathor. Back on the ground floor, equally striking is a calcite crocodile-headed Sobek, cradling Amenhotep III in his arms, and an exquisite votive statue of Mayi offering a crocodile to Sobek carved from black granite.

The new wing presents 'Thebes Glory', the centrepieces of which are the unwrapped mummies of Ahmose I and (possibly) Ramses I (whoever he was, his face is extraordinary). Ahmose I was one of several pharaohs unearthed among a stash of royal mummies discovered in 1881, hidden in a communal grave by the priests of the 21st Dynasty – an attempt to keep the remains safe that proved successful for nearly 3000 years. Nearby, look out for the military decoration belonging to Ahmose's mother, an incredible necklace comprising three giant flies made of solid gold. Also of interest in the main Thebes Glory room is a relief of Amenhotep III making war on his chariot, as well as Tutankhamun's royal bows. From here, as you move to the upper level, note the statues of doleful slaves prostrate with their hands behind their back or held by their hair by Ramses VI. The upper level is dedicated to scribes and the art of writing, and includes the architect's original plans for the tomb of Ramses IX.

Mummification

The ritual of mummification reached its zenith during the New Kingdom at the same time as the Luxor and Karnak temple complexes were being built. It was developed because the ancient Egyptians believed that in order for a person to reach their heavenly aspect or *Ka* in the afterlife, it was essential that both their name and body survived thereby sustaining their cosmic double or *Ka*, which was transported from one life to the next. In order to achieve this, the mummification ritual developed into an extremely complex means of preserving bodies. The dead were placed in tombs together with any food and utensils thought necessary to accompany the person's *Ka* for the journey to the underworld.

Although we know quite a bit about the most commonly used New Kingdom mummification methods, others are still being revealed. For example, a recently opened princess' tomb in Giza revealed that the body had been hollowed out and lined with very fine plaster.

The mummification method found in and around the Valley of the Kings, however, usually involved removing the brain through the nose (it was discarded because the heart was thought to be the centre of intelligence). The entrails and organs were then extracted and stored in jars, known as Canopic jars, while the corpse was soaked in natrun salts for 40 days until it was dehydrated, at which point the embalming process began. In an attempt to recreate its original appearance the body was packed and then painted red if male and yellow if female. Artificial eyes, made of polished stone or jewels were inserted into the eye sockets and the face was made up before the body was wrapped in gum-coated linen bandages and placed in its coffin.

On the highest floor, between three memorable busts of Akhenaten, is the Wall of Akhenaten, 283 sandstone blocks found inside the middle of the Ninth Pylon at Karnak. Here Akhenaten and Nefertiti are shown worshipping Aten, amid scenes of life in the temple. Also on display on this floor are a few choice exhibits from Tutankhamen's tomb including funerary bed and two model barques.

Museum of Mummification

ⓘ *Daily 0900-1400, 1600-2100 winter, 0900-1400, 1700-2200 summer; Ramadan 1300-1600 only. E£50, students E£25. Cameras not permitted.*

Right on the banks of the Nile this museum tells the story of mummification, as practised by the ancient Egyptians, as an integral part of their religious belief in the afterlife. This museum, considered to be the first of its kind in the world, contains a comprehensive display. Exhibits include several human, reptile and bird mummies as well as stone and metal tools used in the mummification process. A well-preserved mummy of a 21st Dynasty high priest of Amun is of interest. It is well set out and worth a short visit. Note the examples of canopic jars for storing the liver, lungs, stomach and intestines.

Karnak Temple complex

ⓘ *Daily 0600-1730 (last tickets sold an hr before closing, but it's recommended to get there by 1600 at the latest), E£70, students E£35. Cameras free. Tickets are purchased by the new visitor centre (which has some interesting old photos on display) on the south side of the vast plaza in front of the temple. To get to Karnak, you can walk or bike the 2.5 km north along Sharia Karnak, but it is probably better to save your energy for the site itself. Microbuses (50 pt) with Karnak en route are found around the train station (look for the yellow signs on the dashboard, yell out 'Karnak', if they're going, they'll stop for you).*

Calèches and private taxis from town officially cost E£20-25. If they wait (2 hrs) and bring you back, it's E£45 and some baksheesh. Expect to bargain hard. If you can face it, it is worth getting up early to be first there and avoid the big tour parties. Allow half a day to see in detail. If possible return in the evening for the Sound and Light show (E£100, students E£60, children aged 6-15 E£75, under 6 free). There are 3 shows daily with a late-night slot for a fourth to accommodate large tour groups. In winter, shows happen daily at 1830, 1945, 2100 (and 2215). In summer, 2000, 2115, 2230 (and 2345). Check at the tourist office, www.soundandlight.com.eg or T095-238 6000 for the latest schedules as the languages vary.

Karnak Temple, the largest pharaonic monument in the country after the Giza Pyramids covering almost half a square kilometre, is a rambling complex of towering pillars and mighty pylons. Known in earlier times as Iput-Isut 'the most esteemed of places', the extent, scale and quality of the remains is astonishing. And they presumably would have been even more impressive, had not many of the blocks been filched by 19th-century *pashas* to be used in the construction of sugar cane factories nearby. Still, as Flaubert said, Karnak gives 'the impression of a life of giants', and as you stand dwarfed by the massive masonry it becomes easy to believe in the vastness of the ancient city of Thebes. The complex's temples vary greatly in style because they were constructed over 1300

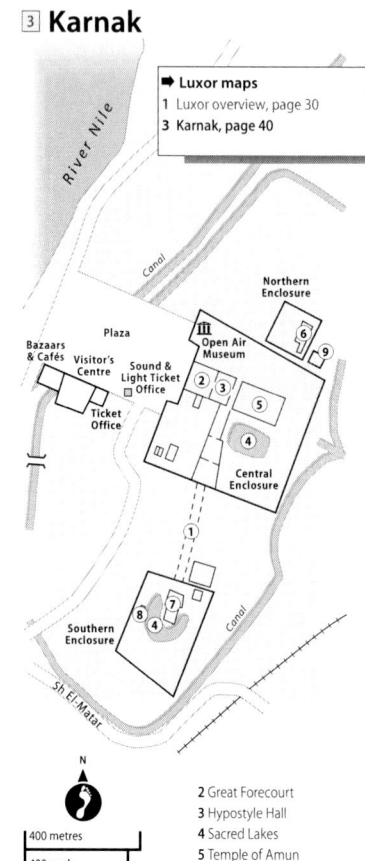

3 Karnak

➡ **Luxor maps**
1 Luxor overview, page 30
3 Karnak, page 40

1 Avenue of Ram Headed Sphinxes
2 Great Forecourt
3 Hypostyle Hall
4 Sacred Lakes
5 Temple of Amun
6 Temple of Montu
7 Temple of Mut
8 Temple of Ramses III
9 Treasury of Tuthmosis I

40 • **Luxor & around** Luxor & the east bank

years and every great pharaoh made his mark. Their only common theme is worship of Amun, Mut and Khonsu, who make up the Theban Triad of gods.

Karnak central enclosure - Temple of Amun

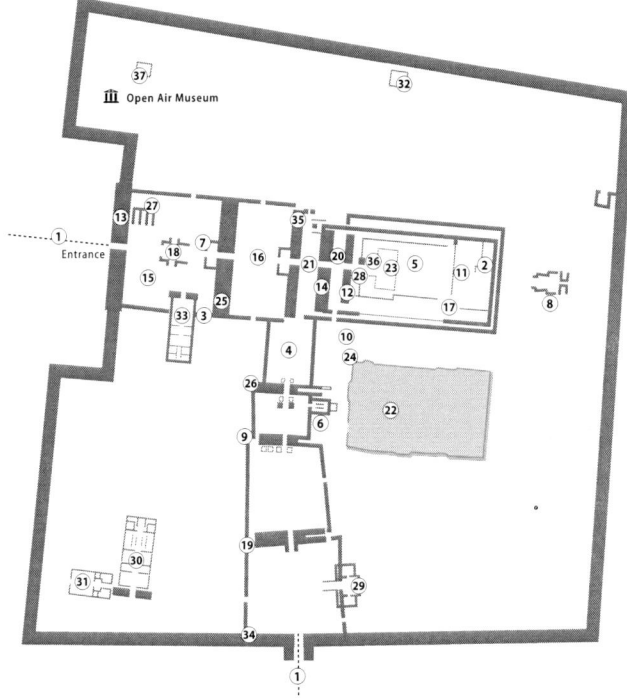

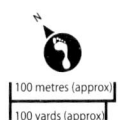

- 1 Avenue of ram-headed Sphinxes
- 2 Botanical vestibule
- 3 Bubastite portal
- 4 Cachette court
- 5 Central court
- 6 Chapel of Tuthmosis III
- 7 Colossus of Ramses II
- 8 Eastern Temple of Ramses II
- 9 Eighth pylon
- 10 Fallen Obelisk of Hatshepsut
- 11 Festival Hall of Tuthmosis III
- 12 Fifth pylon
- 13 First pylon
- 14 Fourth pylon
- 15 Great forecourt
- 16 Hypostyle hall
- 17 Karnak Table of Kings
- 18 Kiosk of Taharqa
- 19 Ninth pylon
- 20 Obelisk of Hatshepsut
- 21 Obelisks of Tuthmosis
- 22 Sacred lake
- 23 Sanctuary of sacred boats
- 24 Scarab statue
- 25 Second pylon
- 26 Seventh pylon
- 27 Shrine of Seti II
- 28 Sixth pylon
- 29 Temple of Amenhoptep II
- 30 Temple of Khonsu
- 31 Temple of Opet
- 32 Temple of Ptah
- 33 Temple of Ramses III
- 34 Tenth pylon
- 35 Third pylon
- 36 Vestibule
- 37 White Chapel of Sesostris

Temple of Amun At the heart of the complex is the enormous Temple of Amun, which was altered, extended and added to by successive rulers. Although the heretical Akhenaten, who converted to the world's first monotheistic religion and moved the capital from Thebes to Tell El-Amarna, replaced the images of Amun with representations of Aten, these were later erased by his successors and Amun's images were restored. The Temple of Amun is approached via the **Avenue of Ram-Headed Sphinxes (1)**, which used to link it to the Temple at Luxor. The imposing **First Pylon (13)** is 130 m wide and each of the two unfinished towers are 43 m high and, although incomplete, nothing else quite matches its enormous scale. Moving towards the inner core of the temple, which is the oldest section, one is moving back in time through successive dynasties. The entry towers are thought to have been constructed by the Nubian and Ethiopian kings of the 25th Dynasty (747-656 BC) while recent work has revealed that several levels were built during the later Greek and Roman eras.

Arriving through the First Pylon, you come to the **Great Forecourt (15)**, begun in the 20th Dynasty (1200-1085 BC) but completed some time later. Immediately on the left is the very thick-walled rose-coloured granite and sandstone **Shrine of Seti II (27)** (1216-1210 BC) which was a way-station for the sacred barques of Amun, Mut and Khonsu as they were taken on ritual processions. The outer façade portrays Seti II making offerings to various deities. In the middle of the Great Forecourt are the 10 columns of **Taharga**, which once supported a 26.5 m high kiosk or small open temple.

To the right of the forecourt is the small **Temple of Ramses III (33)**, which would have stood in solitary splendour in front of the **Second Pylon (25)** when it was first built in honour of Amun. Like the Shrine of Seti II, it was used as another way-station for the sacred barques. Part of an inscription in the interior reads: "I made it for you in your city of Waset, in front of your forecourt, to the Lord of the Gods, being the Temple of Ramses in the estate of Amun, to remain as long as the heavens bear the sun. I filled its treasuries with offerings that my hands had brought."

To the left of the Second Pylon is the 15 m high **Colossus of Ramses II (7)** with his daughter Benta-anta standing in front of his legs. On the right of the pylon is the **Bubastite Portal (3)** named after the 22nd-Dynasty kings from the Delta town of Bubastis. Inside the Second Pylon, blocks and statues from the destroyed temple to Aten were discovered, which are now centrepieces of the Akhenaten displays in Luxor and Cairo museums.

Passing through the Second Pylon brings you to the immense and spectacular **Hypostyle Hall (16)**, which is probably the most overpowering part of the whole Karnak complex. Its 134 giant columns were once topped by sandstone roof slabs, the 12 largest are a gigantic 23 m high and 15 m round and make up the central processional way to the chambers. The other 122 smaller columns, which have papyrus bud capitals and retain some of their original colour at the higher levels, cover the rest of the hall. They are decorated by dedications to various gods, but particularly to the many different guises of Amun and the Theban Triad, and are also inscribed with the cartouches of the pharaohs who contributed to the hall. The south side was decorated by Ramses II with vivid but cheap and simple concave sunk-reliefs, while the north is attributed to Seti II whose artists painstakingly carved delicate convex bas-reliefs on the walls. Ramses is shown, on the south side of the internal wall of the Second Pylon, making offerings before the gods and seeking their guidance, while on the left is a beautiful representation of Thoth inscribing Seti's name on a holy tree.

Seti II is depicted on both sides of the Third Pylon but the south wall running along the right of the hall was mainly decorated by Ramses II. He is shown being crowned by Horus and Thoth and then being presented to Amun. The **Third Pylon (35)** was constructed by Amenhotep III on the site of several earlier shrines that were moved to the Open Air Museum within the walls of Karnak. On the inner east face is a text of tribute and a scene showing the gods' sacred boats. Amenhotep III built a small court to enclose four **Tuthmosid Obelisks (21)** in the narrow gap between the Third and Fourth Pylon, which at that time represented the entrance to the Temple. Of the four, only one pink granite obelisk (23 m high, weighing 143 tonnes and originally tipped with electrum) built by Tuthmosis II now remains and the stone bases and some blocks from two other obelisks built by Tuthmosis III are scattered nearby.

Moving towards the earlier centre of the temple is the limestone-faced sandstone **Fourth Pylon (14)**, built by Tuthmosis I. Texts describing later restorations are recorded on both sides by Tuthmosis IV to the left and Shabaka to the right. Just inside is a small **Transverse Hall** that was originally a hypostyle hall before the temple was extended outwards. Only 12 of the original papyrus bud columns and one of two 27 m and 340 tonne rose-granite **Obelisk of Hatshepsut (20)**, which once stood at the entrance, now remain. In the 16th year of the reign of Hatshepsut (1503-1482 BC), the only woman to rule Egypt as pharaoh, these two obelisks were transported from Aswan where a third unfinished one still lies in the quarry (see The Unfinished Obelisk, page 119). The tip of the second obelisk, which fell to the ground, is now lying near the Sacred Lake. The surviving erect obelisk is decorated along its whole length with the following inscription – "O ye people who see this monument in years to come and speak of that which I have made, beware lest you say, 'I know not why it was done'. I did it because I wished to make a gift for my father Amun, and to gild them with electrum." Her long-frustrated and usurped infant stepson Tuthmosis III, who had plotted against her during her reign, took his revenge by hiding the obelisks behind walls almost to the ceiling, which actually preserved them from later graffiti.

The east wall of the Transverse Hall is the **Fifth Pylon (12)**, which has been attributed to Hatshepsut's father Tuthmosis I. Beyond is another hall and then the badly damaged sandstone **Sixth Pylon (28)**. The world's first imperialist, Tuthmosis III, inscribed it on both sides with details of his vanquished enemies and his victory at the Battle of Megiddo or Armageddon. Past the pylon is a **Vestibule (36)**, which is flanked by two courts and is dominated by two granite pillars with carvings showing Tuthmosis III being embraced by Amun, and the lotus and papyrus symbols of Upper and Lower Egypt. A seated statue of Amenhotep II is against the west wall and on the north side are two colossi of Amun and Amunet, although their faces resemble Tutankhamen who had them built. The Vestibule leads to the Granite Sanctuary built by Alexander the Great's moronic half-brother and successor Philip Arrhidaeus (323-317 BC). The ceiling is covered with golden stars on a dark base while the walls depict scenes of Philip with the god Amun. The exterior walls are decorated in a similar fashion.

North of the Sanctuary beyond the granite door is a series of small chambers built by Hatshepsut but later altered by Tuthmosis III. Some of the rooms were walled up by her son to conceal Hatshepsut's influence and consequently the bright colours have been very well preserved, although Hatshepsut's face has been cut away whenever it appeared.

Further to the east is Tuthmosis III's **Festival Hall (11)** which, with its central tentpole-style columns symbolizing the tents used during his campaigns, is unlike any other Egyptian building. It was built for his jubilee festivals that were intended to renew the pharaohs' temporal and spiritual authority. Access is via a small vestibule that leads to the central columned hall. The columns in the central aisle are taller than the side ones and would have supported a raised section of the roof thereby permitting sunlight to enter. The hall was later used as a Christian church and early paintings of the saints can still be seen on some of the columns.

Off to the southwest is a small chamber where the original stela known as the **Karnak Table of Kings (17)**, minus Hatshepsut, was found. The original is in the Louvre in Paris, the one on display here a replica. The series of interconnecting chambers beyond is dedicated to the Theban Triad and further north is an attractive chamber known as the **Botanical Vestibule (2)**. Its four columns have papyrus capitals and are carved with the unfamiliar plants and shrubs discovered by Tuthmosis III during his Syrian campaign. Surrounding the small chamber on the far east wall is the small and badly decayed **Sanctuary of Amun**, built by Hatshepsut and originally decorated with two raised obelisks on either side of the entrance – only the bases now remain. The nearby **Chapel of Sokar**, which is dedicated to the Memphite god of darkness, is better preserved.

To the south of the main temple, the **Sacred Lake (22)** (200 m x 117 m) has been restored to its original dimensions but has become stagnant since the inundation that used to feed the lake by underground channels from the River Nile ceased after the construction of the Aswan Dam. Today the lake is totally uninteresting but it has the Sound and Light Show grandstand at the far end and a café on the north side. A Nilometer is attached to the lake and there is a statue of a giant scarab beetle that childless women walk around five times in order to ensure that they soon bear children.

While the main temple runs from west to east there is a secondary axis running south from the area between the third and fourth pylons. It begins with the **Cachette Court (4)**, which received its name after the discovery between 1903 and 1906 of 17,000 bronze statues and 780 stone ones that had been stored in the court during the Ptolemaic period, the best of which are now in the Egyptian Museum in Cairo. The reliefs on the outside wall of the Hypostyle Hall, northwest of the court, depict Ramses II in battle starting with the second Battle of Kadesh. Facing this, on the outer (western) wall of the Cachette Court, is a copy of the earliest known international peace treaty. The **Treaty of Kadesh** was drawn up between the Egyptians and the Hittites in 1258 BC, when both sides needed to stop warring with each other in order to focus on fighting more immediate threats. Ramses II promises King Hattusilis III that he will not "gouge out their eyes, kill his children, destroy his house, cut off his tongue, ears, feet or any other part of his body". Other less gory agreements still form the foundations of peace treaties today, such as the sanctity of messengers, repatriation of refugees, and the promise of mutual assistance should either be threatened by a third party. On the east walls, close to the **Seventh Pylon (26)**, is a replica of a stela now in the Egyptian Museum showing the only reference to Israel during pharaonic times. The Seventh Pylon was built by Tuthmosis III and shows him massacring his prisoners before Amun. In front of the façade are parts of two colossi of Tuthmosis and in the courtyard to the left is the small chapel of Tuthmosis III.

Restoration work continues on the nearby **Eighth Pylon (9)** and others further along, but it may be possible to have a quick look in return for a small tip to the guard, either early or late in the day when there are fewer people. The Eighth Pylon was built by Tuthmosis II and Hatshepsut and contains extensively restored reliefs and cartouches. As in many other places, Hatshepsut's name has been erased and replaced by that of Tuthmosis III, while Akhenaten's name was erased by Seti I. The south side of the pylon has four of the original six **Seated Colossi**, two of which are Tuthmosis II and one is Amenhotep I.

The **Ninth Pylon (19)** and the **Tenth Pylon (34)** were built by Horemheb (1348-1320 BC) using materials from the demolished Aten Temple. The Tenth Pylon has two colossi of Ramses II and his wife Nefertari usurping the original colossi of Amenhotep III. On the south side of the pylon are two quartzite colossi of Amenhotep III. The pylon, part of the outer enclosure, marks the start of the ram-headed sphinx-lined road to the southern enclosure.

In the far southwest corner of the central enclosure are two fairly well preserved temples, but they are of limited interest. The **Temple of Khonsu (30)** was built by Ramses III and Ramses IV and dedicated to the son of Amun and Mut. Many of the reliefs show Herihor, high-priest of Amun, who ruled Upper Egypt after Ramses XI (1114-1085 BC) moved his capital to the Delta and delegated power to the high-priest. In the courtyard Herihor's name is inscribed on every pillar and all the scenes depict him venerating the gods and making offerings to them. The **Temple of Opet (31)**, the hippopotamus-goddess, is normally closed to the public as excavations are ongoing.

Southern Enclosure To the south, enclosed by a mud-brick wall are the much overgrown remains of the Temple of Mut and associated buildings (worth a quick visit). The entrance is in the centre of the north wall. Outside the enclosure and to the east are the ruins of a temple and to the west remains suggested as a barque sanctuary. Inside the enclosure, in a central position between the entrance and the Sacred Lake, and orientated north-south, stands the

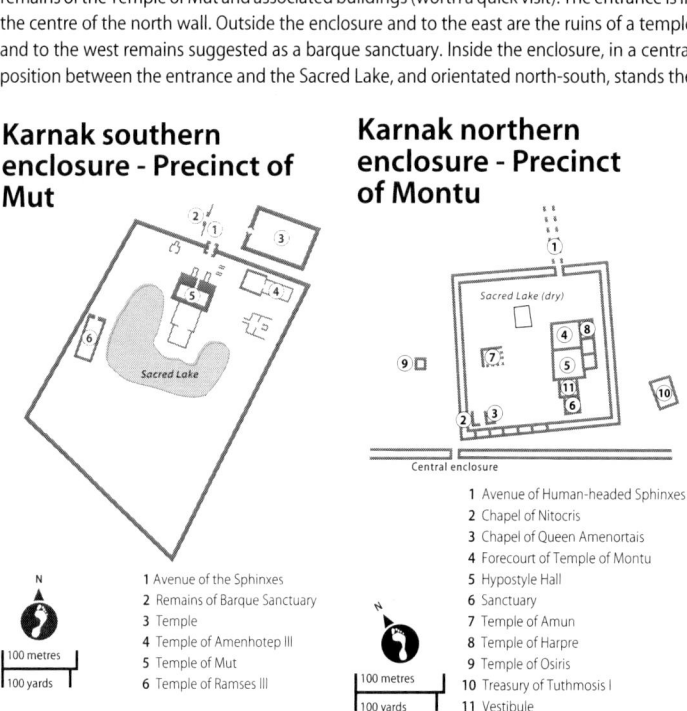

Karnak southern enclosure - Precinct of Mut

1 Avenue of the Sphinxes
2 Remains of Barque Sanctuary
3 Temple
4 Temple of Amenhotep III
5 Temple of Mut
6 Temple of Ramses III

Karnak northern enclosure - Precinct of Montu

1 Avenue of Human-headed Sphinxes
2 Chapel of Nitocris
3 Chapel of Queen Amenortais
4 Forecourt of Temple of Montu
5 Hypostyle Hall
6 Sanctuary
7 Temple of Amun
8 Temple of Harpre
9 Temple of Osiris
10 Treasury of Tuthmosis I
11 Vestibule

Temple of Mut (5), consort of Amun. Little remains of this construction accepted as the work of Ptolemies II and VII except a number of diorite statues of the lioness-headed god, Sekhmet. To the northeast is the **Temple of Amenhotep III (4)**, later restored by Ramses II. Little remains except the bases of the walls and pillars and the feet on wall decorations. To the west of the Sacred Lake stands the **Temple of Ramses III (6)** with some military scenes on the outer walls and a headless colossus on the west side.

Northern Enclosure On the north side of the central enclosure, the **Temple of Ptah (32)** (currently closed for excavation) leads on to Karnak's northern enclosure, which includes two temples, a sacred lake (now dry) and some chapels. The **Temple of Montu**, the god of war, was built by Amenhotep III, some of whose cartouches survive, and restored by Ramses IV. He left his mark too. Also in this small enclosure (150 sq m) to the west is a **temple to Amun (7)**. At the southern wall, six small gateways give access to six small chapels of which the **chapels of Amenortais and Nitocris (2 and 3)** are the best preserved.

To the east outside the enclosure is the **Treasury of Tuthmosis I (10)**; to the west stand the remains of a **Temple of Osiris (9)**.

Open Air Museum ⓘ *daily 0700-1700, E£25, students E£15*. To the northwest of the complex, this museum contains 1300 blocks from the foundations of the Third Pylon and 319 stone blocks reassembled into Hatshepsut's **Sanctuary of the Barque**. Another barque sanctuary built by Amenhotep I is also on display, but the most beautiful monument is the lovely 12th Dynasty (1991-1786 BC) **White Chapel** built by Senusert I (1971-1928 BC), which is divided into four rows of five pillars and includes some wonderful convex bas-reliefs and an interesting geographic list of the Middle East. The rest of the chapel is dedicated to offerings to a phallic Amun-Min who is embraced by Senusert.

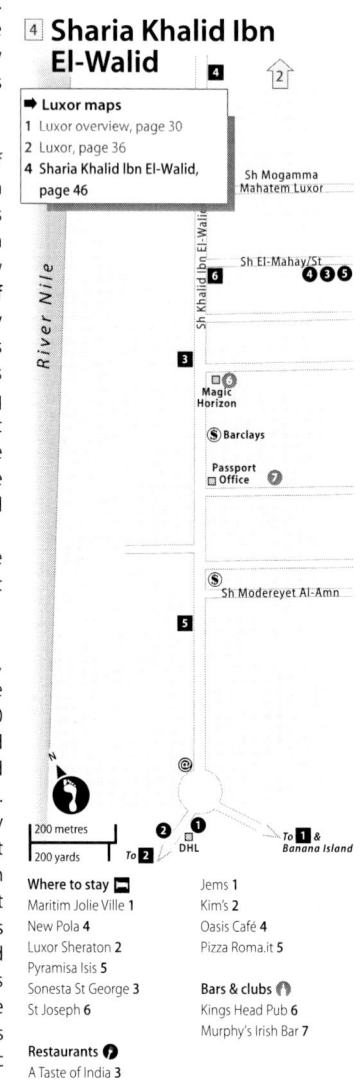

Sharia Khalid Ibn El-Walid

➡ **Luxor maps**
1 Luxor overview, page 30
2 Luxor, page 36
4 Sharia Khalid Ibn El-Walid, page 46

Where to stay
Maritim Jolie Ville 1
New Pola 4
Luxor Sheraton 2
Pyramisa Isis 5
Sonesta St George 3
St Joseph 6

Restaurants
A Taste of India 3
Jems 1
Kim's 2
Oasis Café 4
Pizza Roma.it 5

Bars & clubs
Kings Head Pub 6
Murphy's Irish Bar 7

◉ Luxor and the east bank listings

For sleeping and eating price codes and other relevant information, see pages 11-15.

● Where to stay

Luxor has thousands of beds – from the most luxurious to the dingiest of crash-dives. As a result, when tourism wanes due to the intense heat of summer or tension in the region, competition is fierce. Prices get sliced, sometimes in half, and bargaining is the norm. If you're travelling in peak season (Nov-Feb), it's wise to book ahead; otherwise, shop around. The 5-star hotels are mostly located along the Nile, some quite far from the town centre. Mid-range hotels tend to be scattered both north and south of Sharia Mahatta, the central vein that runs perpendicular to the Nile from the train station. Most offer swimming pools and rooftop terraces with bars. Budget hotels are concentrated around the town centre, and virtually all include breakfast and most breakfasts consist of the same thing: bread, jam, cheese, tea or coffee, and a boiled egg. In the listing that follows, it is only noted if breakfast is extraordinary or not included. Note that there are some lovely budget to mid-range hotels on the west bank, so also see the listings on page 87.

East bank *p31, maps p36 and p46*

€€€€ Iberotel Luxor, Sharia Khalid Ibn El-Walid, T095-238 0925, www.iberotel egypt.com. With an emphasis on friendly service, this upscale hotel feels relaxed and has good restaurants and pleasant terraces. Essential to get a Nile-view room unless you want to look down on the foyer. The pool floating on the Nile is an added bonus and there are good recreational facilities. They have a floating restaurant every Thu with an Oriental show from 1930-2200 (E£200) or 3 day trips a week to Dendara for E£425 per person on Sun, Tue and Fri (Tue is the quietest).

€€€€ Luxor Hilton Resort & Spa, New Karnak, north of town with free courtesy bus, T095-237 4933, www.hiltonworldresorts.com. Reopened late 2008, after a 2-year multi-million-dollar refurbishment, the Hilton offers a truly de luxe experience. Decor is contemporary chic, there are 7 bars and restaurants to indulge at, and 2 Nile-side pools (1 with submerged sun-loungers). Undoubtedly the most glamorous and modern place to stay on the east bank.

€€€€ Luxor Sheraton Hotel and Resort, Sharia El-Awameya, T095-237 4544, www.sheraton.com/luxor. A well-managed hotel with 298 rooms in main building with views of Nile (more expensive) or bungalows in garden (very comfortable). Shopping arcade, disco, tennis courts, heated pool, *feluccas* to rent. The service is consistently excellent and although it caters mainly to tour groups, it's possible to get a good deal as an independent traveller.

€€€€ Maritim Jolie Ville, Kings Island, T095-227 4855, www.jolieville-hotels.com. Enormous and deservedly popular resort with 326 rooms in 21 bungalow pavilions (more being built, which will take it up to 645 rooms). Currently being renovated to 5-star status but it remains homely, among lush flowering gardens and a wealth of birdlife on a beautiful island 4 km south of Luxor. A good choice for families, under 12s sleep free. Connected to mainland by bridge where the taxis to town line up or there's a free shuttle bus. Good restaurants, infinity pool and separate relaxing pool (children not allowed), spa, fitness centre and tennis.

€€€€ Pyramisa Isis, Sharia Khalid Ibn El-Walid, T095-237 0100, www.pyramisa egypt.com. Large hotel with high standard rooms and public areas that are quite slick. Rear rooms have good balconies looking onto the river and pool, the Italian restaurant comes recommended, there's also Chinese dining, plus 2 decent swimming pools by the Nile. Much better room rates online can make it a great deal.

€€€€ Sofitel Winter Palace, Corniche El-Nil, T095-238 0422/5, www.sofitel.com. The oldest (from 1886), and most famous luxury hotel in Luxor whose guests have included heads of state, Noel Coward and Agatha Christie. Classic rooms are rather small (for the price) in the old building, either overlooking the Nile or the verdant garden full of towering old palms, and there are magnificent suites (top price almost €2000). But what you're paying for really is the history and the exquisite public spaces, such as the Victorian lounge with its creaky parquet floor, chandeliers and Orientalist art. Rooms by the luxuriant garden are cheaper in the adjacent **Pavilion Winter Hotel** and a new building modelled in the colonial style is being built, but won't be finished until 2012 at least. The terrace bar is in splendid position overlooking Corniche and river, plus there are numerous other dining and drinking options, and a terribly chic pool. Breakfast costs extra and is expensive.

€€€€ Sonesta St George Hotel, Corniche El-Nil, T095-238 2575, www.sonesta.com. A modern 7-storey building, the interior is all marble and glittering lights, generally bustling and busy. The lower level terrace overlooks the Nile and there's a fabulous pool for guests' use only. 10 restaurants and bars to choose from, of which the **Mikado** Japanese restaurant comes highly recommended for its food if not its atmosphere. Quality sport and fitness centre and all the 5-star amenities you desire.

€€€ El-Luxor, Corniche El-Nil, T095-238 0944, www.el-luxor-hotel.com. A popular choice that has an especially convenient location, with good facilities in the airy rooms and an excellent breakfast. Rooms overlook the Nile or the garden. The attractive pool is open to non-guests and there's a good choice of restaurants and bars. There is an extra charge for the gym.

€€ Domina Inn Emilio Hotel, Sharia Youssef Hassan, T095-237 6666, emilio group@emiliotravel.com. Refurbished rooms all have satellite TV, music system, a/c, mini-bar and inoffensive white-wood furnishings. Most have balconies, and those on the upper floor have views over the Avenue of the Sphinxes. There's a small bar in the foyer and by the pool, 2 restaurants, disco, and a real bonus is the clean and popular pool on the roof. In winter, it's wise to make reservations as the place swarms with European groups.

€€ Philippe Hotel, Sharia Dr Labib Habashi, T095-237 2284, www.philippeluxorhotel.com. Another Luxor hotel that has undergone a renaissance, and the lobby and refitted rooms are now almost swanky. Some have slight Nile views (which you pay more for), some look onto **Windsor's** pool next door, all include TV, a/c, and fridge. Some rooms have remodelled bath, some have balcony. They vary significantly in size so look around before booking if possible, and a few of the singles contain so much huge furniture you can hardly open the door. Pool is only OK, but the terrace and bar surrounding it are attractive for a sunset drink.

€€ New Pola, Sharia Khalid Ibn El-Walid, T095-236 5081, www.newpolahotel.com. A blank rather unappealing tower from the outside, however rooms are much larger than average, freshly tiled with plain and inoffensive furnishings, balcony, fridge, a/c and TV. Good value at E£200 per double. Nicer at the front, but bear in mind that Nile views are across the busy road. There's a small square rooftop pool with plenty of sun-loungers and folks enjoying a beer.

€€ St Joseph, Sharia Khalid Ibn Walid, T095-238 1707, www.xanga.com.stjos. A mid-range and somewhat tacky hotel that attracts Brits and groups. That said, it is social and fun with a busy rooftop pool area covered with astroturf, with good views and rooms that are priced right at US$35 per double. Free Wi-Fi, good amenities and located near Luxor's nightlife.

€€-€ Boomerang, Sharia Mohamed Farid, T019-136 1544, www.boomerangluxor.com. Excellent new hostel with high standards, close to the railway station in the little traveller enclave that's formed on Mohamed Farid. Clean rooms with quality beds (mattresses steam-cleaned regularly) all have their own bathrooms (often across the corridor), a/c, satellite TV and balconies. There are some suites; dorm beds cost E£30. Tours offered, free Wi-fi or use of PC is E£5 per hr. Very pleasant Australian-Nubian management and a family atmosphere also makes it suitable for those travelling with children. Smoking permitted only on the rooftop, where there is also a sun-deck. Good buffet breakfast. Highly recommended.

€ Anglo Hotel, Midan Al-Mahatta, T095-238 2133. If you want to be bang next to the station this is an old-style hotel that's decent value. Rooms are simple, furniture the bare minimum, soft pillows, some have inside bathrooms, all have a/c and TV, only 1 has both private bath and balcony. There's a basement bar, open 2000-0200, or they'll bring beer to your room for E£10. It does have a dubious reputation, however, perhaps not the best choice for lone women. Breakfast is E£5 extra per person.

€ Fontana, Sharia Radwan, off Sharia Televizion, T095-228 0663, www.fontanaluxorhotel.com. Doubles with private bath E£45, singles E£30, subtract E£5 for shared bath. Rooms are simple and clean, ones at the front have balconies, some have a/c. Clean spacious bathrooms include toilet paper and towels. Loquacious Mr Magdy Soliman and his staff are helpful; there's free use of the washing machine and Wi-fi. If you're getting a night train, you can store bags and have a shower before departing at no extra charge. Good in that the breakfast is served as early as 0500 or as late as 1100, lunch is available, and there are bikes and motorbikes for rent. If you call ahead they will arrange a free taxi for you from the station.

€ Happy Land, Sharia El-Kamar, near Sharia Televizion, T095-227 1828, www.luxorhappyland.com. With doubles from E£55-80, singles E£40-70 (dependent on location, a/c, minibar, private bath, etc) the Happy Land remains a stalwart of the backpacker scene. Rooms really are spotlessly clean, sheets and towels are changed daily, and bathrooms have toilet paper. 8 of the 24 rooms have balconies and it's a quiet area. Free Wi-Fi and use of washing machine, nice rooftop terrace where an excellent breakfast is served, there's even a jacuzzi tucked away up there. Luggage storage and use of facilities for guests after check-out. Note that they don't have touts at the station, so ignore people there who claim to work for Happy Land.

€ Little Garden Hotel, Sharia Radwan, off Sharia Televizion, T095-227 9090, littlegardenlxregy@hotmail.com. A quaint yet modern hotel that has the slight aura of a villa, popular with Egyptian couples. Rooms are simple and clean, bathrooms fresh, beds large and comfy. The pricier suites have huge terraces, but don't go for the traditional-style domed rooms on the roof, which are stale in comparison. The garden is more of a patio, but lovely, with fruit trees and flowers. Rooftop restaurant serves Oriental food and has party nights with dancing and dinner (call for timings as there's no set schedule). Internet E£10 per hr for guests.

€ Nefertiti, Sharia El-Sahaby, off Sharia Karnak in the tourist bazaar, T/F095-237 2386, www.nefertitihotel.com. Doubles with a/c, TV, fridge and private bath (E£160) are very clean, with towels and linens replaced daily. Attractively refurbished throughout in an Arabesque style, this centrally located hotel offers a great rooftop (sun-lounging area) with an awesome view of the avenue of the sphinxes and the Nile. At night, the surrounding streets are filled with lively local *ahwas*, including the famed Oum Koulsoum with great *sheeshas*. Breakfast buffet is a step above most and food from their street-side restaurant is also available in the room or on the roof, there's a pool table, *tawla* (backgammon), free Wi-Fi and basic weight room equipment. Family-like warm atmosphere offers a nice respite for weary travellers; this place is highly recommended.

€ Oasis Hotel, Sharia Mohamed Farid, T010-380 5882, www.luxoroasis.com. Blue is the theme throughout this cheap option, which has a lovely rooftop perfect for a relaxing breakfast (included), or the free 'sunset tea'. They also have extremely cheap meals and beer. Unfortunately, many rooms are rather cell-like (particularly the singles), but some have private bath and a/c. Wi-Fi free and tours available, balloon rides are E£400.

€ Seven Heaven 3, Sharia Mohamed Farid, T095-236 2671, www.sevenheavenhotel.com. Previously the **Nubian Oasis**, now managed by the family who own the popular Seven Heaven in Dahab. All rooms have private bath and it's cheap with a/c rooms for E£50 or with fan for E£20 (pay per room, not per person). The recently renovated rooftop terrace is a good spot to hang out, use of the washing machine is E£1 per item, breakfast is E£5-10, free Wi-Fi/internet and use of the kitchen. If you don't mind a few murals and want to meet other travellers, come here.

Camping

Rezeiky Camp, Sharia Karnak, T095-338 1334. Offers cheap tent sites and not-so-cheap a/c rooms. On site, there's a swimming pool, internet café, washing machine and garden with bar and restaurant, serving different Egyptian meals nightly at reasonable prices. It's a bit of a hike to town.

Restaurants

East bank *p31, maps p36 and p46*
Luxor has plenty of fairly cheap Middle Eastern restaurants that have virtually identical menus (kebab, chicken, moussaka) concentrated on Sharia Al-Mahatta and nearby Sharia Al-Adasi. They tend to be inexpensive, safe and pretty good. There's also a growing European expatriate community that has introduced some delicious new mid-range eateries to Luxor in recent years; these places are found on or around Sharia Khalid Ibn El-Walid and are likely to serve alcohol.

Expensive restaurants and fine-dining seem to be generally confined to 5-star hotels. Try the **Sonesta St George** for Japanese, the **Sheraton** for Italian, and the **1886** in the Old Winter Palace for French (formal dress compulsory, men must wear jacket and tie).

€€€ Le Lotus Boat, at Iberotel Hotel. Well-organized dinner cruises every Thu offering international cuisine and an Oriental show from 1930-2200 (E£200), book to get a good seat. Also day cruises with a high-quality lunch while travelling to Dendara for E£425 per person on Sun, Tue and Fri (Tue is the quietest).

€€€-€€ Kim's, Sharia Khalid Ibn El-Walid, T095-238 6742. An unprepossessing canteen environment, but chock-full of Koreans enjoying authentic dishes that really hit the mark. Go early as everyone clears out by 2100. Efficient service and generous portions, you will struggle to eat your main after snacking on all the *kimchee*.

€€€-€€ Metropolitan/Kebabgy, Corniche El-Nil (on the river, near the Winter Palace), T095-236 9994. Very much geared towards tourists, and the setting by the Nile with outdoor tables and plenty of shade pushes the price up. That said, they are always busy and you can enjoy a good range of dishes both Egyptian and Western along with an alcoholic beverage. Kebabgy has more of a cosy evening feel, with feluccas around, whereas Metropolitan is more café-style and close to the cruise boat moorings.

€€€-€€ Sofra, 90 Sharia Mohammed Farid, T095-235 9752, www.sofra.com.eg. Daily 1000-2330. A sweet restaurant with a largely Egyptian menu that incorporates some Mediterranean influences. Housed in an old period building with Arabesque decor and antiquey tiled floors, most people choose to dine on the rooftop but there is also a little downstairs garden and interior. It not only has class but the food is excellent and comes highly recommended by all-comers and local ex-pats. Perfect for a guaranteed good meal out, and feels pretty special for Egypt.

€€ Ali Baba Café, Sharia Karnak, enter on side street. Simple rooftop restaurant that offers a lovely view of Luxor temple, particularly at sunset and in the early evening when the temple is lit up. The food is standard Egyptian fare, but the servings are quite small. Stella and local wine are cheap.

€€ A Taste of India, Sharia St Joseph Hotel, T095-228 0892. For the last 10 years, they've been serving up decent Indian and international cuisine in an Asian-style setting. British management means you are going to be familiar with the dishes and the helpful waiters are accurate with their descriptions of the menu. It's as good as Indian food is going to get in Luxor and makes a nice change.

€€ Chez Omar, Midan Youssef Hassan, near the *souk*, T095-236 7678. Open 0800-0300. This place offers decent food and fast, friendly service alongside Bob Marley prints, a/c and even tablecloths. Lit up with green lights at night, it's a good place to breathe after a long day. Considering the alternatives and the fact it is tourist-oriented, it's still pretty cheap, for example E£45 gets you a 5-course dinner including soup, salad, rice, vegetable, dessert and a meat of your choice.

€€ Jamboree, Sharia El-Souk, T012-781 3149, www.jamboreerestaurant.com. Open 0800-2300. In pleasing new premises above the *souk*, with an outdoor terrace, the menu features omelettes, soups and sandwiches as well as traditional Egyptian food, plus fish, chicken, steaks and a good vegetarian selection. Sunday roast available if you pre-book. Entrées include an excellent salad bar. The food is tasty and good for unsettled stomachs. Also on offer are milkshakes and Movenpick ice cream, but no alcohol.

€€ Jems, Sharia Khalid Ibn El-Walid, T012-226 1697, on the 2nd floor. The atmosphere isn't quite as quaint as neighbouring restaurants but guests love the food and keep coming back. The policy is, if you return more than once in the course of the week, you are offered a modest discount that gets bigger every time you return. There are set vegetarian meals, a hodgepodge of Middle Eastern and British fare and an extensive bar. The *shish tawook* comes highly recommended. Tables by the window offer good views of the action on the street.

€€ Lotus, in the heart of the *souk* on the 2nd floor. Serves a selection of Middle Eastern and European dishes including spinach cannelloni, fish and chips and a variety of vegetarian options. Large windows look down on thriving alleyways. 15% discount for students. The service is good and the chocolate mousse delicious.

€€ Oasis Café, ShariaSt Joseph, T017-595 4667, www.oasiscafeluxor.com. A hip café and gallery is an unusual find in Luxor, the Oasis has attractively painted walls adorned with lovely paintings. Unfortunately the food is not quite as special as the surroundings, but if you crave Western-style sandwiches and salads it fits the bill. Otherwise just go for a coffee to absorb the refined yet causal ambiance.

€€ Pizza Roma.it, Sharia St Joseph, T011-879 9559, www.pizzaroma-it.com. Open 1200-2300. For an authentic pizza or other Italian dish, this bright modern café-style establishment is where you should head. Italian-Egyptian run, it's on a street where many of Luxor's 'foreign' food restaurants are found.

€€-€ Abou El-Hassan El-Shazly, Sharia Al-Adasi (corner with Mohamed Farid), T016-342 9164. Open 0900-0400. Great value local food in a sanitary setting that appeals more to Egyptians than tourists. Outdoor seating on the street corner or a/c interior, recognisable by the painted green chairs and maroon tablecloths. Excellent tagines (E£15-25), chicken and fish meals (E£25) and lots on the BBQ (E£25-45). Surprisingly good for vegetarians, ask about options (which change daily and aren't on the menu).

€€-€ Mish Mish, Sharia Televizion. Serves up tasty cheap pizza with fluffy crust, although the local cheese doesn't melt like mozzarella a medium should fill you up. Also serves pastas, sandwiches and standard Middle Eastern dishes. A longtime popular eatery among backpackers.

€€-€ Quick Restaurant, Sharia Televizion, T095-227 2970, www.quickpizzaluxor.com. Open 1000-0400, also delivers. Next door to **Mish Mish**. Pies, pizza, burgers, fish, chicken and grills in a fast-food style environment, all very reasonably priced (from E£20-70).

€€-€ Abu Ashraf, Sharia Mahatta, halfway between the station and the *souk*. Open 0900-0200. Sells tasty *koshari*, *shish kebab*, roasted chicken, and lots of cheap salads. Nothing on the printed menu exceeds E£20 (and you can further negotiate the price though some of staff are a bit sniffy) and the place is clean.

€ El Zaeem, Sharia Yousseff Hassan. Open 24 hrs. Egyptian staples are either taken away or eaten upstairs in an a/c marble setting. Tourist prices apply on the written menu (at least double what locals pay) though you can try and argue it out with the man on the till. Then you might get a *fuul* sandwich or *koshari* for E£1-4.

Bars and clubs

East bank *p31, maps p36 and p46*
The Nile Terrace at the **Winter Palace** will always beckon for a historic sunset drink, or the **Royal Bar** inside the hotel has plenty of period atmosphere. In the winter, all 5-star and most 4-star hotels have some kind of 'live' music, belly dance or disco. In the summer, they're less frequent, it depends how many people are in town. Quite a few 'authentic' pubs have sprung up over the last few years, generally British-themed, which are mostly centred around Sharia Khalid Ibn El-Walid and are close enough to one another to warrant an evening tour of Luxor pub life. In addition to pubs, a few hotels have rooftop bars offering great views of the town and Nile, particularly at sunset. Besides the bars, Luxor is a lovely town to stroll around at night. There are dozens of *ahwas* scattered around where local men smoke *shisha*, sip tea, watch loud Arabic movies and play dominoes and *towla* (backgammon) into the wee hours, and don't frown at the presence of a tourist.

Esquire, Sharia Ali Ibn Abi Taleb, T012-332 8563. This place has more class than most and is easily walkable from the centre of town. Waxy wood and brass, a huge bar to prop up, quite a diverse menu with English traditionals such as cottage pie as well as Egyptian dishes. Beer is E£12-15 or there's a range of spirits on offer, happy hour daily 1700-1900 when beer goes down to E£10, quiz nights on Tue and Thu at 2030, and premier league matches shown. Food is served until 2300 and the bar stays open till 0100.

The King's Head Pub, Sharia Khalid Ibn El-Walid, T095-228 0489. The king in question is Akhenaten in the most longstanding and happening pub in town. It's a true taste of England except that the place stays open until people are ready to go home (at least until 0200) and serves dozens of cocktails with specials like 'Sex on a felucca'. There's a free pool table in the back. The menu is extensive and includes a wide variety of hot and cold *mezza* (E£15), curries, sandwiches and English standards (fish and chips E£47). Stella E£13, cocktails E£29.

Murphy's Irish Bar, Sharia El-Gawazat, near the passport office off Sharia Khalid Ibn El-Walid, T095-238 8101, www.murphyirish pub.com. Open 1000-0230. Huge 2-floor pub with pool table and football on the TV upstairs.

1980s music wafts in the background quiet enough to hear yourself speak, comfy chairs and lots of wood, not too pricey with Stellas going for E£14. Several whiskies are available and there's an extensive pub menu that includes a veggie burger, a variety of jacket potatoes and loads of soups, salads and pastas. The disco in the basement gets going at about 2230 and feels more like a regular Western club than most in town.

Saint Mina Hotel bar, Sharia Cleopatra, T095-237 5409. Open 1900-0200. Down in the dingy cellar of the Christian-run hotel, this functional bar has a very local vibe and some of the cheapest Stella in town.

Sinbad, Sharia Al-Karnak, in front of the (now closed) **Luxor Wena Hotel**, T010-302 9523. Great for an garden drink under the trees decked with fairy lights and there's always a few people around, everyone is welcome in this friendly spot. The food is very average (Western pretenders mix with Egyptian dishes) but nothing is too pricey and beer is cheap (E£8). Good apple sheesha E£5.

Festivals

East bank p31, maps p36 and p46

The **Egyptian International Marathon** happens on 14 Feb each year, on the west bank.

The **Moulid of Abu El-Haggag** happens during the first 2 weeks of the month before Ramadan (*Shabban*). Luxor's biggest *moulid* has parades, processions, stick-fighting, *zikrs* and all the other traditional entertainments that you don't get to see very often as a tourist.

The **Opet Festival**, which recreated the ancient festival celebrating the pharaoh's rebirth as the son of Amun when barques (boats) were carried along the Avenue of the Sphinxes from Karnak to Luxor temple, used to happen on 4 Nov each year. It was unsure whether this would continue to occur at the time of research; best to check with the tourist office.

Shopping

East bank p31, maps p36 and p46

Shopping in Luxor can be stressful. A leisurely meander through the *souk* is almost impossible when countless kitschy souvenirs are being thrown in your face and everyone is hollering at you to have a look. But there is a lot to look at. Spices, dried herbs and nuts and lots of colourful scarves are all over the place. Local alabaster carved into vases (E£40, small), clay pots and tagine are cheap (E£5, medium size).

Aisha, on Sharia Youssef Hassan, opposite the Emilio Hotel, www.aisha-crafts.com. Open daily 1030-1500, 1800-2230. A wide array of tasteful crafts, scarves, throws, lamps and glassware, as well as Bedouin jewellery. A good place to start, without any hassle, and although the prices are 'fixed', significant discounts will be offered as you browse.

Fair Trade Center, Sharia Karnak, by Luxor Temple, T010-034 7900. Open from 0900-2230 every day. This non-profit organization with an excellent range of tasteful goods from all over Egypt is also very worthwhile.

Habiba, in the *souk*, Sharia Sidi Mahmoud (near Lotus restaurant), T095-235 7305, www.habibagallery.com. Open 1000-2200 daily. Some lovely pieces including cotton goods, jewellery, scarves and lighting.

There are duty-free shops near the Emilio Hotel and by the plaza at Karnak Temple. On the southern end of the Corniche around the strip of 5-star hotels, there are some upscale stores that promise no hassle and sell beautiful gold jewellery and high-quality Egyptian cotton clothing. For the independent traveller, there's an abundance of fresh fruit and vegetables around the *souk* in the **Sharia Televizion market** on Tue. Those who crave Western food and snacks should head to **Arkwrights** food store, Sharia St Joseph, T095-228 2335, which is "open all hours" and has plenty of treats that you might be missing. Generally the further away from the river, the lower the prices and the less the hassle.

Bookshops

Aboudi Bookshop, by Luxor Temple. Open 0930-2330. May be the best bookshop for non-Arabic readers outside Cairo. It offers an extensive collection of fiction and historical books in English, German and French. It also has lots of maps and guidebooks to specific areas in Egypt and a decent selection of cards and gifts.

Al-Ahram, by the Museum of Mummification on Corniche El-Nil. Open 0800-2200. Has a good selection of books, also maps and cards and newspapers.

Gaddis Bookshop, by the **Winter Palace** on Corniche El-Nil, T095-372142. Open 0800-2130. Books in English, French and German plus lots of gift items, in an intriguingly olde-worlde environment.

Foreign newspapers are sold in a kiosk in the middle of the street outside the **Old Winter Palace Hotel**. There is a high chance that these will also be offered for sale by street vendors along the Corniche where the cruise ships are moored.

▲ What to do

East bank *p31, maps p36 and p46*

Balloon flights

Becoming an ever more popular activity as competition brings down prices, making it an option even for budget travellers. These days the skies over the west bank are thick with balloons each dawn, a spectacular sight in itself. Actual flight time is a maximum of 45 mins, but drifting over the Valley of the Kings and Theban temples is a truly memorable experience in the magical morning light. You can also spy down on the farmers starting work in the fields, women cooking on fires, and rooftops where washing and dates lie drying. The mountains are positively glowing by the time the trip comes to an end and the blue of the Nile is unbelievable. All companies will pick you up from your hotel on the morning of your flight at 0500-0530, most include a breakfast on the boat as you cross the Nile in the dark. Then you ascend into the gloom to a height of 300 m. If you chose to take a trip organized through one of the budget hotels it would be wise to check that the operating company has insurance, certification and offer a full refund if the flight is cancelled due to unsuitable weather conditions. There are a few companies with offices on Sharia Khalid Ibn Walid, or pick up a flyer in any high-end hotel. Budget hotels, such as those on Sharia Televizion and Mohamed Farid, offer balloon tours for around E£400 per person.

Calèche

Horse-drawn carriages are all over the place (you can't avoid them if you try), often in queues. Go to the one in front, when he's done, he will return to the end of the queue. E£10 should be enough to get you across town; the official rate is E£30 for an hour's ride, but you'll be lucky to get this.

Cruise boats

Regular Nile cruises operate between Luxor and Aswan for 2-5 days (standard tour) or 7 days (extended tour). The quality of operator and cruise ship will, of course, be largely dependent on the price paid. If the cruise is taken as an all-inclusive package, it is recommended that, if possible, one is chosen where the overall itinerary is under the day-to-day control of a tour manager who is a direct employee of the cruise company. The local management of cruises can be sub-contracted to Egyptian travel agents who, should difficulties arise with the tour, may consider themselves primarily as guides and show marked reluctance to take on any wider responsibility or be fully accountable for solving problems of a more challenging nature.

Luxor with kids

Luxor has the potential to both amaze and daze. Don't be tempted to try and squeeze in dynasty after dynasty of tomb sightseeing, but focus instead on a few of the most enigmatic sites. Highlights include the tombs of Ramses I and Ramses VI – both of which have burial chambers with elaborately painted scenes of animal-headed gods. Older children may enjoy the challenge of reaching the tomb of Tuthmosis III with its steep shafts and challenging passageways designed in an (unsuccessful) attempt to thwart tomb robbers. You'll find that a series of early-morning excursions to the west bank has less 'whinge potential' than a single, long, hot day trip. Spend the afternoons relaxing by a pool and then set off again when it's cooler to visit local Luxor beauties like the Great Hypostyle Hall – a forest of 134 towering pillars at Karnak. A great way to reach this spectacular complex is to take one of the local horse-drawn carriages.

It is easy to arrange a cruise on arrival in Luxor. There are scores of agents along the Corniche. Enquire at a few, try to see the actual boat if possible, and check their programmes – bottom-end cruises probably won't include all the sights.

Most cruises go from Luxor to Aswan, with the journey sometimes in reverse, or a trip both ways. Starting from Aswan you are travelling with the current so the trip will be shorter, and it has the disadvantage of being against the wind which can make relaxing on the top deck almost impossible.

An typical itinerary will offer the following popular features: **Luxor**: visits to the west bank (Valley of the Kings, Valley of the Queens, Colossi of Memnon, Temple of Queen Hapshetsut), Luxor and Karnak Temples (plus at least one alabaster factory shop!). Option of Sound and Light show at Karnak. **Esna**: Temple of Khnum. **Edfu**: Temple of Horus – access by *calèche*. **Kom Ombu**: Temple of Horus and Sobek. **Aswan**: Felucca boat outing to Kitchener Island, trip to Nubian village on Elephantine Island, Unfinished Obelisk, High Dam, Temple of Philae (plus at least one papyrus factory shop!). Option of Sound and Light show at Philae. **Dendara**: Temple of Hathor (this may not be on all itineraries).

Esna lock closures Cruises from Luxor to Aswan can be disrupted by the twice-yearly closure of the lock at Esna for maintenance. Closures usually occur for 2 weeks in Jun and Dec and prospective travellers are strongly advised to check these dates beforehand. When the lock is closed, ships are moored at Esna and passengers are transported by coach to those points on the itinerary inaccessible by river. This can significantly reduce the pleasure of a cruising holiday. A second lock has opened at Esna that does much to ease the pressure of cruise traffic. Passage through is now a speedier process – in the past, boats were sometimes waiting up to 20 hrs to get through during peak tourist periods.

Meals Expect 3 good meals per day, often buffet style. Meal times are likely to operate to a fairly inflexible timetable. Free tea, coffee and soft drinks are available at any time. The bar will be open most of day as this is where they make most of their money. Special menus can usually be organized.

Social life and entertainment Almost inevitably at some stage during the cruise there will be an evening dinner at which travellers will be encouraged to dress in local Egyptian costume – a *gallabiya* party. Other evening entertainment may include discos, live Egyptian/Nubian music and performances by belly dancers, jugglers and acrobats.

Cabin accommodation Cabins at water level will offer limited views and, depending on position, may be more affected by engine noise and fumes than others. A supplement can be paid for a cabin on an upper deck. Top-level cabins may have a sun deck as their roof. It's best to obtain a plan of the vessel before you book your cabin. Bear in mind that when the ship is moored there may not be a view from the cabin whatever its level. Ships can often be berthed 6 or 7 abreast and access to the shore is gained by walking through one ship after another. Expect to be issued with a boarding pass when going ashore.

Feluccas

Feluccas are numerous on this most beautiful stretch of the Nile. Travel is limited to the southward direction, but this also has the most attractive scenery. Sunset is the best time to ride but bring a sweater and protection against mosquitoes (E£40 per hr if you're a hard bargainer). It is a lovely journey to nearby **Banana Island**, where you can stroll through the papaya and orange plantations (give the owner of the island E£5), it's about a 2-hr round trip. Longer *felucca* trips start from Aswan and head north with the current, see box, page 115.

Seaplane flights

Get an even higher view of Luxor in the early morning from a small seaplane, contact T010-079 3310/010-070 7429, flights last about 25 mins and cost US$85 per person including a drink.

Swimming

An exceptionally important activity after a hot day's temple exploring, especially in the summer. Some hotels with pools offer day use for a fee. At the cheaper end of the spectrum, the pool on the roof of the **Emilio Hotel** is largest and cleanest with plenty of sunbathers, E£30. The best deal in town is at the **El-Luxor**, which has a splendid pool with lots of loungers in a palm garden, day use E£50 per person. The pool at the **Iberotel**, E£75, is a bit blank and functional but scores points for actually floating on the Nile.

Tour operators

You can buy ISIC (student) and ITIC (teacher) cards from **Jeddah Tours**, 1st floor, Sharia Ahmed Orabi, T095-238 2163, for E£95; take 2 photos and a copy of your passport. To obtain an ISIC card you will need a letter from your place of study; for a teacher's card you will just have to sign a form. Open daily 0900-2300 (half-hr break from 1600-1630), on Fri from 1030. The process takes less than 10 mins and can save you a fortune.

Travel agencies and tour operators are concentrated on the Corniche by the **Winter Palace**. The lesser-known agencies often offer the best deals. Half- or full-day tours include Dendara, Aswan and Abu Simbel, Abydos, *felucca* and camel trips, and west bank tours.

Carlson Wagonlit Travel, Corniche El-Nil, Old Winter Palace, T095-2371, alaa_luxor5@yahoo.com. Wide range of tours, discounts given on the advertised prices which are already cheaper than most.

Nawas Tours, Souk Marhaba, Sharia Ahmed Orabi, T095-237 0701/2. A cheaper agency selling Hurghada–Sharm ferry tickets, and day cruises to Dendara.

Thomas Cook, Corniche El-Nil, next to the **Winter Palace Hotel**, T095-237 2402, www.thomascookegypt.com. Has a wide variety of quality tours around Luxor and all Egypt.

Dahabiya trips

These traditional sailing boats, some of which are renovated original crafts, are a fantastic, if pricey, way to cruise the Nile. It's advisable to book a *dahabiya* cruise before arriving in Egypt, as they are often chartered by private groups and spaces are in any case limited by the small size of the vessels. Below is information on several recommended boats:

Assouan, El-Nil, Meroe and **Malouka**, www.nourelnil.com. Some of the largest *dahabiyas* on the Nile, these replica vessels are perfect down to the finest detail, while plumbing and conveniences are state of the art. The highly persona-lized service, charming crew members and utterly tasteful decor are especially noted by past guests. Departing from Esna for Aswan on Mondays, for five nights, the *Assouan* and *El-Nil* have a few standard rooms that are slightly more affordable (€1100-1500 per person in a double room).

El Bey, El Hanem, Zahra, Nesma, Amber and **Musk**, www.dahabiya.com. These small boats each measure 38 m by 6 m and accommodate up to 12 people. Each two-person air-conditioned cabin has been individualized with colonial finishes, and themed to match the name of the ship. There's no alcohol licence but guests are welcome to bring their own on board so they can enjoy cocktails on the top deck. Sailings are every Saturday from either Luxor or Aswan and last seven days.

Royal Cleopatra, www.nubiannile cruises.com. Resembling a yacht, the *Cleopatra* is in fact a converted *sandale*, a *felucca* that used to carry cargo along the Nile. Sleeping up to six guests in two gorgeous wood and white staterooms, some meals are eaten al fresco on shore. An Egyptologist guides you through the sites between Esna and Aswan, and cruising can be four, five or seven days. A five-day cruise costs US$2225/2695/3650 per person, depending whether it's triple/double/single occupancy.

Vivant Denon, www.dahabeya.net. Built in 1889, this vessel has been beautifully restored by Didier Caille to sleep six passengers in four cabins. Cruises generally run between October and April, and though it is possible to charter for summer sailings the fact there is no air conditioning on board has to be considered. In-depth tours are given of all the sites, with the itinerary and destinations tailored to group requests. Cabins are not sold separately, the boat is rented in its entirety. *Vivant Denon* is only available for a few weeks per year; sailings are on Saturdays and last one week.

Lazuli, www.lazulinil.com. Three boats with five or six cabins, some rooms have private balconies. Mod-cons such as air conditioning, internet and TVs are provided and decor is slightly more contemporary.

Royal House Boat, www.royalhouse boat.com. With only two cabins and one suite, the Royal House boat is certainly exclusive. Rooms have plasma screens, satellite TV and fancy bathrooms with jacuzzis. Excursions are guided and there is 24-hour butler service. High season price is €500/650 for a standard/suite cabin. Sailings are from Esna every Tuesday for five nights.

⊙ Transport

East bank *p31, maps p36 and p46*
Note Check all times – timetables are often a printed figment of someone's imagination.

Air
EgyptAir, next to the Winter Palace Hotel, T095-238 0581/2, open 0800-2000 and at the airport, T095-238 0588, offers frequent daily flights, particularly in the winter high season, to **Cairo**, **Aswan**, and **Abu Simbel** via **Aswan**. 3 flights a week go to **Sharm El-Sheikh**. Fares change depending on the season. Book your tickets well in advance.
Luxor Airport : T095-237 4655.

Bus
Tourists are no longer restricted to convoys in order to travel between **Luxor** and **Aswan**. You can now negotiate microbuses in order to reach the temples of Esna, Edfu and Kom Ombo, but **do not** leave Luxor after 1800 as it officially requires a private convoy (arranged through a travel agent).
Local Microbus: a cheap (50 pt) and easy way to get around town and to the Karnak Temple. Call out your destination to microbuses passing by. A popular route, Sharia Karnak–Sharia Mahatta–Sharia Televizion, includes the train station to Karnak temple.
Long distance Buses at 0830, 1030 and 1430 leave from Zanakta terminal, T095-232 3218, a 50 pt micro ride from the town centre or E£30 in a taxi. Buses leaving at 1630, 1830 and 1930 also depart from next to the railway station, before calling at the bus terminal. Reserve tickets in advance if possible, or buy at least 30 mins before departure. Currently, there is 1 bus daily to **Cairo** at 1830 (10 hrs, E£100). 1 bus daily to **Dahab** at 1630 (14-17 hrs, E£130) via **Sharm El-Sheikh** (13-16 hrs, E£120). 1 bus daily to **Port Said** at 1930, via the **Red Sea Coast** (E£75). 5 buses per day go to **Suez** (8 hrs, E£60-70) via **Qena** (1 hr, E£5) and **Hurghada** (4 hrs, E£35-45).

Cycle hire
Cheap and fairly roadworthy cycles can be found at plenty of budget hotels, and along Sharia Mahatta or Sharia Televizion for E£10-15 per day.

Motorcycle hire
Motorcycles (around E£100-150 per day) are available for hire from bike shops and hotels on the east bank, ask around or try the **Fontana** or **Everest** (T016-1331 5443) hotels. It is a fantastic way (probably the best) to head off and explore the west bank and gives you a chance to explore outlying areas of Luxor town.

Taxi
Local Taxis congregate around the train station and can easily be hailed from all major thoroughfares; E£5-10 around town; E£30-40 to the airport.
Long distance Private taxi: sample charges: E£325 direct to **Aswan**; E£350 round trip to **Dendara** and **Abydos**. To **Kharga** should cost a maximum of E£600.
Service taxi from the terminal just off Sharia El-Karnak, halfway between the Luxor town centre and Karnak temple, these are quicker and more convenient than trains or buses.

Train
Foreigners are technically restricted in their choice of trains, and you will not be allowed to pre-book tickets for the majority of trains (although you can just turn up at the station and pay on board). To **Cairo**, there is now only 2 'secure' trains, with a/c and restaurants on board, though a further 9 trains make the journey each day (the tourist office, opposite the station, has a list of the times). 1st/2nd-class trains to **Cairo** (10 hrs, E£167/90) leave daily at 2230 and 2330. If you are travelling as

a family or group, you can buy 4 seats (E£167 each) in a Nefertiti Cabin (which seats 6 privately) and the other 2 won't be sold. It is essential, particularly in the high winter season, to reserve your seat at the station a few days before you travel (it is possible to reserve up to 15 days in advance).

Privately run **sleeper** trains depart daily to **Cairo** at 1940, 2040 and 2230 (9-10 hrs, US$60 per person, US$45 children 4-9 yrs, payable in US$ or euro only). There is 1 daily 2nd-class direct train to **Alexandria** at 1530 (16 hrs) but it stops absolutely everywhere en route; better to take a train to Cairo and switch as trains run almost every hour between Alexandria and Cairo. 1st/2nd-class 'secure' trains to **Aswan** (3 hrs) leave daily at 0735, 0935, 1810 and stop in **Esna** (45 mins), **Edfu** (1½ hrs) and **Kom Ombo** (2 hrs). To get to **El-Quseir** or **Marsa Alam** it's best to take a train to **Qift** from where buses leave for the East Coast at 1100, 1430 and 1700 (on to El-Quseir, 2 hrs, E£15; Marsa Alam, 3 hrs, E£30). There are also regular service taxis from Qift, which you will have no problem boarding if you miss the bus.

Directory

East bank *p31, maps p36 and p46*

Immigration Passport Office: Sharia Khalid Ibn El-Walid, opposite Hotel Steinberger, T095-238 0885, visas extended, Sat-Thu, 0800-1500, come around 0900 to get a visa processed same day. **Medical services Hospital: General Hospital**, Corniche El-Nil, T095-237 2025. **Luxor International Hospital**, Sharia Televizion, T095-238 7192-4, best in town.

West bank and Theban Necropolis

On the west bank, depending on your interest, if you hire a car it takes a day to cover the major highlights or up to two full days to visit in its entirety. Obviously, it takes longer if you are on foot (using microbuses to get around where possible) or by bike. Although the west bank is dominated by the Theban Necropolis and the Valley of the Kings, there are also some fascinating temples and monuments above ground worth exploring, in particular the Ramesseum and Medinat Habu, which are not on the standard itineraries of large tour companies. In addition, the Tombs of the Nobles have fewer visitors but some of the most colourful and interesting paintings and they really shouldn't be missed.

Arriving in west bank and Theban Necropolis

Getting there and around

Direct road access from Luxor to the west bank is possible for coaches, minibuses and cars via the Nile Bridge, about 7 km south of town. It takes 30-40 minutes to get from the centre of Luxor to the Valley of the Kings via the bridge. The quicker and easier way for independent travellers to get to the west bank is by public ferry (E£1 for foreigners, 25 pt for Egyptians), which leaves from in front of Luxor temple. The ferry runs 24 hours a day, although you will be waiting a while for it to fill up if it's late at night. Alternatively, you can hire a private motorboat or *felucca* (E£5) to take you across.

Bike Bikes (E£15-20 per day) are readily available on the west bank, someone will probably offer you one on exiting the ferry or just head to the couple of hire places on the main street, past the minibus station. Or you can rent one on the east bank, where it's slightly cheaper, and take it on the ferry with you. It is probably the best way to see the west bank (apart from motorbike), allowing you to visit the major sites in a full-day and have time to relax as well. Be aware that it's a steady uphill gradient all the way to the Valley of the Kings, a bit tough and definitely not recommended in the thick of summer, though coming back down is a breeze. Guards at the various sights will keep an eye on your bike for you. You may want to offer a couple of pounds of *baksheesh* for the favour, but it's not strictly necessary.

Donkey Travelling by donkey can be memorable, if a bit hard on the bum. A short excursion is fun, but it is not a serious means of transport for sightseeing. It does afford some amazing views as you climb up to the Valley of the Kings. For a morning meander, expect to pay about E£50. It's best arranged through one of the budget hotels and usually involves taking the public ferry across the Nile and meeting your donkey there.

Organized tours Many tourists and travellers alike opt to explore the west bank with an organized tour. Most tours also include a certified guide who can elucidate some of the mysteries and secrets of the ancients and their civilization. In the summer, the pricier tours offer the respite of an air-conditioned coach. The disadvantage is that you're being trucked along with a herd of other folk and your time in each place is dependent on your guide and group rather than your own inclination. Tours can be booked from any of the countless

The singing colossus of Memnon

The northern gigantic sandstone colossus was broken off at the waist by the earthquake in 27 BC after which it was reputed to sing at dawn. This phenomenon, which was most likely caused by the wind or the expansion of the broken stone in the morning sunlight, attracted many visitors including the Roman emperors Hadrian in AD 130 and Septimus Severus (AD 193-211). The latter decided it should be repaired, after which it never sang again.

---

travel agents along the Corniche on the east bank (there is a dense handful near the Winter Palace, see Tour operators, page 56 for listings). For a tour of the west bank's highlights from a reputable travel agent expect to pay E£250-350 per person. West bank tours are also offered (sometimes aggressively) by virtually every budget and mid-range hotel in town, with transport in minibuses (generally not air conditioned). Cost fluctuates significantly with the season and is always negotiable. Aim to pay about E£150-200 per person (excluding tickets) for a guided tour of the highlights. If you want to hire a private guide, everyone has a brother who's a tour guide. Ask for leads at the tourist office or try your hotel, and make sure whoever you end up with is licensed.

Taxi If you want to see the sights at your own pace and have a ride, you can hire a taxi for a few hours. Rather than hailing one from the east bank, it's a lot cheaper and faster to take the public ferry across the Nile and pick one up from the landing. You will be bombarded with offers. Expect to pay about E£180 to be shuttled around the major sights for four to five hours, or E£50-60 to take in three sights (eg the Valley of the Kings, Deir El-Bahri and Medinat Habu). Bargain hard.

Walking If it's cool enough, walking around the west bank sights is just about feasible. Public transport, in the form of pickups or microbuses, can get you from the ferry to the main ticket booth for 50 pt. Except for the Valley of the Kings, which is 8 km from the Colossi by road, all main sights are within 3 km of the Colossi, which are about 1.6 km from the ferry landing. Getting back can be harder, and you might have to wait a while for a passing vehicle. It's tough to find a pickup that will get you all the way to the Valley of the Kings (unless it is early morning and the locals are on their way to work), but you could hire a taxi for that leg of the trip for E£15-20. Otherwise, it is a breathtaking walk over the mountain to the Valley of the Kings from Deir Al-Medina (one hour, take the stairs to the left of the car park for a steep ascent past the police post, then follow the track to the right) or from Hatshepsut's Temple (45 minutes, just head up the track behind the temple). Obviously this can be done in reverse, starting up the valley slopes above the tombs where would-be guides hang around and insist you'll get lost (you won't, dismiss them harshly if you are not interested). The walk is worth doing for the stunning views of the valley, tombs and temples.

Tickets and visiting information

Although 63 tombs have been discovered so far, many are closed to the public, some for restoration and others for rest. A system has been devised to reduce wear and tear on the more popular tombs – by closing them at intervals. The changes happen so often that the guards who work in the Valleys have a hard time keeping up. A list of open tombs is displayed by the ticket booth at the Visitor Centre. There are always at least 11-12 tombs

5 West Bank

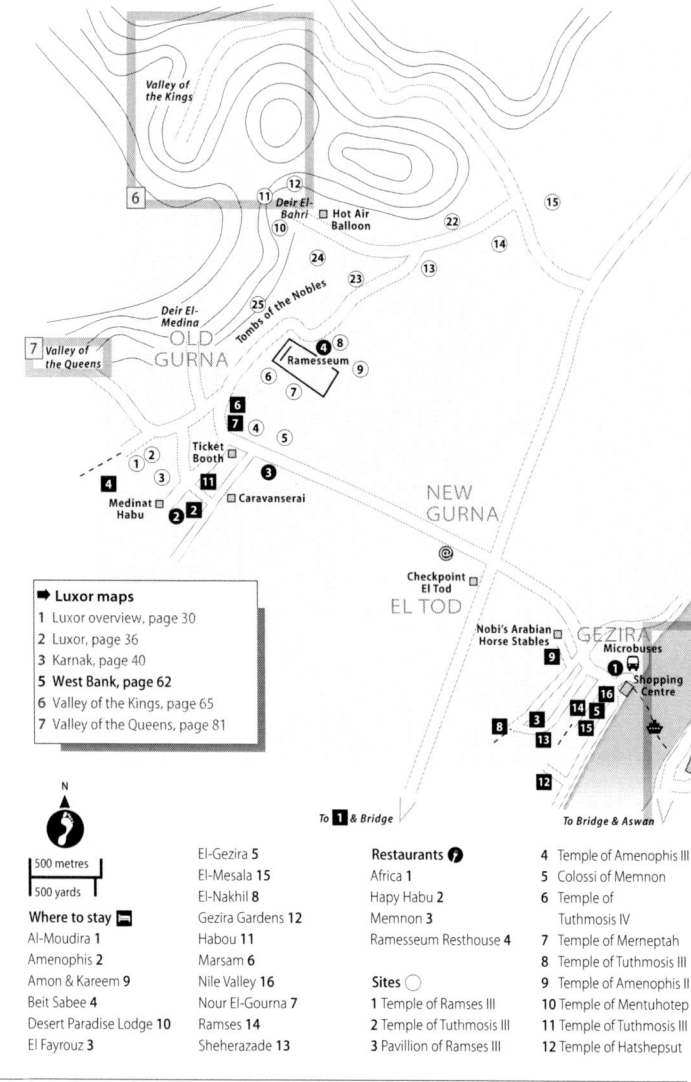

Luxor maps
1 Luxor overview, page 30
2 Luxor, page 36
3 Karnak, page 40
5 West Bank, page 62
6 Valley of the Kings, page 65
7 Valley of the Queens, page 81

Where to stay
Al-Moudira 1
Amenophis 2
Amon & Kareem 9
Beit Sabee 4
Desert Paradise Lodge 10
El Fayrouz 3
El-Gezira 5
El-Mesala 15
El-Nakhil 8
Gezira Gardens 12
Habou 11
Marsam 6
Nile Valley 16
Nour El-Gourna 7
Ramses 14
Sheherazade 13

Restaurants
Africa 1
Hapy Habu 2
Memnon 3
Ramesseum Resthouse 4

Sites
1 Temple of Ramses III
2 Temple of Tuthmosis III
3 Pavillion of Ramses III
4 Temple of Amenophis III
5 Colossi of Memnon
6 Temple of Tuthmosis IV
7 Temple of Merneptah
8 Temple of Tuthmosis III
9 Temple of Amenophis II
10 Temple of Mentuhotep
11 Temple of Tuthmosis III
12 Temple of Hatshepsut

62 • Luxor & around West bank & Theban Necropolis

open in the Valley of the Kings and three open in the Valley of the Queens. The Ministry of Tourism tries to ensure at least a few of the more remarkable tombs are always open. Expecting to see every single tomb and temple on the west bank is impractical unless you intend to visit every day for a week. If you don't have a guide and want to know which open tombs are most worth seeing, ask at the ticket booth. Make sure you bring a supply of water and snacks, as they are expensive around the sights.

Tickets to the Valley of the Kings, the Valley of the Queens, and Deir El-Bahri (Hatshepsut Temple) can all be bought outside the sites. Tickets for Tutankhamen's, Ramses VI's and Ay's tombs are also bought at the Valley of the Kings, though from a separate booth after the Visitor Centre. Tickets to everything else, including the Tombs of the Nobles, Deir El-Medina, Medinat Habu and the Ramesseum must be bought in advance at the 'old' ticket booth 200 m after the Colossi of Memnon. Booths are open from 0600-1600. Sites are open 0500-1600 winter, 0600-1700 summer. There are discounts for those with ISIC or ITIC cards of up to 50% to all sights, the last window at the old ticket booth is reserved for students. Photography of all sorts is prohibited inside all tombs. Note that flash photography can seriously damage the pigment in the tombs. Resist all temptation. There is no charge to see the Colossi of Memnon.

Tourists from cruise ships tend to congregate at the Valley of the Kings between 0700 and 1000, so avoid this period if at all possible. Lunchtime is definitely the quietest time, although it is the hottest time of the day it is recommended to time a visit for 1300-1400. It can't be stressed enough that the difference between a magical experience and one where you don't notice any tomb art because you are trying to survive being jostled by bus-loads of people hangs on what time you go.

13 Site of Ramesside Temple
14 Temple of Amenophis I & Ahmes Nefertari
15 Temple of Seti I
16 Great Temple of Amun
17 Temple of Montu
18 Temple of Ramses III
19 Temple of Amenophis II
20 Temple of Mut
21 Luxor Temple
22 Nobles' tombs at Dra'a Abul Naga
23 Nobles' tombs at El-Khokha
24 Nobles' tombs at El Asasif
25 Nobles' tombs at Sheik Abd El-Gurna

Luxor & around West bank & Theban Necropolis • 63

Theban Death Rites and the Book of the Dead

In order to fully appreciate the Theban Necropolis in the soft limestone hills opposite Luxor it is important to understand a little about the celebration and rituals of death in Ancient Egypt.

The *Book of the Dead* (see box, page 66) is the collective name given to the papyrus sheets that were included by the ancient Egyptians in their coffins. The sheets contained magic spells and small illustrations to assist the deceased in the journey through the underworld to afterlife. In total there are over 200 spells though no single papyrus contained them all. Some of the papyrus strips were specially commissioned but it was possible to buy ready-made collections with a space left for the relevant name.

Some of these spells came from the Pyramid texts. They were the oldest references to this passage from one life to the next. They were found on the walls of pyramids constructed during the fifth to seventh Dynasties (2494-2170 BC). Later the text and descriptions of the rituals that were involved were written on the actual coffins of commoners, not kings. The spells were written in vertical columns of hieratic script. Eventually lack of space on the sarcophagi led to only the ritual prayers and offerings being listed. When papyrus began to be used during the New Kingdom (1567-1085 BC) written texts were enclosed in the coffin and they became known as the *Book of the Dead*. Many copies of the writings, including the *Book of the Caverns* and the *Litany of Re*, were subsequently discovered.

The ancient Egyptians believed that at sunset the sun-god Re descended into the underworld and voyaged through the night before emerging at dawn to sail his barque across the heavens until sunset when the whole cycle began again. This journey was believed to be replicated by the dead pharaoh who descended through the underworld and whose heart, which was believed to be the centre of intelligence (see box, page 39), would be weighed in the Judgment of Osiris to determine whether or not he would be permitted to continue his journey to the afterlife.

The burial ceremony was elaborate with priests performing all the necessary rites, including sacrifices, in order to ensure that the deceased had a rapid passage to the next life. The tomb, together with everything the pharaoh might need, including slaves, was then closed, plastered over and stamped with the royal seal. In order to protect the royal tombs from graverobbers, they were fitted with false burial chambers and death-traps most of which, unfortunately, did not work.

Colossi of Memnon

These two gigantic sandstone colossi, which are located on the main road 1.6 km from the river 200 m before the 'old' ticket booth, represent Amenhotep III (1417-1379 BC). Although the faces and crowns have been eroded the two colossi make a strange spectacle seated in splendour on the edge of the fields and it's worth stopping on your way past. They are particularly mesmerising at dusk, when a couple of little eateries opposite provide the perfect spot for a sunset drink. The Colossi once stood in front of Amenhotep III's mortuary temple, which collapsed and was plundered for stone long ago. However, excavations begun in the last few years are now uncovering a wealth of statutory hidden beneath the earth. This temple site is strictly off-limits while work continues, but you can observe some of the megaliths from the roadside (many remain cloaked in protective sheeting).

Valley of the Kings

ⓘ *www.valleyofthekings.org, entry is E£80, students E£40, and gives you access to 3 tombs of your choosing, except for Tutankhamen's tomb, which costs E£100/50 extra (closed between 1300-1400) and Ramses VI's which is E£50/25. The visitor centre has film footage, running on a loop, showing the emptying of Tutankhamen's tomb and a scale model of the valley, which is quite useful for getting your bearings. Video cameras must be left in the cloakroom (free). The tuf-tuf train from here (cost E£4 per ride) saves the tiresome 300-m walk up the valley in the heat.*

Also known as Wadi Biban El-Muluk, the Valley of the Kings is one of many necropoli in the limestone hills on the west bank. The area first became a burial site during the New

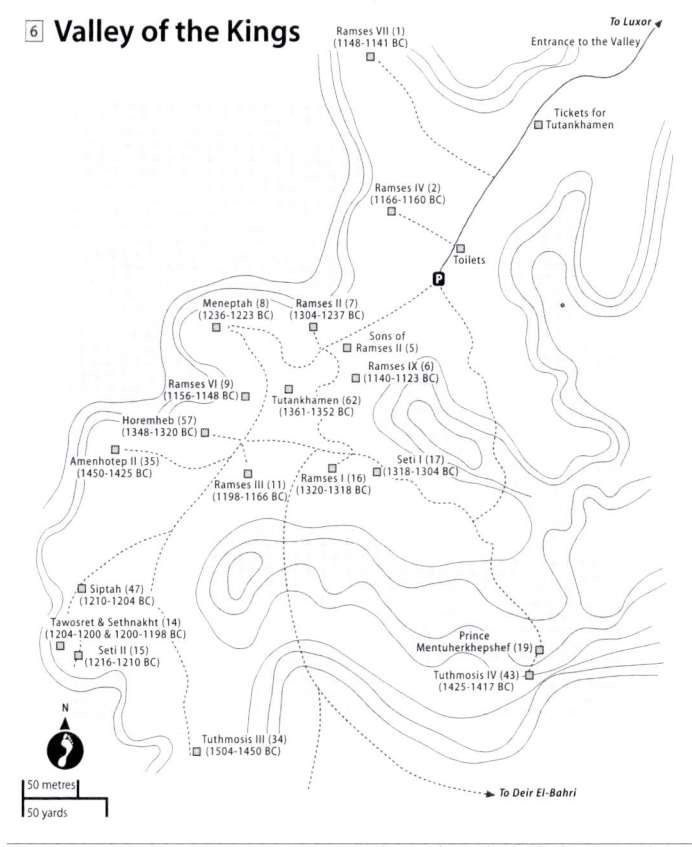

6 Valley of the Kings

Books of the afterlife

The Egyptians believed that the journey to the afterlife was through *Duat*, the underworld, and to combat the monsters and other evils there, a series of prayers and some magic spells were necessary. These were written in the *Book of the Dead*, which also contained a map of *Duat*.

Book of the Dead Called *The Book of Coming Forth by Day* by the Egyptians. This is a collection of mortuary texts, spells or magic formulas that were placed in tombs and intended to be of help in the next world. They are thought to have been compiled and perhaps edited during the 16th century BC. They included texts dating back to around 2000 BC (Coffin Texts) and 2400 BC (Pyramid Texts). Selected sections were copied on papyrus by scribes (illustrated versions cost more) and sold for inclusion in one's coffin. Many selections have been found and it is estimated that there were approximately 200 chapters. Extracts appear on many of the antechamber walls of the Ramessid tombs. Nearly 12 chapters are given over to special spells – to turn the deceased into any animal shape.

Book of Am-Duat Called *The Book of the Secret Chamber* by the Egyptians. It deals with the sun's journey through the underworld during the 12 hours of the night. Selections are found in many tombs. Full versions are inscribed on the walls of the burial chambers of Tuthmosis III and Amenhotep II.

Book of Gates Refers to the 12 gates that separate the hours of the night and first appears on tombs of the 18th Dynasty. The inscriptions in the tomb of Ramses VI give the most complete version. This has the same journeying theme as the *Book of Am-Duat* but the *Duat* is not comparable other than for the fact that is has 12 segments.

Book of Caverns A full version of this is found in the tomb of Ramses VI.

Litany of Re This deals with Re in all his 75 different forms.

Books of the Heavens Describes the passage of the sun through the 24 hours of the day and includes the *Book of the Day*, the *Book of Night* and the *Book of the Divine Cow*. These texts were first used during the New Kingdom and there are several pieces inscribed in the tomb of Ramses VI.

For further details refer to *The Ancient Egyptian Book of the Dead* by RO Faulkner.

Kingdom rule of Tuthmosis I (1525-1512 BC) in the hope that the tombs would be safe from looters. The kings' tombs are not actually confined to the single valley and it is believed that there may be others still waiting to be discovered. Those already discovered are numbered in the chronological order of their discovery rather than by location. Although some are simple and comparatively crude the best are incredibly well preserved, stunningly decorated and a testament to the intricate craftsmanship of the workers. Most of the discovered tombs are in the east valley but the Tomb of Ay in the west valley (Valley of the Monkeys) is worth a visit, see page 73.

The tombs generally follow two designs. The early 18th Dynasty (1567-1320 BC) tombs are a series of descending galleries followed by a well or rock pit that was intended both to collect any rain water and deter thieves. On the other side of the pit there were sealed offering chambers and then the rectangular burial chamber built at right angles to the descending galleries. The later tombs, from the late 18th to the 20th Dynasties

(1360-1085 BC), were built in the same way but the galleries and burial chambers were on the same axis, being cut horizontally but deeper, straight into the rock face.

Note There was obviously no need, originally, for light in the tombs and today the authorities maintain the lowest possible light levels. Take a torch, it will enable you to read this book, admire the outstanding wall decorations and illustrations, and avoid tripping on the uneven ground!

Ramses VII 1148-1141 BC (1)
This later style, single horizontal plane, and poorly preserved tomb lies in a small valley to the right after the entrance gate and is seldom visited by tourists. Above the outer door Ramses VII's names are displayed with a scabbard and disc. The walls are lined with scenes from the *Book of Gates*. The most interesting area is the Burial Chamber with its granite sarcophagus still in place. The picture on the ceiling portrays the constellations and calendar of feasts while the sky goddess Nut spans the area. The inner chamber contains scenes of Ramses making offerings to the gods.

Ramses IV 1166-1160 BC (2)
Nearer is the tomb of Ramses IV; although his huge sarcophagus was reburied in Amenhotep II's tomb by the priests, it has been returned. Do not be discouraged by the Coptic and Greek graffiti (note the saints with halos by the entrance on the right side) because the colours of the inner tomb are truly fantastic. The first two corridors contain poorly preserved reliefs of the *Litany of Re*, while the Hall and Burial Chamber are decorated with parts of the *Book of the Dead* and a golden Nut spans the bright blue ceiling. The sarcophagus lid shows Ramses IV protected by images of Isis and Nephthys and the pink granite sarcophagus is inscribed with magical texts. This is the only tomb for which the original plans, drawn on papyrus, still survive (now in the Turin Museum).

Prince Mentuherkhepshef (19)
Discovered by Belzoni in 1817 in the southeastern extremity of the east valley is a tomb that rarely receives visitors. Intended as a final resting place for a king (Ramses VIII) but truncated and occupied by Prince Mentuherkhepshef, one of the sons of Ramses IX, there is no burial chamber as such. The entrance is remarkable for its width (3.6 m), while the door jambs are decorated with serpents. The glass-covered walls of the 3-m-wide corridor each bear seven images of Prince Mentuherkhepshef making offerings to the gods, including Khonsu, Osiris and Ptah. The paintings, particularly of Prince Mentuherkhepshef although now rather damaged, are renowned for being among the most technically excellent in the Valley of the Kings and exhibit the Ramsesian school to great advantage. His wraps of linen clothing create transparent layers and he wears a forelock to signify his youth.

Tuthmosis IV 1425-1417 (43)
This large tomb was discovered in 1903 by Carter, but others had been there before and everything moveable had been taken. Many of the walls and pillars are undecorated and the impression is rather austere. The well room has scenes of Tuthmosis paying homage to to the gods and receiving the key of life from various deities including Hathor. The antechamber has illustrations of a similar theme and both have a ceiling of yellow stars on a dark blue sky.

Ramses IX 1140-1123 BC (6)

Immediately to the left of the barrier, this tomb is typical of the later long, deep style that became the established style by the end of the New Kingdom. The reliefs on the corridor walls depict Ramses before the gods and the four pillared Offerings Chamber leads to the richly decorated Burial Room, but the sarcophagus is missing. The ceiling in yellow on a dark blue background depicts a scene from the *Book of the Night* with jackals, watched by Nut, drawing the barque through the skies to the afterlife.

Meneptah 1236-1223 BC (8)

Set back against the cliff face on the other side of the road is a long steep 80-m tomb with a wonderfully preserved false Burial Chamber. The ceilings of the five corridors are decorated with flying vultures and other forbidding reliefs. Looters abandoned the sarcophagus lid here, which portrays scenes taken from the *Book of Gates* and the *Book of Am-Duat* similar to those in the antechamber. Steep steps lead down to the Burial Chamber where the rest of his pink granite sarcophagus lies, decorated with intricate designs from the *Book of Gates*. It is claimed that Meneptah was pharaoh during the time of the Exodus.

Ramses VI 1156-1148 BC (9)

Note – A separate entry ticket is required. The discovery of this tomb, which was usurped from his predecessor Ramses V and enlarged to become one of the longest in the valley, shed light on some aspects of pharaonic beliefs that were not previously understood. The corridor displays reliefs from unknown and long-since lost *Books*. Egyptologists were fascinated at their revelation of pharaonic concepts, more usually associated with India, of reincarnated birth into a new life. One does not, however, have to be an expert to appreciate the graphic designs and the colours beyond the graffiti drawings in the first two corridors.

The themes on the corridor ceilings are predominantly astronomical while the walls are largely devoted to the *Book of Gates* and the entire version of the *Book of Caverns*. In the Offerings Hall there is a relief of Ramses making libations before Osiris, while the pillars are devoted to the pharaoh making offerings to other gods including Amun. Descending deeper

Tomb of Ramses VI (9)

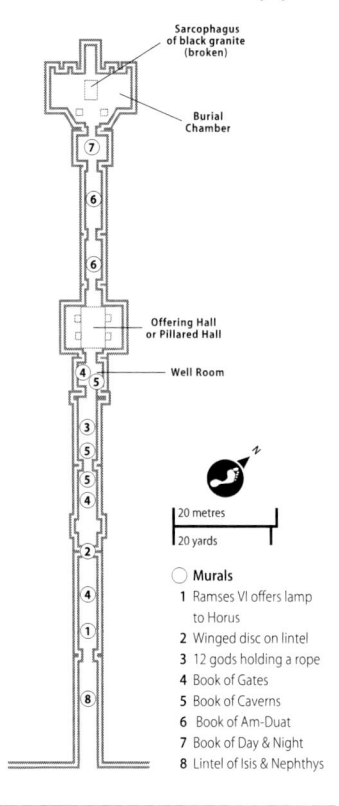

Murals
1. Ramses VI offers lamp to Horus
2. Winged disc on lintel
3. 12 gods holding a rope
4. Book of Gates
5. Book of Caverns
6. Book of Am-Duat
7. Book of Day & Night
8. Lintel of Isis & Nephthys

within the tomb, the passage leading to the Burial Chamber is guarded by serpents of Nekhbet, Neith, Meretseger and Selket. Further on illustrations from the *Book of the Dead* predominate. Just before the entrance to the Burial Chamber, cryptographic texts adorn the ceiling. Astronomical scenes from the *Book of Day* and the *Book of Night* cover the ceiling and the sky goddess Nut observes from above. The sarcophagus, shattered by grave robbers centuries ago, lies broken in the centre of the room.

Ramses III 1198-1166 BC (11)

Also known as 'Tomb of the Harpists', this particularly beautiful and exceptionally large tomb is unusual because, unlike those of most pharaohs, it contains scenes from everyday life. It was originally intended for Sethnakht (1200-1185 BC), but the angle of digging was such that it coincided with another tomb and was abandoned. Later Ramses III restarted the work by digging into the rock face from a different angle. The lintel with a disc and Re shown with a ram's head accompanied by Isis and Nephthys can be seen at the entrance. Ten side chambers, which were for storing objects that the pharaoh would require after his death, lead off from the entrance corridor. In the last on the left is the famed depiction of the two harpists, the lyrics of the song are carved into the entrance wall. The final section of the tomb is closed because of a collapsed ceiling.

Ramses I 1320-1318 BC (16)

Despite being the founder of the 19th Dynasty, his short reign meant that this Ramses did not merit a larger tomb but it still has beautifully ornate and sophisticated designs that are preserved on the blue-grey foundation. The granite sarcophagus in the burial chamber is decorated with yellow while the wall relief depicts scenes of the pharaoh with local deities and divisions from the *Book of Gates*. The eastern wall of the entrance corridor is decorated with 12 goddesses depicting the hours of the night. This is one tomb not to be missed if open when you visit.

Tomb of Tuthmosis III 1504-1450 BC (34)

Hidden away high up a side valley furthest from the main gate this is one of the oldest tombs, and its distinctive location makes it feel quite special and different. Though it is particularly stuffy and sweaty after the long ascent and descent, there is a pleasing spacious lightness to the chambers and its simple design is balanced by the interesting layout. After the second steep corridor, it veers sharply to the left into the antechamber. The walls here are lined with lists of 741 deities who are portrayed as tiny stick figures. The burial chamber, shaped, unusually, like a cartouche, is entered down a set of oval shaped steps. The walls here are dominated by sections of the *Book of Am-Duat* with an abridged version also inscribed on two pillars. Tuthmosis III is depicted on one of the pillars with his mother standing behind him in a boat. A beautiful carving of Nut, effectively embracing the mummified Tuthmosis with her outstretched arms, lines the inside of the red granite sarcophagus. His mummy is in the museum in Cairo.

Siptah 1210-1204 BC (47)

The interesting tomb of Siptah, a monarch of the late 19th Dynasty, was discovered by Edward Ayrton in 1905. The stair entry leads to a long corridor plastered and painted with formal scenes of the Litany of Re on the right and left, with images of Mut and a fine representation of Siptah before Re-Horakhte. The intermediate corridors leading, via the antechamber, to the Burial Chamber are undecorated. Inside the burial chamber are four rough-hewn pillars and a red granite sarcophagus bearing jackal and demon figures. The tomb was disturbed at one time – possibly during the 21st Dynasty – and the mummified body of Siptah was found in a cache of royal mummies in the tomb of Amenophis II (35) in 1898, the withered left foot of the King clearly visible.

Tawosret 1204-1200 and Sethnakht 1200-1198 BC (14)

Sited close by the tomb of Tuthmosis I, this is one of the longest (112 m) axial tunnels in the Valley of the Kings – belonging to Tawosret, wife of Seti II from the 19th Dynasty. The monument was taken over by Sethnakht, the first ruler of the 20th Dynasty, who lengthened the tomb and removed the remains of Tawosret, it is suggested, to the cache in Tomb KV35. The original ownership of the tomb is still apparent in the first corridor, with male deities bearing female designations, but many scenes of Tawosret before the gods were usurped by Sethnakht. In the barrel-domed burial chamber of Tawosret itself there are scenes from the *Book of the Dead*, the ceremony of the opening of the mouth and the *Book of the Gates*, together with a finely drawn scene of facets of the Sun God Re as a disc and ram-headed eagle from the *Book of the Caverns*. Beyond is the extended royal tomb of Sethnakht along broad corridors decorated with unpainted scenes from the *Book of the Secret Chamber*. In the blank burial chamber of Sethnakht his reconstructed granite sarcophagus lies in place.

Seti II 1216-1210 BC (15)

The tomb of Seti II has been open since antiquity. It was a hastily completed monument but is important in that it has a number of innovations that became standard practice in subsequent tomb building. The wall niches in the antechamber to the first pillared hall are much more pronounced than in earlier tombs while the entrance is cut into the hill face lacking the previously used wall and stairway. The burial chamber is crudely adapted from what was to have been a passage to a larger room that was never excavated. There are conventional decorations on the entrance doorway of Ma'at, the goddess of truth and beauty, and scenes from the *Litany of Re* are shown in a variety of reliefs on both the left hand wall of the first and second corridors. Beyond the first corridor the walls are unplastered and generally painted in an attractive but peremptory fashion. The antechamber has an unusual format of figures of deities among which the king is shown riding on a panther and hunting in a papyrus boat. In the pillared hall itself there are formal scenes from the *Book of the Gates* and above the damaged sarcophagus is a fine picture of Nut, goddess of the sky, with outreaching wings. The mummy of Seti II was among the kings found in the cache of royal mummies at the tomb of Amenophis II (**35**).

Amenhotep II 1450-1425 BC (35)

When this tomb, one of the deepest in the valley, was opened up again by Victor Loret in 1898 a trove of grisly and invaluable treasure was found. Here for once the tactics of building false chambers and sunken pits actually worked and the pharaoh's mummified body was found inside the sarcophagus, along with another nine royal mummies that had been removed from their original tombs for safety's sake. Amenhotep's mummy was originally kept in the tomb but after a nearby theft it was removed to the Egyptian

The curse of Tutankhamen

Tutankhamen's tomb's fame and mystery was enhanced by the fate of several of those who were directly connected with its discovery. The expedition's sponsor Lord Carnarvon, who had first opened the tomb with his chief archaeologist Howard Carter, died shortly afterwards in April 1923 from an infected mosquito bite. Howard Carter supposedly protected himself by not entering the tomb until he had performed an ancient ritual. A subsequent succession of bizarre deaths added weight to British novelist Marie Corelli's unproven claim that "dire punishment follows any intruder into the tomb". However, such alleged curses have done nothing to deter the tens of thousands of visitors who still visit the site despite the fact that most of the treasures are now in the Egyptian Museum.

Museum in Cairo. Ninety steep steps and a descending corridor lead into a pillared chamber where the tomb's axis shifts 90° to the left, after which the walls and ceiling are decorated. The ceiling is coloured blue with an astronomical star design in yellow and the walls delicately illustrated with passages from the *Book of the Secret Chamber*. Columns show pictures of the king with deities – Anubis, Hathor and Osiris. Further stairs (the air gets hotter and thicker with each one) and a short passage lead to the enormous two-level Burial Chamber. Amenhotep's sarcophagus sits in a sunken area with storage chambers around, the second on the right being where the cache of mummies was discovered. Look in particular for the beautiful image of Isis in sunk relief at the end of the decorative quartzite sarcophagus, still with its lid in place.

Horemheb 1348-1320 BC (57)

After the long, steep and undecorated descent is the Well Room where beautifully detailed reliefs begin. Colourful scenes portray General Horemheb who, despite lacking royal blood later became pharaoh, was the powerful regent behind Tutankhamen's short rule and leader of the Theban counter-revolution against Akhenaten's monotheistic religion. The scenes of Horemheb being introduced to the gods are repeated in the antechamber, which is dominated by the huge red granite sarcophagus. Point a torch inside the sarcophagus for a glance at some bones. Some guides suggest that the base black lines in the sanctuary indicate the first draft of the decorating, while the marks are corrections, as Horemheb died too young for the artists to finish.

Tutankhamen 1361-1352 BC (62)

The tomb owes its worldwide fame not to its size or decoration, being on the whole rather small and ordinary, but to the multitude of fabulous treasures that were revealed when it was opened in November 1922. Even the burial chamber is relatively limited in size, so when Carter broke through the rooms were crammed with an abundance of artefacts. In fact, the scale of the discovery was so vast that it took 10 years to fully remove, catalogue and photograph all of the 1700 pieces. Considering that the boy king reigned for a mere nine or 10 years and was a comparatively minor pharaoh, the lavish funeral objects found seem all the more extraordinary.

The 'lost' tomb

Explored and looted decades ago, dismissed as uninteresting by Egyptologists, and used as a dump for debris from the excavation of Tutankhamen's tomb, Tomb 5 in the Valley of the Kings was about to become a car park. However, the final exploration in May 1995 unearthed a major discovery, certainly the largest and most complex tomb ever found in Egypt and possibly the resting place of up to 50 sons of Ramses II. Excavations are expected to take at least another four years, but the tomb's unusual design is already apparent. Instead of plunging down into the steep hillside, Tomb 5 is more like an octopus with at least 62 chambers branching off from the central structure. There may be more chambers on a lower level and it is hoped that some of the mummies may still be entombed.

No treasure is expected: robbery of the tomb was documented as early as 1150 BC, but the elaborate carvings and inscriptions along with the thousands of artefacts littering the floor, including beads and fragments of jars used to store the organs of the deceased, nevertheless offer a wealth of information about the reign of one of ancient Egypt's most important kings.

Egyptologists have never before found a multiple burial of a pharaoh's children and in most cases have no idea what happened to them. This find thus raises the question of whether Ramses buried his children in a unique way or that archaeologists have overlooked a major type of royal tomb. And where are Ramses' dozens of daughters? Are they buried in a similar mausoleum, perhaps in the Valley of the Queens?

The short entrance corridor leads to four chambers but only the Burial Chamber, which is the second on the right, is decorated. Around the room from left to right glassed-in murals display Tutankhamen's coffin being moved to the shrine by mourners and officials after which his successor Ay (1352-1348 BC) performs the ceremony of the Opening of the Mouth and makes sacrifices to sky-goddess Nut. Tutankhamen is then embraced by Osiris and is followed by his black-wigged *Ka* or spirit. A scene from the *Book of Am-Duat* on the left-hand wall depicts the pharaoh's solar boat and sun-worshipping baboons. The quartzite sarcophagus is still in place, with its granite lid to one side, and inside the innermost solid-gold coffin, containing his mummified remains.

Seti I (17)

Seti I's is regarded as the most developed form of the tomb chambers in the Valley of the Kings. At some 120 m it is the longest, but it is permanently closed for conservation purposes since its decorations suffer from condensation produced by visitors. Throughout the tomb there are paintings/reliefs of fine workmanship on nearly every surface, though not all were completed. Seti's mummy can be viewed in the museum in Cairo while the sarcophagus is in Sir John Soane Museum in London.

Tomb of Ay

ⓘ *E£25, students E£15, you need a car to get there or by foot allow 2 hrs there and back.*
This monument **(23)** in the west valley dates from the 18th Dynasty and was opened up by Bellzoni in 1816, cleared by Schaden in 1972 and opened to the public in recent years. The entry shaft at first has a shallow incline but then after a second flight, steps become very steep. Flat shoes are a necessity here.

Ay (1352-1348) was the counsellor of Tutankhamen and his successor to the throne. The tomb had probably been built for King Tutankhamen but was incomplete at the time of his sudden death. Ay had no claims to royal descent and was not even high-ranking in the priesthood, but his tomb is celebrated for its unusual pharaonic hunting scene in the Burial Chamber.

Only the Burial Chamber is decorated but even here there has been extensive damage to the paintings and the roof is just rough-hewn rock without decoration. Throughout almost all of the tomb the cartouches have been defaced. On the entry wall to the left of the door is the famous hunting scene with the deceased shown clubbing birds and plucking reeds as if he was an ordinary being rather than a deity. On the north wall is a painting representing 12 baboons (hence the name Tomb of the Monkeys) or hours of the night from the *Book of the Secret Chamber*. On the west wall look for the image with Ay before the gods, including Osiris, Nut and Hathor. A well worked but slightly damaged boating scene is shown on the south wall above passages from the *Book of the Secret Chamber*. On the lintel area above the door to the canopic chamber is a fine representation of the four sons of Horus, which you will not see anywhere else in the Valley of the Kings. The sarcophagus, made out of quartzite and nicely tooled in reliefs of deities, was formerly in the museum in Cairo but was transported back to the tomb in 1994. Its lid is intact and there are wings of four goddesses – one at each corner, with wings protectively wrapped round the sarcophagus.

Howard Carter's House

ⓘ *Open 0600-1800 (-1700 in winter), entrance E£20, students E£10, T012-145 2501.*
The most famous of all Egyptian archaeologists lived on site when excavating in the Valley of the Kings, and his house, located by the entrance to the valley, has recently been opened as a museum. Information panels fill you in on the discovery and cataloguing of the tomb, while a 3D hologram of 'Carter' describing his work is a nice feature. Period furniture has been used to reconstruct his bedroom, darkroom, study and other rooms, and facsimiles of his notes and diaries lie around. There is also a lovely garden café, the perfect place for a rest, although it is very expensive.

Deir El-Bahri

ⓘ *E£30, students E£15, cameras and videos free of charge. A tuf-tuf train runs tourists to the temple for E£2, but it's a short walk.*
Meaning 'Northern Monastery' in Arabic, Deir El-Bahri derives its name from the fact that during the seventh century the Copts used the site as a monastery. It is now used as the name for both the magnificent **Mortuary Temple of Hatshepsut** and the surrounding area.

Howard Carter

Howard Carter was born at Swaffham in Great Britain in 1873. When he was only 17 years old he was taken on by the Archaeological Survey of Egypt under Flinders Petrie and became Inspector General of Antiquities in Upper Egypt in 1899 for the Antiquities Service. Carter was responsible for excavation of the Valley of the Kings and discovered the tombs of Hatshepsut and Tuthmosis IV in 1902 for the American Theodore Davis. After a dispute with Davis he moved to Saqqara in 1903 but then left the Archaeological Service to open a studio in Luxor where, in 1907, he met and began his archaeological association with the wealthy Earl of Carnarvon, whose own efforts at excavation had failed. When Theodore Davis gave up his concession to excavate in the Valley of the Kings in 1914, Carter, backed by the Earl of Carnarvon, took it up and continued digging, locating six more royal tombs. In 1922, Carter's last year of sponsorship by Lord Carnarvon, he came across a set of remains of workmen's houses built across a stairway to a tomb. Carter waited for Lord Carnarvon to arrive at the site and then dug away the remaining rubble to reveal the entrance to the Tomb of Tutankhamen. Eventually Carter's men cleared the way to the anteroom, which was full of interesting cloths, furniture and other materials. The burial chamber that Carter found was again packed with valuable objects but none more so than the gold-laden coffins and mummy of Tutankhamen. Carter remained at the site for a further 10 years supervising the cataloguing activity of so great a find. The nearby house that he lived in has recently been opened as a small museum. He died in London in 1939.

Howard Carter will always be known principally as the discoverer of the Tomb of Tutankhamen. But his imprint on Egyptology went far deeper. He was among the first archaeologists, following Flinders Petrie, to apply scientific principles to the recording of his excavations. Remarkably, the treasure trove of objects found in 1922 has still to be studied in full and, to Carter's great disappointment, there were in any case no parchments or manuscripts to explain historical events surrounding the boy king and the court politics of the day.

Queen Hatshepsut was not just the only female pharaoh to reign over ancient Egypt (1503-1482 BC) but also one of its most fascinating personalities. She was Tuthmosis I's daughter and was married to his successor Tuthmosis II but was widowed before she could bear a son. Rather than give up power to the son of one of her husband's minor wives she assumed the throne, first as regent for the infant Tuthmosis III but then as queen. Tuthmosis III, who later hugely expanded the Egyptian Kingdom and was the first imperialist, was only able to assume office when Hatshepsut died 21 years later in 1482 BC. He naturally resented her usurping his position and went on to remove all traces of her reign including her cartouches. Consequently the full truth about her reign and the temples she built both here and at Karnak was only fully appreciated by archaeologists relatively recently. As a woman she legitimized her rule by being depicted with the short kilt and the false beard worn by the male pharaohs.

Hatshepsut's imposing temple, which was only dug out of the sand in 1905, was designed and built in the Theban hills over an eight-year period by Senenmut who was her architect, steward, favourite courtier and possibly the father of her daughter Neferure. Against the rocky cliffs of the Theban hills, the stark clean planes of the terraces, surfaces and ramps appear as brand-new rather than just reconstructed – it is almost impossible to comprehend that the temple is 3500 years old. The temple's three rising terraces, the lower two of which were lined with fountains and myrrh trees, were originally linked to the Nile by an avenue of sphinxes that aligned exactly to Karnak. A pair of lions stood at the top and bottom of the ramp, which leads from the ground level terrace over the first colonnade to the large second terrace.

The scenes on the left-hand side of the first colonnade columns depict the transportation of the two obelisks from Aswan to Karnak temple. Behind its columns on the right-hand side is a relief in which Amun can be seen receiving an offering of four calves from Hatshepsut, whose face has been erased by her son. The original stairs from the second terrace to the second colonnade have now been replaced by a ramp. Hatshepsut's famous voyage to **Punt**, which was known as 'God's Land' by the ancient Egyptians, and various texts to Amun are depicted on the left-hand side of the second colonnade. Voyages to Punt, now believed to be modern-day Somalia, had been undertaken since the Old Kingdom in order to find the incense and myrrh that was required for temple rituals.

Further to the left is the **Chapel of Hathor** where the goddess is depicted both as a cow and as a human with cow's ears suckling Hatshepsut. This area is badly damaged because Tuthmosis removed most traces of Hatshepsut and later Akhenaten came along and erased Amun. The reliefs on the colonnade to the right-hand side of the ramp portray Hatshepsut's apparently divine conception and birth. She claimed that her father was the supreme god Amun who visited her mother Ahmose disguised as Tuthmosis I, just as Amenhotep III made similar claims later on (see Luxor Temple, page 34). Further to the right is the fluted colonnade and the colourfully decorated **Chapel of Anubis**, who is portrayed in the customary way as a man with a jackal mask, but the images of Hatshepsut are once again defaced. Note, however, the frieze of cobras, the colourful bird in the top left-hand corner and the bright blue starred ceiling.

Temple of Hatshepsut

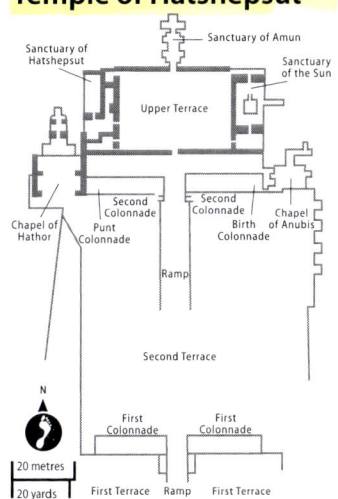

The ramp leading to the smaller and recently restored upper terrace is decorated with emblems of Upper and Lower Egypt with vultures' heads guarding the entrance. The columns were originally round, but were squared off by Tuthmosis III in an attempt to replace her name with his own and that of his father. Beyond the Osiride portico (a line of reconstructed statues of Hatshepsut in Osiride form) to the left is the **Sanctuary of Hatshepsut** with its enormous altar and to the right is the **Sanctuary of the Sun**. In the middle at the back of the whole temple is the **Sanctuary of Amun**, which is dug into the cliff-face and aligned with Hatshepshut's tomb in the Valley of the Kings on the other side of the hill. A huge granite doorway carved with hieroglyphs marks the entrance, but the area is cordoned off. A further burial chamber for Hatshepsut's lies underneath the Sanctuary, but it is unclear whether she was ever actually interred in either place.

Tombs of the Nobles

ⓘ *The tombs are divided into groups, a ticket to each group costs E£12. It's wise to bring a torch to look at shadowy corners and lots of small notes to offer as* baksheesh *(either to take advantage of a guard's knowledge or to be left alone).*

Nobles' tombs are found at a variety of sites throughout Egypt but none are better preserved than those on the west bank. While the pharaoh's tombs were hidden away in the Valley of the Kings and dug deep into the valley rock, those of the most important nobles were ostentatiously built at surface level overlooking the temples of Luxor and Karnak across the river. Their shrines were highly decorated but the poor quality limestone made carved reliefs impossible so the façades were painted on plaster. Freed from the restricted subject matter of the royal tombs, the artists and craftsmen dedicated less space to rituals from the Books and more to representations of everyday life and their impressions of the afterlife. Because, unlike the royal tombs, they were exposed to the elements many of the nobles' shrines have deteriorated badly over time. Although some were subsequently used as store rooms and even accommodation, others are still in relatively good condition and give a clear impression of how they must originally have looked. They are worth visiting for their wealth of vernacular paintings – quite as interesting as the formal sculptures of the great tombs of the Kings and Queens.

The most frequented are the tombs located in the area known as Sheikh Abd El-Gurna (commonly known simply as 'The Tombs of the Nobles'), where a ticket gains entry into three sets of tombs: **Ramoza (55)**, **Userhat (56)** and **Khaemhet (57)**; **Nakht (52)** and **Mena (69)**; and those of **Rekhmire (100)** and **Sennofer (96)**. Further tombs belonging to nobles are open for viewing at **El-Asasif**, **El-Khokhah** and **Dra'a Abul Naga**. The tombs of **Sennedjem**, **Peshdu** and **Inherkhau** are just above Deir El-Medina (see page 83), an archaeological site where the housing of the workmen on the west bank has been excavated.

Tomb of Ramoza (55)

Ramoza was Vizier and Governor of Thebes at the beginning of the Akhenaten's heretical rule in 1379 BC and the tomb illustrates the transition in style between the worship of Amun and Aten. The impressive and excellent workmanship of the shrine is probably because it was built by Ramoza's brother Amenhotep who was the chief of works at the family's home town of Memphis. Only the main columned hall can be entered, the inner hall and false sarcophagus area are separated off. This is one of the few tombs where the forecourt is still preserved and the central entrance leads into a broad columned hall. The tomb was carved out of solid limestone and all the decoration carved on polished rock. On the wall to the right are depictions of Ramoza with his wife and opposite on the back wall

Akhenaten and Nefertiti stand at their palace windows giving a golden chain to Ramoza. On the left-hand wall are scenes of Ramoza and his wife worshipping Osiris. Beyond is an undecorated inner hall with eight columns and the shrine at the far end. There is a second gap on the left of the end wall leading to the actual sarcophagus chamber. Within each hall are entrances to dark tunnels that end with a dangerous 15-m drop to the burial chamber.

Tomb of Userhat (56)

Userhat who, in the reign of Amenhotep II, was a royal tutor and scribe, was buried in a small tomb that was partially damaged by early Christian hermits. At the extremity of the outer hall on the left is a stela showing the purification by opening of the mouth. At the opposite end of this hall look out for the representation of the double python, a symbol of protection.
Note The interesting representation of rural life on the left on the way into the hall, the façade of the snake-headed harvest goddess Renehat on the right of the back wall, and a realistic hunting scene in the desert on the left of the inner hall.

Tomb of Khaemhet (57)

Khaemhet, another royal scribe and overseer of the granaries in the period of Amenhotep III in the 18th Dynasty, adopted a raised relief system for the carved and painted decoration of his tomb-chapel, which is worth seeing for its variety. The tomb is entered through a courtyard off which there two other blocked off tomb entrances. The Khaemhet tomb is made up of two transverse chambers joined by a wide passage. In the outer chamber there are rich reliefs depicting rural scenes, some of the originals now only to be seen in Berlin. The passage has funeral scenes and the voyage to Abydos, while both the transverse chambers have statue niches of Khaemhet and his family.

Tomb of Nakht (52)

Set in the entrance of the tomb is an interesting display including a plan of the tomb, sketches of the reliefs and a replica of the statue of Nakht. Unfortunately the original was lost in 1917 when the SS Arabia, which was transporting it to the USA, was torpedoed by the Germans in the Atlantic. Inside, the tomb is well lit and the decoration protected by glass screens.

Nakht was Tuthmosis IV's astronomer, vineyard keeper and chief of his granaries. He and his wife Tawi were buried in this small shrine with a well-preserved and colourful antechamber which depicts the harvest in intricate detail. On its west wall in the centre is a painting illustrating parts of Nakht's life together with the goddess of the west. On the left of the far wall is a depiction of a funeral banquet at which Nakht (the top half has been badly defaced), is shown seated beside his wife, a cat at his feet is eating a fish and he is being entertained by a blind harpist and beautiful dancing girls. Opposite is an unusual painting of peasants treading grapes while empty wine jars await filling. Here the ceiling is brightly decorated with designs representing woven mats. The marshland scenes on the right-hand (south-facing) section of the antechamber are exceptionally fine – the fish are wonderfully depicted. In the inner chamber there is a deep shaft leading to the inaccessible burial chamber.

Tomb of Mena (69)

This tomb has undergone restoration and, although Mena's eyes have been gouged out by rivals to prevent him seeing in the afterlife, the paintings are in good condition. He was an 18th Dynasty scribe or inspector of the estates in both Upper and Lower Egypt. On the end wall on the right-hand side of the outer hall is a depiction of a series of gods, notably Hathor and Isis. On the adjacent wall is a fine painting of Mena and his wife giving flowers. Opposite is a vignette of the younger members of the family making gifts to their father. In the left-hand limb of the outer hall note the depiction of Mena's wife in an elegant dress and jewellery as she stands with her husband before Osiris. In the inner hall there is a niche for a statue of Mena and his wife. In the inner hall, look out for the finely executed paintings of hunting and fishing scenes on the right-hand wall close to the statue niche, showing crocodiles, wild cats and fish. The brightly coloured ceilings represent woven cloth.

Tomb of Sennofer (96)

At the time of Amenhotep II (1450-1425 BC), Sennofer was, among other things, Mayor of Thebes, overseer of the granaries and gardens, and chief vintner. In the antechamber of this tomb there is an excellently clear set of diagrams etched on the glass showing the layout of the tomb and its decorations, accompanied by explanations. The ceiling is covered in illustrations of grapes and vines, thus the tomb is known as the 'Tomb of Vines'. Within the four-pillared hall Sennofer is shown making offerings to the deities and on his journey into the afterlife, accompanied by his wife Meryt. A double figure of the jackal-headed Anubis looks down on the whole chamber from above the entrance. There is a false door painted on the right-hand wall with the god Anubis and the goddess Isis. Facing the entrance arch look to the right for a depiction of Sennofer's wife, son and daughters. On the north (end) wall Sennofer and his wife cross to the west bank of the river by boat, accompanied by a funeral offering of wine, flowers and food. On the west wall are the goddess Hathor and Osiris in the dark colours of the dead. On the same wall to the left is the funeral furniture for use in the afterlife. Above, note the vultures with wings spread for protection of the tomb. On the pillars are formal representations of mummification, cleansing rites and offerings.

Tomb of Rekhmire (100)

This crucifix-shaped tomb should not be missed because its highly decorative paintings and inscriptions reveal some of the secrets of Ancient Egypt's judicial, taxation and foreign policy. Rekhmire, who came from a long line of viziers and governors, was the vizier at the time of Tuthmosis III's death in 1450 BC when he then served his successor Amenhotep II. Walking left or clockwise around the whole tomb from the entrance wall of the transverse corridor you can see: Egyptian taxes, Rekhmire being installed as vizier, foreign tributes being received from Punt, Crete, Nubia, Syria and Kush; then along the main corridor the inspection of the various workshops, the voyage to Abydos, the various gods of the dead, and the end niche that would have contained a statue of Rekhmire. The ceiling has deteriorated but some of the original plaster work remains, with a continuous line down the centre of the main north-pointing chamber. Look out too for the splendid marsh/woodland scene which, with a small lake and trees, has a warmth and realism that contrasts nicely with the formal and predictable decoration in praise of the gods (notably Osiris) and Tuthmosis III. On the way out along the other corridor wall are pictures of the afterworld and then, back in the transverse hall, illustrations of hunting and fowling, winemaking, Rakhmire's wives and ancestors, and finally more taxes being collected.

Tombs at El-Asasif

ⓘ *Between Deir El-Bahri and the Tombs of the Nobles are the El-Asasif tombs. Tickets are bought at the Deir El-Bahri ticket office, a ticket for the Asasif tombs, E£25, student E£15, gives entrance to Kheruef and Anch-hor's tombs and a separate ticket is required for Pasaba's tomb, E£25/15. The turn-off to the tombs is signed to the left, off the road to Deir El-Bahri, 100 m before the ticket office.*

Kheruef (192) Kheruef's, the Steward of Amenhoptep III's wife Queen Tiye, is one of few tombs at El-Asasif that survived the rapacious activities of tomb robbers, largely because it was filled with compacted debris. Added importance arises from its decoration, which is not only good quality but also unusually illustrates the festivals of the Jubilee, an affirmation of a king's power in the land towards the close of the 18th Dynasty.

The architecture of the tomb is sophisticated, with a short entry tunnel leading into a large open courtyard at the side of which is a four-pillared portico over a decorated wall. In the centre of the west wall there is an entrance (with locked gate) to the 30-pillared hall, where only one fluted column is left standing. This remnant does, however, give some idea of the original grandeur of this chamber before its ceiling collapsed. A doorway leads to an extension to an unfinished second hall, where two pillars are in place.

The decoration of the tomb is worth some attention. To the right, after the entrance under a picture of Amenhotep, are nine vignettes of nations conquered by the pharaoh, each representative of a different race and city. On the portico wall is a set of scenes of stick fighting, sports, dancing and men driving cattle as part of the festival of the pharaoh's jubilee in which Kheruef is keen to show his important role. At the left-hand end of the portico is another set of images showing the king and queen sailing at the end of the jubilee festival and decorated, large-scale figures of Amenhotep III and his queen. There are wonderful impressions of ladies clapping, musical instruments such as flutes being played, and ladies dancing during the jubilee celebrations – all very beautifully and graphically done. Look out for Nubian dancing ladies though the colouring is now faded. These figures are mainly on the bottom two registers, the high levels being scraped and broken and in very bad condition.

At the very end of the blue-ceilinged access tunnel to the pillared hall, on the right-hand side, is a large panel of the king and queen in a boat crossing to Abydos but it is badly damaged. On the right of the corridor, about 2-3 m from the end and about 1 m from ground, is a small cartoon in black of Sinmoôtè, one of the great craftsmen of the period, and it leads specialists to suspect that this area was used as a trial ground for the workers who built the main Hatshepsut temple.

Anch-hor (414) This 26th Dynasty tomb in El-Asasif was prepared for the chief steward of the divine votaress of Amun, and Overseer of Upper Egypt. A long flight of stairs leads down to a set of 10 rooms and an open courtyard. The main chamber has eight square columns and leads to a deep antechamber, and then to a small burial chamber with a niche in the west end. The engravings are uncoloured and often unfinished, but look out for a beautiful gazelle and a heron, plus a unique scene of the art of bee-keeping.

Pabasa (279) Nearer the entrance to Hatshepsut's Temple is the tomb of this 26th Dynasty official. On the lintel above the doorway is a relief of a barque, after which a hall leads to the pillared first court where six pillars are carved with scenes of daily life, such as catching birds, bee-keeping and fruit-picking. The granite sarcophagus of Pabasa is now in the Kelvingrove Art Gallery and Museum in Glasgow.

Tombs at El-Khokah

ⓘ There are some 60 tomb chapels from the Ramessid period at El-Khokha, about 500 m south of the El-Asasif tombs.

Nefersekhru (296) Nefersekhru, whose tomb was discovered in 1915 by Mond, was the scribe of the divine offerings of all of the gods. He married three wives who are all represented in the tomb.

Inside, the single chamber has a ceiling of highly coloured panels in geometric designs probably representing a carpet. To the south of the door on the entrance wall is a formal picture taken from the *Book of the Gates* and scenes of Nefersekhru before the deities. Beautiful paintings on the left of the back wall show the deceased sporting a leopard-skin outfit. The middle panel has three registers, of which the left one, which is more or less intact, shows a wife. Two things of which to take special note are the dominating image of Osiris, the king of the dead – sadly scarred – and the statues of Nefersekhru set in niches in the middle section.

On the right wall at the end is well-executed sculpture of two wives and the deceased sitting on a bench. On the back wall under a lintel is a scene of feasting with the deceased and one of his wives handing out gifts, including flowers, to visitors. There are agricultural scenes on the left-hand side of door on entry to the chamber.

The western side chamber leads to another Ramessid tomb chapel (**295**) of unknown ownership with a shaft in its north eastern extremity. The ceiling of this side room has a spectacular carpet design.

Neferrompet (178) This small but famous tomb temple to the Scribe of the Treasury lies to the right at the bottom of the stairs leading to Nefersekhru's tomb. Also discovered in 1915 by Mond, it dates from the time of Ramses the Great. Made up of two chambers joined by a narrow doorway, lighting in the tomb is good and the walls are protected by glass.

Decoration is typical of the Ramessid tomb type, and in both rooms the friezes portray Hathor's face and Anubis. The first hall has a ceiling with beautiful carpet-like paintings bearing geometrical designs with flowers. The most interesting decoration is a representation of 14 scenes from the *Book of the Gates* with Neferrompet and his wife drinking from the pool, a weighing scene led by Anubis, a harpist singing, and his wife playing draughts. She wears beautiful hair styles and attractive dresses – in places the garment appears so fine that the outline of her arm shows through the cloth. Look for the cat with a bone in the far left-hand corner.

In the second chamber are five panels showing adoration of the gods. There is a much-noted panel showing Neferrompet keeping a tally of offerings given to the temple, which is in excellent condition and illustrates life in the treasury at that time. On the end wall is a series of four statues cut from the rock and decorated, showing perhaps Mutemwia and daughters or possibly priestesses.

Tombs at Dra'a Abul Naga

ⓘ *Opened to the public in 1999, the tombs at Dra'a Abul Naga are about 1 km south of the El-Khokha tombs by road. Some 48 tombs from the 18th Dynasty have been located here, in valleys scattered over a wide area of the desert, of which 2 are open.*

Roy (255) This finely decorated tomb was prepared for Roy, the royal scribe and steward of the estates of Horemheb. It is one of the most beautiful of the all nobles' tombs with remarkable scenes and colouring still intact. The southern wall is decorated with ploughing scenes, flax-pulling and a funeral procession showing grieving friends and mourners led by Anubis. The northern wall is decorated by offering scenes and libations before the deceased and his wife. There is a niche containing stelae with the barque of Re adorned with baboons. On the left side, the deceased is worshipping Hathor in the form of a tree goddess with Ba (the soul) drinking. On the right Roy's wife is worshipping.

Shuroy (13) Also north of the road at Dra'a Abul Naga is the tomb of Shuroy, the head of the brazier bearers. The tomb is worth a visit since the entry chamber is brightly coloured with many scenes in a good state of preservation – as bright as the day they were drawn. The first hall is decorated with sketches of the deceased and his wife adoring divinities, and look on the right side for the gates decorated with demons. The door jambs of the second hall carry sketches of the Shuroy on the right and his wife on the left. The left side of the chamber is decorated with offerings-bearers and a funeral procession, including a child mourner before a mummy, and the deceased kneeling with braziers before Hathor on a mountain. On the right side there are scenes representing offering-bearers before the deceased and his wife and a banquet with clappers and bouquets.

Valley of the Queens

ⓘ *Nefertari's tomb is closed to the general public, due to the disintegration of the paintings as a result of exposure. It can only be viewed these days by VIPs or corporate groups, at enormous expense (E£20,000 plus E£100 per person). A visit to the other tombs in the valley costs E£35/20.*

The 'Valley of the Queens' is a bit of a misnomer, as it is in fact chiefly the burial site of the princes. It was originally known as the 'Place of Beauty' but is now called in Arabic the 'Gates of the Harem' (Biban El-Harem). It was used as a burial site for officials long before the queens and their offspring, who had previously been buried with their husbands,

7 Valley of the Queens

➡ **Luxor maps**
1 Luxor overview, page 30
5 West Bank, page 62
6 Valley of the Kings, page 65
7 Valley of the Queens, page 81

began to be buried here in the 19th Dynasty (1320-1200 BC). It contains more than 80 tombs but many are still unidentified. The tombs are generally quite simple with a long corridor, several antechambers branching off and the burial chamber at the end. The most famous tomb is that of Ramses II's wife Nefertari, the best preserved and most colourful of any tomb in any valley in Egypt. However, now that this is permanently closed except to VIPS and only three other tombs are open, the Valley of the Queens has fallen off most tour bus agendas. Which can make a visit refreshingly quiet, if you have the time, though the appeal of the tombs is certainly more subtle.

Prince Khaemweset (44)

Although the tomb is dedicated to one of Ramses III's young sons, who died of smallpox, it is dominated by the pharaoh himself. The reliefs depict the young boy being led to the underworld by his father who is offering sacrifices and helping his son through the judgement of Osiris to the Fields of Yaru. The side chambers are well preserved, with pastel colours beautiful against a chalk background, and the detail in their clothing (down to the patterns on their sandaled feet) quite exquisite.

Queen Titi (52)

Queen Titi was the daughter, wife and mother of a succession of 20th Dynasty pharaohs called Ramses, but it is uncertain to which one she was married. A corridor leads to a square shrine that branches into three antechambers with the badly preserved burial chamber on the left being dedicated to the four sons of Horus and Osiris. The central chamber features the Queen before the gods and the shrine is dominated by animal deities with pictures of jackals, baboons and guardian lions. The right-hand chamber depicts the tree goddess and Hathor as a cow (now defaced) rejuvenating the Queen with Nile water.

Prince Amun-Hir-Khopshef (55)

Prince Amun-Hir-Khopshef was the eldest son of Ramses III and, again, he died young, but this time possibly in battle at the age of nine. Descent to the tomb is via a stairway into the main hall from which there is a corridor to the burial chamber. The tomb is elaborately decorated with fine illustrations which remain in good condition. The scenes show excerpts from the *Book of the Gates* and Ramses III leading his son in a course around the stations of the gods. An oddity is the sarcophagus which contained the remains of a foetus, now displayed in a glass cabinet in one corner of the burial chamber.

Private tombs

Qurnat Murai

Amenhoptep (Huy) Amenhoptep (Huy) was the Viceroy of Kush in the reign of Tutankhamen. The tomb-chapel is cruciform with a transverse chamber and an incomplete inner chamber with four irregular pillars. The decoration of the transverse chamber is fascinating, showing Nubian royalty in procession delivering rings of gold to Tutankhamen, feathers adorn their bleached hair and they drive a chariot pulled by a cow. Almost all the worthwhile decorations are in the west wing of the transverse chamber, although sections of Hymn to Ptah occur in the small corridor between the two chambers.

Ramses The Great (1304-1237)

Known by the Egyptians as Ramses Al-Akbar (The Great), a name that would no doubt have pleased him, the achievements of Ramses II, arguably Ancient Egypt's most famous king, were majestic. During his 67-year reign, the pharaoh presided over an empire stretching west from present-day Libya to Iraq in the east, as far north as Turkey, and south into Sudan. While his military feats were suitably exaggerated for posterity in the monuments of his day, Ramses also engineered a peace treaty with Egypt's age-old northern rivals, the Hittites, by a strategic marriage to a daughter of the Hittite king in 1246 BC that ended years of unrest. The peace lasted for the rest of the pharaoh's lengthy reign. Ramses II is believed to be the pharaoh of the biblical 'exodus', although Egyptian records make no mention of dealings with Israelite slaves. His massive fallen statue at the Ramesseum inspired Shelley's romantic sonnet *Ozymandias*, a title taken from the Greek version of Ramses' coronation name *User-maat-re*. Egypt's most prolific pharaoh (siring at least 80 children), he was also a prodigious builder. He began building soon after ascending the throne at the age of 25, having discovered that the great temple his father Seti I had begun at Abydos was a shambles. During the rest of his reign he erected dozens of monuments including a temple to Osiris at Abydos, expansions of temples at Luxor and Karnak, and the awe-inspiring cliff temples at Abu Simbel. In an age when life expectancy was 40 years at most, Ramses, who lived to 92, must truly have appeared to be a god.

Deir El-Medina

ⓘ *Tickets available at the main ticket office, E£30, students E£15 for Sennedjem and Inherkhau tombs and the Hathor Temple, and note that there is a separate ticket for the tomb of Peshedu, E£15 student E£8. Cameras must be left outside the tombs.*

The original occupants of this village were the workers who excavated and decorated the tombs in the Valley of the Kings. The neat remains of the 18th-Dynasty town comprise a narrow street, in places little more than a metre wide, with the houses tightly packed on either side. The foundations show how small these dwellings were, and often they were subdivided, but remains of stairs indicate an upper storey and sometimes a cellar. Some houses were a little larger and contained a kitchen.

Above the site of Deir Al-Medina are three tombs open at present, those of Sennedjem, in the 19th Dynasty, Peshedu and Inherkhau, foreman of a construction team in the 20th Dynasty. All are beautifully preserved and have outstanding paintings. Normally guides are not allowed to conduct their groups into the comparatively small chambers, and relatively few visitors in any case makes it a worthwhile visit.

Sennedjem (217) Sennedjem's tomb was found undamaged in 1886 by Gaston Maspero, then head of the Antiquities Service. It is a small, simple, rectangular burial chamber, 6 m by 3 m, with narrow stairs leading into it – note the bare-breasted Mut on the underside of the lintel. On discovery it held intact the mummies of Sennedjem, his wife, son and two daughters-in-law, plus a handsome range of funeral materials – now unfortunately dispersed across the museums of the world. The wall decorations, protected by glass, are first-rate in style and condition, while the domed ceiling is wonderfully decorated with snakes, pictures of the gods and very fetching black and white cow. Clockwise round the chamber are hunting/forest scenes in the lower register and, above, a mummy on a bier with the goddesses Isis and Nephthys protecting it. Also look out for the priest who is clad in a wonderfully detailed leopard skin ensemble. On the side wall Sennedjem and his wife stand before the gods and, on the back wall is the masterpiece of the tomb: the body of Sennedjem lying on an ornamental bier being embalmed by Anubis. On the east wall is a painting of the barque of Re flanked by blue baboons and, below, a view of the afterworld (where the Nile seems to be the centre of life also). The south wall shows Sennedjem and his wife, Iyneferty, facing the Deities of the Gates, their frilly hair is just lovely. Of great appeal is the depiction of the tree of life on the ceiling, from which a goddess is appearing bearing an offering table.

Inherkhau (219) This is another brilliantly painted tomb, accessible down two steep flights of steps to a low-ceilinged anteroom with plastered walls bearing coloured paintings and a ceiling covered with abstract designs, now damaged by efflorescence and exfoliation of the limestone rock. An exit leads down steps under a low lintel to the main vaulted chamber, approximately 5 m by 2 m. On the left-hand side is a painting of a scarab an elegant stork, several Anubis, and a fine depiction of the family with hair left down in funeral form. Also, note the cat of Heliopolis (with the head of a ferocious hare) killing a serpent beneath the holy tree. At the north end, slightly damaged, is a full-scale representation of Inherkhau and his family with offerings. The right-hand side wall also carries more pictures of Inherkhau's family, the children naked and with hair curled round their ears to denote immaturity. The ceiling is vaulted and painted in bright ochre, yellow and gold, bearing cartouches and a detailed list of events in the life of Inherkhau.

Peshedu (3) A short toil uphill brings you to Peshedu's tomb, which is highly decorated and in very good condition. It celebrates the life of the 'servant in the place of truth' and is very light and airy, with the coloured scenes protected by transparent screens. It is entered down a very steep flight of stairs, with a low roof – beware. Eventually, an entrance leads into the first large chamber, which narrows down into a low gateway just 1.5 m high. This is where the wonderful decorations begin – all in good condition on panels on both sides with hieroglyphics above. On the sides of the entry corridor are images of Anubis lying on an altar. Within the burial chamber, the wealth of decoration begins above the doorway where the god Ptah-Sokaris is shown as a winged falcon under the eye of Horus. The two human figures are Peshedu on the right and his son on the left. Inside to the left the upper register shows a beautiful image of a female (probably the goddess of the sycamore) carrying water up the tree and below right are rows of Peshedu's attendants in fine detail. The long left-hand wall carries an image of Peshedu and his wife with two children standing before Horus with passages of *Book of the Dead* around them.

The right wall of the burial chamber shows Peshedu and his child before Re-Horakhte and three other gods. Surrounding these images are passages from the *Book of the Dead*. Inside the burial chamber to the left is the now famous scene of Peshedu beneath a date palm in fruit by the side of the water.

Hathor Temple The Ptolemaic Hathor Temple stands just to the north of the workers' village and gives its name, Deir El-Medina (Monastery of the Town) to the area, as in the early Christian era it was inhabited by monks. Dedicated to Maat and Hathor, whose head atop the square pillars still has blue painted hair, the temple is a peaceful spot. The three shrines to the rear are white-washed and colourful decoration remains on the depictions from the Book of the Dead. Ask if you can go on the roof, via the damaged stairway.

Other temples and sites

The Ramesseum
ⓘ *Tickets available at the main ticket office, E£25, students E£15.*

While most tourists confine themselves to the Valley of the Kings and Hatshepsut's temple, there are a number of other interesting west bank ruins closer to the river. Of these, among the most impressive was the Ramesseum, a 19th-century name for what was effectively a state cult-temple, on the opposite side of the road near the Tombs of the Nobles. Today, only scattered remains and faded reliefs are left of the great temple, which once stood there and reportedly rivalled the splendours of the temples at Abu Simbel. It is still an extremely worthwhile stop that fires the imagination and you will be alone but for the cooing and fluttering of the pigeons. There a sleepy little resthouse where you can get a cool drink, handily near the exit of the temple (see Restaurants, page 90).

Ramses II (1304-1237 BC) built this mortuary temple, on the consecrated site of Seti I's (1318-04 BC) much smaller but collapsing temple, in order to impress his subjects. But he failed to take into account the annual flooding of the Nile. The result was that this enormous tribute to Amun and himself was less eternal than he expected. The first two pylons collapsed and only a single colonnade remains of what would have been the **First Courtyard**. On its south side is a palace where Ramses stayed when he attended religious festivals on the west bank. In front of the ruins of the Second Pylon is the base of the enormous colossus of Ramses, which was originally over 17 m high but it is now much eroded and various parts of his anatomy are scattered throughout the world's museums. The forefinger alone measures more than 1 m in length. The upper part of the body crashed into the second court where the head and torso remain. Next to the three stairways leading to the Hypostyle Hall stood three smaller colossi stood but only a single fragmented one has stood the test of time.

Although it is now roofless, 29 of the original 48 columns still loom tall in the **Hypostyle Hall**. The centre of the roof would have been higher than the sides in order to allow shafts of sunlight to enter. To the left of the entrance is the famous relief of the Egyptian victory over the Hittite city of Dapur during the Battle of Kadesh. Around the base of the west walls some of Ramses' many sons are depicted. At the far end of the hall a central door leads into the Astronomical Room, renowned for its ceiling illustrated with the oldest-known 12-month calendar. Because the temple was dedicated to Amun it is thought to represent a solar year. Two other vestibules, a library and a linen room, lead to the ruined sanctuary, which is the temple's highest point.

Medinat Habu
ⓘ *Tickets available at the main ticket office, E£30, students E£15.*
The Mortuary Temple of Ramses III (1198-1166 BC), which lies west of the Colossi of Memnon at a place known in Arabic as **Medinat Habu**, was modelled on that built by his forefather Ramses II nearby. It is second only to Karnak in terms of its size and complexity and within the enormous enclosing walls are a palace, a Nilometer and several smaller shrines with some pre-dating the temple itself. When Thebes was threatened, as it was during the 20th Dynasty's Libyan invasions, the enclosing walls of the complex were large enough to shelter the entire population. The immensity of the structures that remain are still quite overwhelming and the temple is a true highlight, uncluttered by visitors and a good place to finish a day on the west bank as the sun goes down.

Although Ramses III named his temple the 'House of a Million Years', the smaller shrine that already occupied the site next to the south enclosure walls was in use long after the main temple shrine had fallen into disuse.

To the north, the **Small Temple**, which was constructed by Hatshepsut but later altered by Tuthmosis III who, as ever, erased her cartouche, was built on a platform from which there are good views in all directions. Until the 18th century a grove of acacia trees led to the Colossi of Memnon. The site, known as Jeser Ast or 'Sacred Place', was venerated because it was thought that the waters of chaos had divided and the primeval mound erupted here. During Akhenaten's rule, Amun's images were destroyed but they were later replaced by those of Horemheb and Seti I.

The whole temple complex is entered via the three-storey southeast gatehouse, which is built like a fortified Syrian pavilion and was originally 22 m high. Arriving through it into the large forecourt you can see the small temple to the right, the huge main temple directly ahead, and the small Chapels of the Votressess, dating from the 25th Dynasty (747-656 BC) kings of Kush, just to the left.

The remarkable homogeneity of the main temple's structure reflects the fact that it was designed and built by Ramses III alone rather than being expanded by successive pharaohs. The wonderfully preserved **First Pylon** was originally dedicated to Amun but was also used by Ramses II as a memorial to his Libyan and Asiatic campaigns. It would originally have been larger the one at Luxor, standing 27 m high and 65 m long, but now the north corner and cornice are missing. The images on the left of the Pylon show Ramses slaying Nubian prisoners watched by Amun and Ptah while Syrians are slain on the right. The illustrations are based on genuine wars Ramses III never actually fought either nation.

On the left of the entrance way through the First Pylon, before arriving in the great 48 x 34 m **First Court**, Ramses III is shown worshipping the deities Ptah, Osiris and Sokar. The west of the court is flanked by eight columns and the east by seven Osiride pillars. On the **Second Pylon** the pharaoh is depicted marching rows of prisoners, the third row being Philistines (or Palestinians) wearing feathered headdresses, towards Amun and Mut. The **Second Court** is also made up of a combination of Osiride pillars and columns, and here the intensity of the colours on pillars and on ceiling slabs are especially breathtaking and well-preserved. One scene depicts the Feast of Sokar while the lower register of the back wall is dedicated to the Ramses III's sons and daughters. At the far right end of the hall is a small entrance that has two interesting illustrations. One shows the pharaoh before Seth, but this was later defaced to change him into

Horus, while above the door Ramses is shown kneeling on the symbol of the united Upper and Lower Egypt.

The west door connects to the ruins of the severely damaged **Hypostyle Hall**. Above the door the pharaoh can again be seen kneeling over the symbol of Upper and Lower Egypt and at the base of the entry wall are 13 princesses and 10 princes. The central aisle of the hall would have been raised, in the same way as at Karnak, to allow Re's sunlight to enter.

A multitude of side rooms would originally have led off from the Hypostyle Hall but little now remains because of the severe damage caused by the major earthquake in 27 BC. The best-preserved room is the **Treasury** to the north where the walls are adorned with scenes of the pharaoh making offerings of gold to Amun. Another small room shows him wearing the Osiride symbols of the Atef feathered crown, a crook and flail.

The outer walls are better preserved and some of the reliefs are clearly visible. At the far end of the south wall is a calendar of religious feasts that is believed to be the longest such inscription. Further along is a portrayal of all the benefits with which Ramses III was blessed by Amun, while the rear west wall is dedicated to the pharaoh's victories in battle. In the northeast corner of the enclosure, near the Small Temple, is a small sacred lake where childless women came to bathe at night and pray to Isis that they might conceive. Close by stand the remains of the Nilometer that was originally fed by a canal that branched off from the Nile.

On a more modern theme – the **Monastery of St Theodore** lies to the southwest of the Temple of Medinat Habu and is within easy reach. The religious pictures are quite modern. Theodore was one of the many Christian soldiers who fell foul of Diocletian's oppression.

West bank and Theban Necropolis listings

For sleeping and eating price codes and other relevant information, see pages 11-15.

Where to stay

West bank *p60, map p62*
In recent years, several charming hotels have sprung up on the west bank. Though the area has a lot less action than the east bank, services are completely adequate and for people in search of a more tranquil Luxor experience it is an appealing place to be. Egyptophiles who return frequently to Luxor would not dream of staying anywhere else. The cheap public ferry makes transport across the Nile easy, and runs all night. Prices below include breakfast, unless stated otherwise. Most hotels don't offer TV in the rooms as they are aiming for a more rustic experience.
€€€€ Al-Moudira, Hagar Dabaiyya (5 km from the bridge), T012-325 1307, www.moudira.com. An Arabesque hotel that is palatial, exquisite and far away from everything except serenity. Built with natural materials, each unique room is furnished with antiques, equipped with full amenities and with a divine terrace. Bathrooms are lavish (particularly in the suites) while the pool (heated in winter), courtyards, restaurant and gardens are simply perfect. They can arrange pick-up from the airport (45 mins, E£100), Luxor downtown (E£70) or the ferry (E£30), as well as driver/guide for the sights. Free Wi-Fi in the lobby and a most tasteful gift shop. Probably the loveliest hotel in all Egypt, at prices that are below what you would expect for such a wonderful experience.
€€€ Desert Paradise Lodge, New Gabawy village, north of the Valley of the Kings, T095-231 3036/T016-997 7720, contact@desertparadiselodge.com. This

marvellous little enclave with Swiss-Egyptian owners has 10 raised rooms around a relaxing courtyard of trees. Each large, domed suite has a front and back door, Western-standard bathrooms and wooden furniture. 2 rooms on the upper level have a/c (others not, for environmental reasons) and enjoy a glorious sun terrace. The little pool, upstairs indoor lounge, and restaurant are very homely – it is just a shame that new housing surrounding them has encroached on the fabulous mountain views. Stay for 7 nights and get 1 night free.

€€€-€€ **Beit Sabee**, Medinat Habu, T010-632 4926, www.nourelnil.com. A beautiful traditional mud-brick house with glorious views of the Theban mountains and an outlook onto Medinat Habu (now sadly marred by the wall that the government has built to enclose the west bank sites). The 8 rooms are of varying sizes, very rustic-chic, all en suite with unique furnishings and colour schemes. Attracts a mix of nationalities and age-groups, there is a wonderful rooftop terrace, good-value vegetarian meals are possible, and they can help arrange transport and advise on interesting local excursions. This maison d'hotel is one of those special places.

€€ **Amon**, Gezira, T095-231 0912, www.amonhotel.com. The tropical garden is a major plus point, the restaurant pleasing and modern, balconies lovely, rooftop has loungers. Rooms are boring yet well furnished and feel homely. Single women travellers repeatedly recommend this place.

€€ **El Fayrouz Hotel**, Gezira El-Bairat, T095-231 2709, www.elfayrouz.com. This is a great hotel all round, but it's the secluded garden restaurant that really makes it (see Restaurants, page 90). Rooms are neutral with sizable baths, 1 roof terrace has Bedouin seating, staff are excelllent and free Wi-Fi. Conveniently located on the edge of Gezira El-Bairat village, singles/doubles are E£95/115 or (in the newer rooms, which are nicer and have a/c) it's E£150/180. Many guests have been coming back every year since they opened and wouldn't dream of staying anywhere else, which speaks for itself.

€€ **El Mesala Hotel**, Gezira, T012-351 4523, www.elmesalahotel.com. Opened in summer 2010, this hotel has 8 rooms, 2 suites and 1 flat, all with a/c, fridge and TV. 3 have excellent big balconies overlooking the Nile and Luxor Temple directly in front. Nicely furnished, the bathrooms are particularly good. Shady roof terrace and little front garden, all very well maintained (so far!). The owners (brothers) can help arrange apartments for those who want to spend a week or more on the west bank.

€€ **El-Nakhil Hotel**, Gezira El-Bairat, T095-231 3922, T012-382 1007. Beautiful spacious rooms have brick-domed ceilings, dark red walls and quality furnishings, lit by filigree lanterns, plus high-spec bathrooms (some with tubs). There is an air of peace and refinement throughout, a pleasant garden and Luxor Temple is visible from the rooftop restaurant. Far more chi-chi than other similarly priced options, there is also 1 room with disabled facilities and free Wi-Fi throughout. The only problem is the manager, who can be overbearing (especially with lone women) and you will need to be firm.

€€ **Gezira Gardens**, T095-231 2505, www.el-gezira.com. A well-established place that is of a good standard, the exterior is painted a cheerful white and blue though interior furnishings feel a bit dark and gloomy. Rooms have fridge, TV, a/c, balcony/terrace, plus 8 apartments (sleeping 4, €60). There's a good pool which outside guests can use for E£15, a nice bar and rooftop restaurant. Free Wi-Fi, internet E£15 per hr.

€€ **Kareem**, Gezira, T095-231 3530, www.hotelkareemlxr.com. A particularly clean and freshly decorated hotel with 12 rooms (4 more to come), some have a/c and most have balconies, but there are no fridges, TV or Wi-Fi (PC costs E£2 per 30 mins).

Wonderfully lush views from the shady rooftop (from where you can take dinner). Come here not for Egyptian atmosphere but for quality furnishings and a clean modern feel. Doubles E£210.

€€ Nile Valley, Gezira, T095-231 1477/ T012-796 4473, www.nilevalley.nl. Deservedly popular place, rooms here are bright white with touches of colour, nice new showers, daily cleaning, refurbishments are frequently carried out which keeps things fresh. Decent-sized pool (with bar stools in the water! Non-guests can use for E£50), the usual rooftop restaurant, as well as poolside and a/c dining. Upstairs rooms have balconies.

€€ Nour El-Gourna Hotel, Gurna, opposite the ticket office, T095-231 1430, T010-295812, www.nourelgournahotel.com. Mud-brick and simple, this small hotel is quite charming and has excellent food. The 7 rooms have spotless linens and rustic furnishings, 2 upstairs have balconies (and are more expensive), all are individual. There are views from the upstairs terrace to the Colossi of Memnon, and a village atmosphere. Internet is available (not Wi-Fi). No alcohol served.

€€ Sheherazade, Gezira, T010-611 5939, www.hotelsheherazade.com. There are 2 main differences at this hotel when compared to other west bank offerings: 1 being the extensive garden-restaurant which has actual grass, and the other the unusual architecture with domed public areas that soar to the sky. Garish paintings from the 1001 Nights adorn some walls, there is a honeymoon suite and private rooftop. They charge for Wi-Fi (E£10 per day), most rooms have a/c, the breakfast is superb, and the decor Egyptian.

€ Amenophis Hotel, near Medinat Habu Temple, T095-206 0078, husseinamonphis 17@yahoo.com. A good choice in the upper-budget category, doubles are E£150 and although they're not huge or atmospheric, they are certainly fresh and attractive with especially comfy beds and pillows. Go for a corner room at the front for great views of the fields stretching east and windows and balconies on 2 sides. The location near Medinat Habu is utterly peaceful and rural. They also have an apartment that sleeps 4 for E£300 per night. Free use of PC.

€ El-Gezira Hotel, Gezira, T/F095-231 0034, www.el-gezira.com. This popular hotel is a long-timer on the west bank scene, rooms are looking slightly dated but have fridges, a/c and balconies (on the upper level). Singles are E£100, doubles E£150. The sociable rooftop (where you can have dinner) and garden with water feature are a bonus, and they serve alcohol (beer E£12). They also own the Gezira Gardens nearer the river (see above), where El-Gezira guests can use the pool for free.

€ Habou Hotel, Medinat Habu, T095-231 1611, habouhotel@hotmail.com. Rooms are fairly basic with outside bathrooms, fans, no mossie nets – really it's just a bed with clean sheets. But the upstairs terrace views directly onto the 1st pylon of Medinat Habu at unbeatable (only worth staying on the upper level) and worth some discomfort. Internet available.

€ Marsam Hotel, Gurna, T095-237 2403, T010-3426471, marsam@africamail.com. Popular with archaeologists during the season, austere rooms have reed furniture and are cool, calm, dark retreats. The smaller rooms without bath are one of the cheapest deals on the west bank (single E£65, double E£130 with breakfast), there are also high-ceiling rooms with private bath (E£80/170). Unfortunately the pillows are rock hard, but otherwise all is perfect. The rooftop looks out over fields to the Colossi of Memnon or back to the hills and the garden is a shady relaxing place to be. Bikes are available for hire. An excellent choice with a very special atmosphere.

€ Ramses Hotel, Gezira, T/F095-231 2748, www.ramsesshotel.net, Good value rooms are somewhat garishly decked out but the colourful walls are attractive, all have a/c, TV and fridge (single E£80, double E£120, triple E£160). Tall building means great views from most balconies, there's a sun-deck above the rooftop restaurant, and nice patio out the front. Family-run.

Restaurants

West bank *p60, map p62*

A number of restaurants have sprung up on the west bank, and all the hotels have attractive roofs or gardens where you can dine.

€€ African Garden, opposite the ferry landing, T095-231 1488, T012-365 8722. Open 0800-2400. Serves up the standard Luxor menu of rice, salad, meat/fish and veg for E£35 in a delightful outside courtyard. Surrounded by fruit trees and mint that the friendly staff will pick to accompany your tea. As the menu differs somewhat for English speakers, if there's a local dish you want that you don't see, ask for it. Serves a good traditional Egyptian breakfast. Beer available. Good bathrooms.

€€ El Fayrouz Hotel, Gezira El-Bairat, T095-231 2709, www.elfayrouz.com. Sociable seating among flower and shrubs, varied menu to choose from, pizzas are particularly recommended although everything is reliably good. It's also a great place hang out and have a beer.

€€ Hapy Habu Restaurant, T095-206 0718. About 50 m beyond the entrance to Medinat Habu, this well-maintained little place offers a range of Western dishes as well Egyptian food – great when you fancy a pancake, quiche or light lunch rather than a hot rich stew. The location is idyllic and the garden terrace most relaxing. Recommended.

€€ Nour El Gourna Hotel & Restaurant, Old Gurna, opposite the ticket office, T095-231 1430, T010-295812, www.nourelgournahotel.com. Delicious tagines and stews come in substantial portions – in fact, it's a good idea to negotiate sharing 1 meal between 2. They can accommodate vegetarians, while meat eaters will be treated to duck and pigeon delicacies. A lovely spot under shady reed awnings, and the staff are extremely nice.

€€-€ Memnon Restaurant, next to the Colossi of Memnon, T012-327 8747. A good resting place for a chilled drink as the sun sets on the Colossi (though they might have to dash out on a motorbike to get more beer, it comes with an iced glass). The food is recommended by ex-pats who live on the west bank, with all sorts on offer from pasta to fish, plus great soups and salads (they pride themselves on their *fattoush*), all reasonably priced. You can't fault the view or the tiny flowery garden.

€€-€ Ramesseum Resthouse, by the entrance to the Ramesseum, is perfect for a post-temple drink either inside the cool interior or outside in the shade (beer E£15). Meals are good too, groups occasionally come at lunchtime. Owned by the Abdel Rasoul family – see the articles inside which feature the grandfather who was part of Howard Carter's team.

Shopping

West bank *p60, map p62*

For chic and well-selected items from Egypt and further afield head to **Heavenly Blue**, in the new shopping centre by the ferry, T016-634 7582, open daily 1000-2200. Ingeborg Unseld is an interior designer and her impeccable taste is evident: elegant clothes, great Ramadan lanterns, throws, bags, Lenhert & Landrock photos, and much more. She also showcases local artists and supports west bank craft initiatives. Just behind her shop is **Nour El Nil Boutique**, which has an eclectic selection of goods from the flea markets of Alexandria and Paris, alongside other quirky items from Egypt.

A good place to buy Egyptian handicrafts is **Caravanserai**, near Medinat Habu, T012-327 8771, www.caravanserai.luxor.com, where the owner Khairy sells glassware, pottery, Bedouin embroidery, ethnic jewellery and more. He tries to promote local village industries, in particular. Open daily 0800-2200.

Very worthwhile is a visit to **Balady Handicrafts**, Gurna, T010-543 6085, www.baladyhandicraft.com. A project started by a local family to find gainful employment for kids no longer allowed to tout postcards to tourists on the west bank. Children are trained in potting, weaving and embroidery (after school hours; you can see them at work from 0700-1330 and 1500-1700). The shop sells the attractive products of their labour; each pot carries the name of the child-artist, who receives payment accordingly.

What to do

West bank *p60, map p62*

Cycle hire
Cheap and fairly roadworthy cycles are available in Al-Gezira village on the west bank for slightly more than on the east bank.

Horse riding
Horse riding on west bank has become popular, usually passing through villages and some monuments towards the mountains (E£30 per hr). Camel and donkey excursions are also possible (E£30).
Try **Nobi's Arabian Horse Stables**, Al-Gezira, west bank, T095-231 0024, T010-504 8558, or **Pharaoh's Stables**, T095-231 2263; probably best to call in advance.

Tour operators
QEA, Al-Gezira, west bank, T095-231 1667, T010-294 3169, www.questforegyptian adventure.com. Tailor-made tours of Luxor's east or west banks (1 day) and further afield around Egypt.

Sohag to Dendara

An agricultural and university west bank city, 97 km south of Assiut on the widest point of the Nile, Sohag (pronounced 'Sohaj') has a large Coptic community among its 500,000 population. Although it has a few minor sites, it is not geared towards tourists (who used to be escorted by police on all excursions; this restriction has softened of late) but it does have the advantage of being relatively close to the beautiful temple at Abydos and within a half-day journey from Dendara. Bear in mind, though, that it's possible to visit both these sites on a day trip from Luxor. A new museum, due to open soon in Medinat Nasr, on the east bank right next to the Nile, will showcase the wealth of finds from Akhmim and the surrounding area. It is hoped that around 5000 artefacts will be displayed, including mummies. On the east bank of the Nile, across from Sohag proper, is the village of Akhmim where a towering statue of the ancient queen Meryut Amun was uncovered in 1981. A pleasant two- to three-hour trip can be made to the nearby Red and White monasteries, where exceptional paintings are being restored in the apse of the Red Monastery. Sohag itself is not an appealing city, nor particularly friendly. However, the *souk* is wonderfully authentic and worth a wander if you are in town.

Sohag → *For listings, see pages 100-102.*

The **tourist office** ① *T093-461 0093, Sat-Thu 0800-1400*, is on the first floor of the governorate building in Medinat Nasr, on the east bank near the bridge. They will help arrange a taxi to the monasteries and provide a couple of brochures, but English is not their strong point.

The White Monastery and the Red Monastery
① *6 km west of Sohag, a taxi costs E£40-50, with waiting time, for a visit to both monasteries. Entrance is free, open 24 hrs (supposedly).*

Deir Al-Abyad, the **White Monastery**, has light-coloured limestone walls and was founded in the fifth century by St Pjol although it is attributed to his nephew St Shenute, one of the most prominent figures in the history of the Coptic church. It once had a population of over 2000 monks but today only four permanent mendicants remain. St Shenute worked in the White and Red Monasteries for over 80 years – he is believed to have lived until well over 100 – and introduced both spiritual and social support for the local community as well as medical help. He documented a great deal of Coptic literature on papyri, using the Akhmimic dialect, some examples of which can be seen in the Coptic Museum in Cairo. Stone to build the monastery was brought from ancient sites nearby, especially Arthribis, and hieroglyphs and Hellenistic decoration can be seen engraved on blocks in the walls. The layout echoes that of a pharaonic temple, and in fact the imposing building resembles a temple more than a church. Remove your shoes before entering the soaring interior, which is divided with decorated columns into a central nave and two aisles. A faded image of Christ Pantokrator looks down from above. The three altars are dedicated to St Shenute (in the centre), St George and The Holy Virgin. It is possible to follow the stairs, from the left side of the central nave, to the upper level where the relics of a saint are shrouded in red behind a mashribiya screen. There is a *moulid* every July that climaxes on the 14th. Drinks, snacks and souvenirs can be bought at the shop within the monastery walls.

Three and a half kilometres to the north, on the edge of the village of Awlad Nusayr, is the smaller Deir Al-Ahmar, **Red Monastery,** founded in the mid-fifth century by St Bishoi, a disciple of Shenute. It is built of burnt red brick, hence the name and is said to have been the centre of a monastery of 3000 monks. The nave is open to the sky, with only the eastern end still roofed. The church of St Bishoi has some extraordinary frescoes inside the triconch sanctuary that are being painstakingly restored. The Italian-run project, which began in 2002, is due for completion very soon. Almost every interior surface is covered with paint, mostly dating from the fifth to 10th centuries, including the pillars that are decorated with floral and abstract patterns. As a millennium's worth of soot is removed, glorious images of the virgin and child and the apostles are being slowly revealed on the three apses. In particular, note the rare image of Mary suckling Jesus on the domed ceiling of the left-hand apse; below them, portraits of St Bishoi, St Shenute and St Pjol adorn the niches. Also look out for the images of deer and peacocks, and the pop-eyed rendition of St Basilicus on the far lower niche on the right-hand side.

Akhmim

Across the Nile from Sohag is the interesting ancient town of Akhmim once, though it seems unbelievable now, the capital of the Ninth Nome. Unfortunately, police desperately urge you to leave as soon as you have seen the designated sights and are reluctant to let you wander off down the enticing medieval laneways.

Here stands an imposing statue of **Queen Meryut Amun** ⓘ *daily 0800-1700, E£20, students E£10; if the fees seem a bit steep you can get a good view through the railings*, which was uncovered in 1981 when foundations were being dug for a school. At 11 m tall, she is the tallest statue discovered in Egypt of an ancient queen and was the daughter of Ramses II (who she also ended up marrying). In her left hand she carries a flail and the details of her wig, earrings and necklace are sharply sculpted. Across the road among chaotic excavations lies a massive but neglected and dusty bust of her father, with traces of paint on his headdress and a gorgeously intact beard. His seated legs lie nearby and give a sense of how colossal the complete figure would have been.

Akhmim also has a long and famed history as a centre of weaving going back to the time of the pharaohs, whose palaces were adorned by the fabrics created here while tradition holds that their shrouds were make of Akhmim silk. In the Coptic era, it remained the most prominent centre of weaving and during Roman times local turnips provided the purple hues that dyed the robes of the emperors. Some of this tradition is preserved by a weaving factory, opposite the entrance to Meryut Amun through the green gates, although the designs for sale are 1950s and created on mechanical looms. Fabulous vintage cars (*fuuljahs*) ply the route between Sohag and Akhmim, 50 pt to share (though it's hard to get a seat) or E£7 to hire the whole thing.

Abydos → *For listings, see pages 100-102.*

Getting to Abydos Most people come to Abydos on an organized trip from Luxor in a convoy. If you want to take public transport (and thus arrive alone rather than with masses of others on a fixed schedule) is possible to take a service taxi to the nearby village

The Nile ran red

As the story goes – Re, the sun-god, creator of all men and all things, began to grow old and the men he had so carefully created began to mock him. They criticized his appearance and even complained about his neglect of them. Re was angry at their lack of reverence due to his position; after all, he was their creator. He called a secret council of gods and goddesses (Geb, Shu, Tefnut, Nut and Hathor), where it was agreed that they would destroy all mankind.

The task of destruction was handed to Hathor, the daughter of Re. She seems to have been happy in her work, 'wading in blood' as the story goes. The gods realized, almost too late, that without the men the tasks on earth in the temples would not be performed. It was essential, therefore, to protect those who remained. The drug mandrake was mixed with freshly brewed beer and the blood of the already slain making 7000 vessels in all. This liquid was poured across the land (symbolic of the Nile floods) and Hathor, waking, mistook this liquid for blood, drank it all and was too stupefied to complete her gruesome task.

---

of El-Balyana, halfway between Sohag and Qena, from Sohag (one hour, E£2) or take a train to Qena from Luxor so the police don't stop you, and change there. The turn-off from El-Balyana to Abydos is marked by a police checkpoint, where officers will insist you take a private taxi the remaining 12 km southwest to the temple (E£10). You might want to negotiate a return trip with waiting time, so as not to be at the mercy of the taxis at the other end. If you then want to hire a private taxi on to Dendara, it costs around E£130-150.

Visiting Abydos Abydos is home to the stunning **Temple of Seti I** ⓘ *daily 0800-1700, E£30, students E£15*. It contains some of the most exquisitely carved reliefs of any monument in Egypt, and the detail in faces, jewellery and hairstyles can be utterly transfixing, particularly on the unpainted reliefs. Meanwhile, blocks of white light coming through the holes in the ceiling allow you to admire the extensive colours of ochre, turquoise, umber and colbalt still clinging to the interior walls. As the holiest town of all for the ancient Egyptians, pilgrims were making the journey to Abydos from the Seventh Dynasty (2181-2173 BC) until well into the Ptolemaic era (323-30 BC), and it is still a spiritual visit for many people.

It was the cult centre for **Osiris**, the god of the dead who was known as 'Lord of Abydos' because, according to legend, either his head or his whole body was buried at the site (see Temple of Isis, Aswan, page 128). Abydos, which looked out over the Western Desert, was considered the door to the afterlife. Initially, in order to achieve resurrection it was necessary to be buried at Abydos but the requirement was later changed to a simple pilgrimage and the gift of a commemorative stela. There are cemeteries and tombs scattered over a very wide area in Abydos but there are only a few buildings left standing that aren't too far apart: the Temple of Seti I, the Osirieon (Cenotaph) and the Temple of Ramses II.

The **Temple of Seti I** was constructed in fine white marble by Seti I (1318-1304 BC) as an offering in the same way that lesser mortals would come on a pilgrimage and make a gift of a stela. Most of the work on the temple and its convex bas-reliefs, among the most

Brick-making in Egypt

Sun-dried bricks were made from the dried Nile mud. This mud shrinks a great deal when it dries and has to be protected from the sun and the wind to prevent the brick collapsing even before it is used. To reduce the breakage rate the mud was mixed with chopped straw or reeds.

The Bible tells of the Israelites being forced to make bricks while in captivity in Egypt. Each brick-maker had a daily target with only whole bricks being counted. Making bricks without straw meant more journeys to collect mud as it was then the only ingredient and the bricks were fragile and more frequently broken.

---

beautiful of all New Kingdom buildings, was carried out by Seti I, but when he died his son Ramses II (1304-1237 BC) completed the courtyard and façade. This can be seen from the quality of workmanship, which changes from Seti I's beautiful bas-reliefs to Ramses II's much cheaper, quicker, and therefore cruder, sunken reliefs. It is unusual in being L-shaped rather than following the usual rectangle design and because it has seven separate chapels rather than a single one behind the hypostyle halls.

Temple of Seti I, Abydos

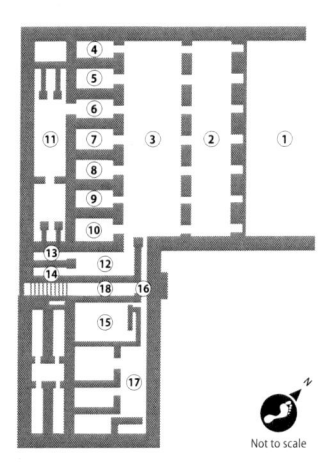

1 First & second court (destroyed)
2 First hypostyle hall
3 Second hypostyle hall
4 Chapel/Sanctuary of Horus
5 Chapel/Sanctuary of Isis
6 Chapel/Sanctuary of Osiris
7 Chapel/Sanctuary of Amun-Re
8 Chapel/Sanctuary of Re-Harakhiti
9 Chapel/Sanctuary of Ptah
10 Chapel/Sanctuary of Seti I
11 Suite of Osiris
12 Suite of Sokar & Nefertum
13 Chapel of Sokar
14 Chapel of Nefertum
15 Hall of the Books
16 Gallery of the Lists
17 Hall of Sacrifice
18 Corridor of the Bulls

The theme of the seven separate chapels is evident in the **First Hypostyle Hall**, built and decorated by Ramses II's second-rate craftsmen, where the columns with papyrus* capitals depict Ramses with the god represented in the corresponding sanctuary. In the much more impressive **Second Hypostyle Hall**, built by Seti, the first two rows of columns also have papyrus capitals but the last row have no capitals at all. On the right-hand wall Seti is pictured before Osiris and Horus who are pouring holy water from vases and making offerings in front of Osiris' shrine as five goddesses look on. The quality of the work in this hall contrasts sharply with the rougher decoration in the outer hall – probably because Ramses had ordered all the most skilled craftsmen to concentrate on his own temple.

Behind the inner hypostyle hall there are seven separate **sanctuaries** that are dedicated to the deified Seti I, the Osiris

Luxor & around Sohag to Dendara • 95

triad of Osiris, Isis and Horus, and the Amun triad of Amun, Mut and Khonsu. Many of the wonderful bas-reliefs are still coloured, which gives a good idea of the temple's original decoration, but some of the finest are unpainted and show the precision and great artistry used in the moulding. The sanctuary furthest to the left is dedicated to Seti and contains a beautiful scene of the Pharaoh being crowned by the goddess of Upper and Lower Egypt. His plaited sidelocks of hair symbolize childhood and are utterly beautiful.

Each of these sanctuaries would have contained the god's barque as well as his stela placed in front of a false door. The sanctuary was locked and only High Priests had access because the Ancient Egyptians believed that the gods lived in their sanctuaries. The daily rituals that were carried out included a sacrifice as well as the dressing and purification of the stelae. Unlike the others, the **Sanctuary of Osiris** does not have a false door at the back of the chapel but connects with the pillared **Suite of Osiris**. It is decorated with scenes from the Osiris myth and has three shrines on the west wall dedicated, with magnificent and incredibly vivid paintings, to Seti, Isis and Horus. The Mysteries of Osiris miracle play would have been performed in the hall and in the unfinished and partially destroyed Sanctuary of Osiris, which is reached through a narrow entrance on the opposite wall.

Back in the Second Hypostyle Hall the temple changes direction on the left-hand or southeast side with two entrances leading to a number of other halls. The nearest is the three-columned **Hall of Sokar and Nefertum**, northern deities subsequently integrated into the Osirian cult, with the separate **Chapel of Sokar** and **Chapel of Nefertum** at the back. Through the other entrance is the narrow star-decorated **Hall/Gallery of Ancestors/Lists** which, very usefully for archaeologists, lists in rows the names of the gods and 76 of Seti's predecessors although, for political reasons, some, such as Hatshepsut, Akhenaten and his heirs, are omitted. The gallery leads on to the **Hall of Barques** where the sacred boats were stored, the **Hall of Sacrifices** used as the slaughterhouse for the sacrifices, and other storerooms: they are currently closed to visitors. Instead it is best to follow the side **Corridor of the Bulls**, where Ramses II is shown lassoing a bull before the jackal-headed 'Opener of the Ways' Wepwawet on one side and driving four dappled calves towards Khonsu and Seti I on the other, before climbing the steps to the temple's rear door and the Osirieon.

The **Osirieon**, built earlier than the main temple and at water level, which has led to severe flooding, is sometimes called the Cenotaph of Seti I because it contains a sarcophagus. Although it was never used by Seti I, who is actually buried in the Valley of the Kings in Luxor (see page 65), it was built as a symbol of his closeness to Osiris. Many other pharaohs built similar 'fake' tombs, which were modelled on the tombs at Luxor, in Abydos but were eventually buried elsewhere. The Osirieon is the only remaining visible tomb but is unfortunately largely inaccessible because of the inundation of sand and the flooding caused by the rise in the water table.

The small **Temple of Ramses II** (accessed via the track to the right of Seti I's temple, someone will fetch the key), is naturally an anticlimax after the scale and sheer beauty of the Temple of Seti I. However, it was originally a very finely built shrine, erected in 1298 BC for Ramses' *Ka* or spirit in order to give him a close association with Osiris. The workmanship is better than in most of Ramses II's monuments because it was probably decorated by craftsmen trained in his father's era. Although the temple was reportedly almost intact when first seen by Napoleon's archaeologists, it has since fallen into ruin except for the lower parts of the limestone walls which are still surprisingly brightly coloured. Ramses' chunky feet and calves are all that remain of the statutory in the main courtyard.

Qena → *For listings, see pages 100-102.*

The town of Qena, just 58 km north of Luxor, despite being the provincial capital, is not very welcoming to foreign visitors. Services are lacking, and often unavailable to tourists. Though the town has undergone a makeover at the hands of a progressive governor (complete with rubbish bins), it's not particularly friendly and police escorts can't be dodged for long. The main reason for stopping in Qena is to see the magnificent temple at Dendara about 8 km from the centre of town but also worth a look if you make it here is the lovely Abdur Rahim mosque on the main road in town.

Arriving in Qena
Getting there and around From the train station, the adjacent bus station and the southbound service taxi depot, on either side of the main canal, Sharia El-Gumhoriyya leads southeast to a major roundabout and the town's main street, to the west end of which is the northbound service taxi depot, near the River Nile. To get to Dendara from the centre of Qena, tourist police generally insist that independent travellers hire a private taxi to take them to the temple and back. If you can dodge security, service taxi pickups (50 pt) bound for Dendara converge at a depot by the large intersection near the Nile. ▶▶ *See Transport, page 102.*

Dendara
ⓘ *Summer 0700-1800, winter 0700-1700 but they stop admitting visitors an hour before closing time, E£35, students E£20, use of cameras and video recorders free.*

Dendara was the cult centre of Hathor from pre-dynastic times and there are signs of earlier buildings on the site dating back to Cheops in the Fourth Dynasty (2613-2494 BC). Hathor, represented as a cow or cow-headed woman, was the goddess associated with love, joy, music, protection of the dead and, above all, of nurturing. Her great popularity was demonstrated by the huge festival held at Edfu when her barque symbolically sailed upstream on her annual visit to Horus to whom she was both wet-nurse and lover. As they reconsummated their union the population indulged in the Festival of Drunkenness, which led the Greeks to identify Hathor with Aphrodite who was their own goddess of love and joy.

The **Temple of Hathor**, built between 125 BC and AD 60 by the Ptolemies and the Romans, is the latest temple on a site begun by Pepi I in the Sixth Dynasty (2345-2181 BC). The enclosing wall around the temple is of unbaked bricks laid alternately convex and concave, like waves of a primeval ocean – an extraordinary sight in itself. The huge, well-preserved temple dominates the walled Dendara complex which also includes a number of smaller buildings. Even though it was built by non-Egyptian foreign conquerors it copies the earlier pharaonic temples with large hypostyle halls leading up, via a series of successively smaller vestibules and storerooms, to the sanctuary at the back of the temple. There are also two sets of steps leading up to and down from the roof sanctuaries.

At the front, the pylon-shaped façade is supported by six huge Hathor-headed columns with blue painted headdresses, and reliefs showing the Roman emperors

Tiberius and Claudius performing rituals with the gods. Through in the **Hypostyle Hall** there are 18 Hathor-headed columns, capitals of which are sistra-rattles associated with music and dance. The magnificent ceiling, which is illustrated with an astronomical theme showing the mystical significance of the sky, has retained much of its original colour. It is divided between day and night and illustrates the 14 days' moon cycle, the gods of the four cardinal points, the constellations, the zodiac, and the elongated goddess Nut who swallows the sun at sunset and gives birth to it at dawn. It is currently being restored and is, therefore, slightly obscured by scaffolding; intense blue and white colours are being revealed.

The next room, which is known as the **Hall of Appearances** and is supported by six columns, is where the goddess appeared from the depths of the temple as she was transported on her ritual barque for the annual voyage to Edfu. On either side of the doorway there are scenes of offerings and the presentation of the temple to the gods.

Around this Hall are six small rooms (all lit by sunlight from holes in the roof). The first on the left was the laboratory, used for the preparation of balms and the nine oils used to anoint the statues. It has several inscriptions, with the recipes and instructions for their preparation. The next two rooms were used as store-rooms for offerings such as flowers, beer, wine and poultry. The second room, called the Nile Room, has an exit to the back corridor and the well outside. Next is the first vestibule, which was known as the **Hall of Offerings** because it was there that the priests displayed the offerings for the goddess on large tables. The food and drink was then divided among the priests once the gods had savoured them. On the left a stairway leads to the roof sanctuary. The second vestibule, called the **Hall of the Ennead**, contained the statues of the kings and gods that were involved in the ceremonies for Hathor while her wardrobe was stored in the room on the left. This leads on to the **Sanctuary of the Golden One**, which contained Hathor's statue and her

Temple at Dendara

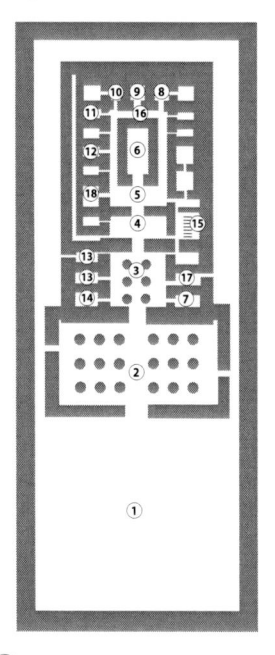

N
Not to scale

1 Court
2 Pronaos/First Hypostyle Hall
3 Second Hypostyle Hall/ Hall of Appearances
4 First Vestibule/ Hall of Offerings
5 Second Vestibule/ Hall of Ennead
6 Sanctuary of the Golden One
7 Treasury
8 Per-Neser Chapel/ House of Flame
9 Per-Ur Chapel/ Shrine of Egypt
10 Per-Nu Chapel
11 Sacred Serpent
12 Seat of Repose
13 Harvest Rooms
14 Laboratory
15 Stairs to roof
16 Stairs to crypts
17 Nile Room
18 Hathor's Wardrobe

ceremonial barque that was carried to the river each New Year to be transported on a boat upstream to the Temple of Horus at Edfu. The south and north walls of the independently roofed sanctuary depict the pharaoh in various phases of the ceremony. The so-called **Corridor of Mysteries** around the outside of the sanctuary has nine doors that lead to 11 small shrines with 32 crypts, including the crypt where the temple's valuables would have been stored. Make sure to enter the **Per-Neser Chapel** where a trapdoor gives access to one of these crypts, consisting of a two-pronged corridor covered with delicate carvings.

The walls of the stairway from the left of the Hall of Offerings to the **Roof Sanctuaries** (which, unlike anywhere else, have been completely preserved), depict the New Year ceremony when the statue of Hathor was carried up to the roof to the small open **Chapel of the Union with the Disk** to await the sunrise. The scenes on the left of the stairs represent Hathor going up while those on the right show her returning down. In the northwest corner of the roof terrace is **Osiris' Tomb**, where ceremonies commemorating Osiris' death and resurrection were carried out. In the east corner there are two rooms with the outer one containing a blackened plaster-cast copy of the original **Dendara Zodiac** ceiling that was stolen and taken to the Louvre in Paris in 1820. The Zodiac was introduced to Egypt by the Romans and, although Scorpio's scorpion is replaced by a scarab beetle and the hippo-goddess Tweri was added, this circular zodiac held up by four goddesses is virtually identical to the one used today.

The views from the uppermost level of the roof terrace are superb, however the area is now cordoned off since an American tourist toppled over the side when taking a photograph a few years ago. However, if you express enough interest and there aren't any other people around, police/guardians may allow you up. From the roof, the overall scale and layout of the temple buildings, the extensive outer walls and the intensively cultivated countryside surrounding Dendara can really be appreciated. From the northern edge of the upper terrace there are good views looking down on to the sanatorium, the two birth houses and the Coptic basilica (see below).

Back downstairs and outside the temple, on the exterior south wall, there are two giant damaged reliefs depicting Cleopatra (the only surviving relief depicting Cleopatra VII in the whole of Egypt) and her son Caesarion, and beyond a number of small ruined buildings surrounding the main temple. At the back is the **Temple of Isis** that was almost totally destroyed by the early Christians because of the fear that the worship of Isis as the universal Egyptian goddess might spread (a custodian will appear to magically open up the two rooms). At the front of the main temple to the right is the **Roman Birth House**, or Mammisi, which has some particularly beautiful carvings covering its façade and south walls. The **Sanatorium**, between the Mammisi and the main temple, was where pilgrims who came to Dendara to be healed by Hathor were treated and washed in water from the sunken stone-lined **Sacred Lake**, now drained of water and with date palms poking out the top. Between the two birth-houses is a ruined fifth-century **Coptic Basilica**, one of the earliest Coptic buildings in Egypt, which was built using stone from the adjacent buildings.

⊙ Sohag to Dendara listings

For sleeping and eating price codes and other relevant information, see pages 11-15.

Where to stay

Sohag *p92*

Sohag is not a particularly appealing town and sees few foreigners, but it's recommended to phone ahead as hotels are tend to be very busy.

€€€€-€€€ Hotp Hotel, Medinat Nasr (on the east bank), T019-992 7332/3. By far the swankiest choice in Sohag, the Hotp (or 'Hotep') is a cruise boat permanently moored on the east bank of the Nile. Unfortunately, a bridge dominates the view, but the 48 rooms (doubles US$130) are attractively furnished in a modish style with black wood, bright fabrics and modern facilities. Bathrooms are tiny, as you would expect on a boat, but most rooms are quite spacious (except for the standard singles, US$70). Suites (US$180) are very similar to the doubles and not worth the extra money.

€€ Al-Safa Hotel, on the west bank 1 km north of the station, T093-230 7701. Western-style clean rooms, those at the rear have balconies overlooking the Nile, with TV, a/c and fridge. Nothing spectacular but comfortable and not bad value, has popular patio coffeeshop by the water, decent restaurant and good breakfast is included. Free Wi-Fi.

€€ Nile Hotel, Medinat Nasr (on the east bank), T093-460 6253-5. Sohag's newest hotel (they are still building the upper storeys) has an ornate exterior, spacious public areas and decent rooms with the amenities you would expect for the price (single E£200, double E£300). Furniture is a bit dark and they have a propensity to cover the light wood floors with unattractive rugs, but the rooms with balconies to the Nile are pleasant as is the riverside garden coffeeshop. The restaurant is very reasonable. Breakfast included.

€ Andalos, opposite the train station, T093-233 4328. Rooms are clean with private bath, hot water, towels and soap. Noisy, but still the best choice near the station. The manager is nice, with limited English.

€ Cazalovy Hotel, on the east bank, T093-460 1185. Includes breakfast, but rooms could be cleaner.

€ Merit Amoun Hotel, on the east bank, T093-460 1985. 30 rooms, being renovated at the time of writing so should be a better alternative.

€ Sara Plaza, no English sign, it's the tall orange and blue building with a neon sign on top, to the left on exiting the train station. Fairly sanitary rooms have a/c and private bath, breakfast included. Hot water is not reliable, but quite quiet because rooms are so high up.

€ Youth hostel, 7 Sharia Port Said 1.5 km from station, T093-232 4395. Not much English spoken, a bed is E£15. Parking.

Abydos *p93*

It is possible to stay close by the temple at Abydos if you want to imbibe some of Seti I's spirit and its promised 'high energy'.

€€ House of the Companions, to the right of Ramses II's temple, T010-331 2188 (Amir). Large airy rooms for rent with all meals included, singles E£150 or doubles E£240. Various healing, meditation and purification programmes are available. Worth phoning ahead, there is a genuinely intense atmosphere and you get to experience the beauty of the temple at all hours if you can deal with a dose of mumbo-jumbo.

Qena *p97*

Visitors are discouraged from staying in Qena, not so much by the police these days but more by the poor choice of hotels. If you are determined, the best bet is:

€ New Palace, Midan Mahata, Qena, T096-532 2509. 75 rooms, far from palatial, it's still the best of the options. Rooms are overpriced and depressing, but clean enough, all have TV and some have balcony. With a/c, en-suite and breakfast, singles are E£120, doubles E£150, or with a/c, shared bath and no breakfast E£80/100 (women won't be enamoured by these bathrooms, which have urinals in). There are also 5 small singles with en-suite but no a/c for E£60. Staff are kindly. Located behind the Mobil garage near the train station.

Restaurants

Sohag *p92*

Finding decent food is an issue in Sohag.
€€ Nile Hotel, the restaurant is quite pleasant and meals are very reasonably priced, with grills, chicken, fish and plenty of salads and soup.
€€ Safa hotel has a pretty decent restaurant and serves up good fish soup.

There's also a decent kebab place in Midan Aref, not far from the station as well as the usual scattering of *fuul*, *taameyya* and *koshari* stands around the train station.

Abydos *p93*

€ Cafeteria Hadika Al-Pharoni, in front of the temple. OK meals are served up for between E£10-20, if you negotiate.

Qena *p97*

Besides *koshari* and *fuul* stalls, there are a few small cheap restaurants, including:
€ El-Prince, **Hamdi** and **Maradona** and **Omar Kyam** (which is probably the best), all located on the main street in town.

Shopping

Akhmim *p93*

Hussein El-Khatib & Sons. Sat-Thu 0800-2000. Produce silk and cotton textiles that are for sale in their showroom beneath the weaving factory. For sale by the metre (E£75 for silk/cotton mix) or pre-packaged as place settings, or bed covers (E£100-150). Worth stopping by, the designs are unusual.

Transport

Sohag *p92*

Bus

The bus depot, T093-233 2021, is a 5-min walk south from the train station. There are daily buses to **Cairo** (8 hrs, E£40-45) at 0900, 1000, 1100 and 1830. There are also buses to **Assiut** at 0630, 0900, 1200 and 1300 (2 hrs, E£5).

Taxi

Service taxis run north as far as **Assiut**, from the depot near Midan Opera, on the north side of town. Services for the south leave from the southern end of Midan Al-Aref, going to **Qena** (3 hrs) via **El-Balyana** (for Abydos, 1 hr, E£2) and **Nag Hammadi**. Some also go direct to **Luxor** and **Aswan**, though it's an uncomfortable journey. Be forewarned that bus and taxi travel for foreign visitors may be restricted.

Train

Travel by train is preferable, and offers the least restrictions. All trains travelling between **Cairo** and **Luxor** stop in Sohag. You should be allowed to get on any train and then pay on board, which costs a bit extra, but if you try to buy a ticket in advance you will only be sold ones for the tourist trains.

Qena *p97*

Bus
There are 2 a/c **Superjet** buses to **Cairo**, via **Hurghada** and **Suez**, as well as service to other Red Sea destinations like **Safaga** and **El-Quseir**. Though buses also go to Nile Valley hub towns like **Assiut**, **Sohag** and **Minya**, they are more easily accessed by train.

Taxi
Service taxis, if open to foreign travellers, make a quick and easy way to travel. Southbound service taxis to **Luxor** and all points in between depart from the square just across the canal behind the railway station. 500 m away there are service taxis to **Safaga** and **Hurghada**. Northbound service taxis along the west bank to **Sohag** via **Nag Hammadi** and **El-Balyana**, can be caught from the depot near the river in the southwestern part of town. Microbuses circulate around town, passing the train station on route.

Train
At least 6 daily trains northbound to **Cairo** via **Sohag**, **Assiut**, **Minya** and **Beni Suef**, and south to **Luxor** (40 mins) and **Aswan**.

Contents

- 104 Getting around
- 104 Best time to visit

105 South of Luxor to Aswan
- 113 Listings

117 Aswan
- 118 Places in Aswan
- 123 The west bank
- 132 Listings

140 Lower Nubia
- 140 Lake Nasser Temples
- 147 Abu Simbel
- 153 Listings

Footprint features

- 107 Horus – The first living god-king
- 113 What colour is a camel?
- 115 Felucca trips
- 119 The souk
- 127 The great dams of Aswan
- 131 David Roberts – painter of Egypt
- 143 Fishing on Lake Nasser
- 144 Worship of the Nile crocodile – Crocodylus niloticus
- 146 Cobras
- 148 Burckhardt the explorer
- 151 A bit of Nubian lingo

South of Luxor

At a glance

✪ Getting around Cruise boats are popular between Luxor and Aswan. You can also cruise on Lake Nasser. *Feluccas* sail from Aswan to Edfu and flights head to Abu Simbel.

⏱ Time required Allow 2-3 days for Aswan.

☀ Weather Perfect for winter sun. Stiflingly hot between May and Sep.

✘ When not to go The Sun Festival at Abu Simbel attracts hoards of people on 22 Feb and 22 Oct. Avoid if you dislike crowds.

• 103

Getting around

Travel in Upper Egypt, at present, is fairly straightforward. With no terrorist attacks since 1997, there is little to worry about. The last surviving tourist convoy in Egypt operates between Aswan and Abu Simbel and this is expected to be dispensed with in the near future. Despite this local authorities prefer foreigners travelling overland in Upper Egypt to travel in groups when venturing between the major sights. As such, accompanying a tour (which is sometimes just a ride) is often the easiest and most hassle-free way to go. There are many options, catering to both piaster-pinching backpackers as well as tourists with more resources, see pages 138 and 155. However, if you are few in number and take a chance boarding buses, service taxis and trains, the benefits of not arriving at a temple with hundreds of other tourists makes the extra effort worthwhile. While there should be no problem getting out of smaller towns on microbuses (such as Kom Ombo, Edfu, and so on), problems may arise when drivers remember the restrictions of the past. Generally speaking, calm persistence will get you onto your chosen form of transport. For information on *felucca* trips on the Nile, see page 115.

Best time to visit

Most people visit the area between October and March, and around Christmas in particular. There is a running joke in Aswan, 'we have the best weather in the world ... in the winter.' And it's true. In December, temperatures average a lovely 30°C. Come July, though, they rise to a scorching 40°C. Be prepared.

South of Luxor to Aswan

The main road follows the Nile along its east bank from Luxor, past Edfu (115 km) on the west bank, before continuing via Kom Ombo (176 km) to Aswan (216 km). There is an alternative, less crowded and less scenic route along the west bank from the Valley of the Kings to Esna (55 km) and Edfu before having to cross the river to continue the journey along the east bank to Aswan. Most visitors make this journey by river in one of the many floating hotels that moor at the sites along the way (see information on Nile Cruisers and *felucca* trips, pages 56 and 115). Egyptian village life, often obscured from the road and not easily appreciated from the window of a speeding car, can be seen on this relaxing journey that many deem the highlight of their trip though Egypt.

Getting there
There are no longer official restrictions on foreigners travelling in this area so any form of available transport can be used to get around. Coming from Luxor it is possible to take the train or bus, hire a private taxi (about E£300-400 to go from Luxor to Aswan) or even take microbuses (though note that these are few and far between on a Friday). ▸▸ *See Transport, page 114.*

Mo'alla Cemetery
ⓘ *Before visiting this site buy your tickets at the kiosks on Luxor's west bank, at the Luxor Museum kiosk or be prepared to pay an informal fee of some E£20 to the guardian. Travelling from Luxor, after the Nagga Abu Said station take the first turning left, cross the bridge over the canal then take the unsurfaced track that swings left towards the cliffs and the cemetery.*
There are rock-cut tombs in the cemetery of Mo'alla on the east bank 40 km south of Luxor dating from the First Intermediate period. Four tombs are located here, cut into the cliffs. All entrances face the west and the Nile.

The tomb of Ankhtifi (1) Ankhtifi was one time governor of the area between Edfu and Armant. He was a very important man in his time and noted for feeding the people in neighbouring areas during a time of famine. The tomb is of a slightly irregular shape and cut directly into the rock, shaped to fit in with the harder veins in the rock strata. On entry there is a rectangular chamber that originally had 30 pillars in three rows of 10, some round and others hexagonal in form. Most pillars are decorated with fine plasterwork and those pillars near the doors carry the best examples of coloured hieroglyphs. An amusing scene on the wall immediately to the right of the entrance door shows a huge fish being caught by spear, and there is a small picture of the deceased and his beautiful wife in very good condition, about 50 cm sq. Other interesting scenes of daily life include lines of animals carrying food to relieve a local famine and a row of spotted cattle to indicate Ankhtifi's wealth. The burial chamber lies at a lower level at the rear of the main hall.

Tombs 2 and 3 These comprise small chapels cut into the rock, but very little decoration remains – mind your head as you go down into the chambers.

The tomb/chapel of Sobekhotep (4) This monument to another regional governor lies a short way to the north in the cemetery. It is entered (or seen into) via a metal door. There are vestiges of decoration on the door jamb but the best known decoration is on the back wall where there are representations of trees and a man taking animals as offerings. The three pits inside the grill have over them a picture of the owner in full size carrying a staff and on the right a scene with eight women.

Esna

This small market town lies about 55 km south of Luxor on the west bank of the Nile, and (as with any Egyptian town) feels like a bustling place. Besides its Temple of Khnum, it's mainly known for the sandstone dam across the river, built in 1906 at about the same time as the first Aswan Dam. Cruise ships and barges usually have to queue a while for their turn to pass through the barrages, though waiting time has been considerably reduced by the building of a second lock. It's a typical dusty town, not geared towards tourists save for the souvenir-sellers, and there is not much to keep you here once you've finished at the temple. The narrow lane ways around the back of the temple, away from the 'souvenir street' do, however, afford an insight into the life of a typical Upper Egyptian town and are worth a short stroll. There are also a few attractive but crumbling villas by the side of the Nile. Have a look for the 600-year-old doorway to a *caravanserai*, to the right of the entrance down to the temple, set slightly back from the street. You can be in and out in under two hours, which will keep the local police force happy. If you do stop off to see the temple after a *felucca* trip (most of which finish 30 km south of Esna), you'll find stalls serving simple food in the *souk*. Service taxis and buses stop about 10 minutes' walk from the temple, which is in the centre of town, walk to the river and then south along the Corniche to the ticket kiosk.

The **Temple of Khnum** ⓘ *daily 0600-1700 winter, 0600-1800 summer, E£20, students E£10,* lies partially exposed in a deep depression in the centre of town. The excavation began in the 1860s but could not continue because the area above was covered in houses. Also, over the centuries since its construction, the annual Nile flood has deposited 10 m of silt over the temple site so that in fact all that is visible today is the **Hypostyle Hall**. This comes as a disappointment to some visitors, and consequently many tours no longer include Esna on their itineraries. The only part of the temple that can be seen is Ptolemaic/Roman, built on the foundations of a much older shrine which was also dedicated to the ram-headed deity Khnum. He was believed to have created man by moulding him from River Nile clay on a potter's wheel. Later, when Amun became the principal deity, Khnum had an image change and, in conjunction with Hapy, came to be regarded as the guardian of the source of the Nile.

The hypostyle hall's **Outer Facade** is decorated from left to right with the cartouches of the emperors Claudius, Titus and Vespasian Inside the lofty hall 18 columns with capitals of varying floral designs support the **Astronomical Ceiling** which, although once a beautiful and complex spectacle, is barely visible today because it was blackened by the wood fires of a Coptic village once housed within the temple. In places various deities and animals, including winged dogs, two-headed snakes and the pregnant hippo-goddess Taweret can be seen intermingled with signs of the zodiac. The hall's columns are inscribed with texts detailing the temple's various festivals. On the right side (as you enter the temple), look out for the cross-legged pharaoh, frogs on top of a capital representing

Horus – the first living god-king

Horus, who was originally the Egyptian sky-god and falcon-god, was later identified as the son of Osiris and his sister Isis. He subsequently avenged his father's murder by his uncle Seth in an epic fight at Edfu in which Horus lost an eye and Seth his testicles. It was not until Isis intervened that Horus prevailed as good triumphed over evil. Osiris pronounced his judgment by banishing Seth to the underworld and enthroning Horus as the first living god-king.

Each pharaoh claimed to be an incarnation of Horus and the annual Festival of the Coronation, at Edfu's now-destroyed Temple of the Falcon in front of the main temple's grand pylon, followed by a crowning ceremony in the temple's main forecourt, symbolized the renewal of royal power.

the goddess Heqet and the square pillar engraved with countless crocodiles. Around the northern outer walls at the back of the temple are texts to Marcus Aurelius while Titus, Domitian and Trajan slay their Egyptian enemies on the eastern and western outer walls.

Al-Kab
ⓘ *0800-1700 summer, E£30, student E£15.*
Al-Kab, 32 km south of Esna, was known in antiquity as Nekheb – home of the vulture goddess Nekhbet. It was a pre-dynastic settlement, although the remains that you see today are mostly from the New Kingdom era. A series of tombs of the high priests/scribes are dug into a hillside close to the road, while the ruins of the temple are enclosed within a huge 5000-year-old mud-brick wall found across the railtracks near to the river. Four of the tombs are open to the public and some rich colouring remains in a couple of them, while the scenes of daily life (fishing, fowling, fixing nets, etc) mingle with the graffiti of early travellers (Belzoni made his mark here in 1817).

Edfu and the Temple of Horus
ⓘ *0700-1800 winter, 0700-2000 summer, E£50, student E£25. Sunset is a good time to visit, when the crowds vanish and you also have the option to stay for the Sound and Light Show (at 2000, 2100 and 2200). The temple is west or inland from the river along Sharia Al-Maglis and can be reached by calèche (10 mins, E£30), some of which are drawn by bony and badly treated horses, which await the arrival of the tourist cruise ships. Taxis and pickups linger around the train station on the east bank, quite close to the Nile bridge; the service taxi terminal at the town-side west end of the bridge is a 20-min walk or short ride to the temple. Intercity buses drop their passengers on Sharia Tahrir or the parallel Sharia El-Gumhoriyya about halfway between the bridge and the temple.*

Edfu, 60 km south along the west bank almost equidistant from Luxor (115 km) and Aswan (106 km), is the site of the huge, well-preserved Ptolemaic cult Temple of Horus – the most complete in the whole of Egypt. The almost-intact ceilings and wealth of carvings make it more immediately impressive than many older pharaonic cult temples and, as it replicates their architectural design in any case, gives a strong impression of what they would have looked like in their prime. Edfu Temple (as it is generally known) was the focus of the ancient city of Djeba. It was begun in August 237 BC by Ptolemy III

Temple of Horus

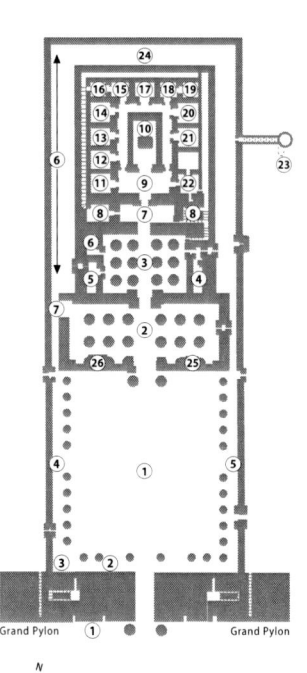

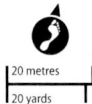

1. Court of offerings
2. First hypostyle hall
3. Second hypostyle hall/festival hall
4. Offering hall: liquid offerings
5. Offering hall: solid offerings
6. Laboratory
7. First vestibule/hall of offerings
8. Stairs to roof
9. Second vestibule/Sanctuary of Horus
10. Main sanctuary dedicated to Horus with altar
11. Chapel of Min
12. Chamber of Linen
13. Chamber of the Throne of the Gods
14. Chamber of Osiris
15. Tomb of Osiris
16. Chamber of the West
17. Chamber of the Victor (Horus)
18. Chapel of Khonsu
19. Chapel of Hathor
20. Chapel of the Throne of Re
21. Chapel of the Spread Wings
22. Sun Court
23. Nilometer & well
24. Passage of victory/ambulatory
25. Library
26. Chamber of Ungents

○ **Murals** see text

and took 25 years – and several Ptolemies – to complete. The decoration took another five years and then a revolt in Upper Egypt meant it was not until February 176 BC that the opening ceremony actually took place under Ptolemy VII. Further additions were still being made into Ptolemy XIII's reign. Like Esna's Temple of Khnum, it was completely buried (except for its huge pylons) under silt and sand and its top was covered with houses until the 1860s but, unlike Esna, the whole site has been excavated. It had been severely damaged by the town's inhabitants and it was not until 1903 that the excavation work was finally completed.

The complex is entered from the ticket office at the south end of the Great Pylon. Just to the southwest is the small east-west axis birth house called the **Mammisi of Horus**, which was built by Ptolomy VII and VIII. The inner sanctuary is surrounded by a peristyle of foliage-capped columns, topped by pilaster capitals showing the grotesque figures of Bes, god of joy and birth. His frightening appearance was thought to dispel evil and to protect women in labour. Each year there was a performance of the miracle play that represents Horus' birth at the same time as the birth of the divine heir to the throne of Egypt. At the southwest corner of the birth house there are reliefs of Isis suckling Horus (in infancy) and an erect Amun. On the pillars of the colonnades in the forecourt Hathor beats a tambourine, plays the harp and suckles Horus (in adolescence).

The main temple is entered through a gateway in the huge **Grand Pylon** on either side of which are grey granite statues of the hawk-god Horus. A tiny Ptolemy stands in front of the left-hand statue. On the left outer wall of the pylon Ptolemy XIII (88-51 BC), who was also known as Neos Dionysus and had usurped the pylon from its original builder Ptolemy IX (170-116 BC), is shown killing his enemies before Horus and Hathor **(1)**. The right wall has the same illustration in mirror image. On its inner wall the barge of Horus tows the barque of (no sails are required as the waterborne procession is downstream.) Celebrations for the gods' arrival are seen at **(3)**. The pylon also contains the usual guardians' quarters and stairs up to the roof.

The giant **Court of Offerings** is lined with 32 columns with paired capitals behind which, on the west side, Ptolemy IX makes offerings to Horus, Hathor and Ihy, their son **(4)**, and on the right (east) Ptolemy X appears before the same three **(5)**. At the north end of the court is the **First Hypostyle Hall**, built by Ptolemy VII (180-145 BC), with its 18 once brightly painted columns supporting the roof. There are three different types of capital, repeated on either side of the hall. Before the entrance of the Hall stand two further statues of Horus, in grey granite, the larger on the left being a popular spot for photographs. At the entrance to the Hypostyle Hall is the small Chamber of Unguents to the left with reliefs of flowers and recipes for consecrations (you will need a torch to examine the interior) and a small library, where the names of the guests for the day's festival would be kept, to the right. Here many rolls of papyrus were found. The foundation ceremonies are illustrated on the walls of the hall.

Leading north from the hall is a narrower 12 slender columned hypostyle hall, known as the **Festival Hall**, the oldest part of the building dating back to Ptolemy III (246-222 BC) and completed by his son, where offerings entered the temple and were prepared. Recipes for offerings are found on the walls of the laboratory. These were then carried through into the **Hall of Offerings** where the daily offerings would have been made at the many altars and tables bearing incense, juices, fruit and meat. From here there are steps to the roof that were used for the procession up to where the **Chapel of the Disc** once stood. The stairs are illustrated with pictures of the priests carrying the statues of the gods to the roof to be revitalized. The roof offers an excellent view of the surrounding area, but the gates are permanently locked and baksheesh will not gain access.

The Offerings Hall leads to the inner vestibule called the **Sanctuary of Horus**, where engravings show Ptolemy IV making offerings to the deities while others show Horus and Hathor in their sacred vessels. Within is a low altar of dark syenite on which stood the sacred barque (a replica is now in place) and behind it the large upright shrine of Aswan granite where the statue of the god was placed. The sanctuary is virtually a separate temple, surrounded by a series of 10 minor chambers, which are intricately carved.

Not to be missed is the ambulatory, where you can access a sunken well and Nilometer below the eastern wall. Horus' defeat of Seth, who is portrayed as a hippopotamus, is illustrated in the middle of the west wall of the ambulatory **(6)**. Note how the hippo gets smaller and smaller as the tale is repeated to the north. On the same side where the ambulatory narrows to the south the pharaoh helped by gods pulls close a clap net containing evil spirits portrayed as fish, birds and men **(7)**. There are some interesting water spouts jutting from the top of the interior wall, some in better repair than others, carved as lions' heads.

Silsila

In between Edfu and Kom Ombo as limestone gives way to sandstone and the river narrows, the ancient quarries of Silsila come into sight on the west bank of the river. In use from the 16th to the first century BC, the quarries were the source of tonnes of sandstone used in temple building. Convicts were used to cut the huge blocks from the cliffs then they were transported on the Nile to sacred sights around Egypt. You can still see holes carved into the rock where the ancient boats were moored. The cliffs are decorated with graffiti and stelae, and small temples with false doors and statues were also hewn into the surrounding rock. The cliffs of Silsila are particularly beautiful around sunset and attractively lit up at night. The colourful **Temple of Horemheb** ① *open 0700-1600 winter, 0700-1700 summer, entry into the temple E£25, students E£15*, has some interesting carvings, note the slaves tied up on the left side of the entrance hall and Horemheb being suckled by the gods on the side wall. If you're on a boat and have the chance to stop, it's definitely worth exploring, even after hours. As the cruise boats cannot dock here, *felucca* and *dahabiya* travellers get the place to themselves. Arriving by land is a bit more of a challenge, it's really only worth the trek if you have a lot of time and a lot of interest: the closest town is Faris, from there, you will need to take a ferry to west bank where you can hire a private taxi for E£20 to bring you to the temple.

Silwa

About 30 km south of Edfu is the small but colourful Nubian village of Silwa. Many of the houses are decorated with unusual paintings depicting stick-fighting and men riding horses. The residents are friendly and welcoming, and if you are in a taxi or private car it is well worth a photo stop here.

Kom Ombo

Kom Ombo was the ancient crossroads where the Forty Days Road caravan route from western Sudan met the route from the eastern desert gold mines. It was also the place where African war elephants were trained up for use in the Ptolemaic army. Sixty-six kilometres south of Edfu and only 40 km north of Aswan, today this small east bank town is known for its sugar refinery, which processes the cane grown in the surrounding area. It is also now home to many of the Nubians who were displaced by the flooding following the construction of the Aswan High Dam. Tourists stop here to visit the Temple of Sobek and Horus that stands directly on the banks of the Nile, 4 km south of the town. If you are staying overnight in Edfu, the temple is particularly attractive at dusk when it is floodlit and many of the beautiful reliefs are shown at their best, especially in the first and second hypostyle halls. Taking a torch with you at this time of day is wise. There is a café on the bank in front of the temple, where you also find the ticket booth. A new museum displaying mummified crocodiles found at Kom Ombo has been built, but was not yet open at the time of research, and beyond this there are few shops and restaurants.

Kom Ombo Temple, is the more usual name given to the small but beautiful **Temple of Sobek and Horus** ① *daily 0700-1900 winter, 0700-2000 summer, E£30, students E£15*. To reach the temple, leave the service taxi to Aswan at the turn-off 2 km south of Kom Ombo town from where the signposted 'tembel' is only 1.5 km away. In the town itself, buses and service taxis stop on the north–south Sharia 26th July, 300 m apart. Cheap pickups to the temple can be caught from behind the white mosque, one block away from the Luxor–Aswan road on Sharia El-Gomhoriyya, for E£10. These days most visitors arrive by *felucca*, *dahabiya* or cruiser.

The temple faces the Nile at a bend in the river and is unusual because it is dedicated to two gods rather than a single deity. The left-hand side is devoted to a form of Horus the Elder or Haroeris known as the 'Good Doctor', his consort Ta-Sent-Nefer ('Good Sister') and his son Horus the Younger, who was known as Pa-Heb-Tawy ('Lord of the Two

Lands'). The right-hand side of the temple is dedicated to the crocodile-god Sobek-Re (here identified with the sun), his wife in another form of Hathor, and their moon-god son Khonsu. Sobek was an appropriate choice, given the fact that the nearby sandbanks were a favourite basking ground for crocodiles until the construction of the Aswan Dam. A healing cult developed here and pilgrims who came to be cured would fast for a night in the temple precinct before participating in a complex ceremony with the priest of Horus in the heart of the temple.

The present temple, like many others along this stretch of the Nile, is a Graeco-Roman construction, built of sandstone. Ptolemy VI started the temple, Neo Dionysus oversaw most of the construction while Emperor Augustus added some of the finishing touches. Its proximity to the Nile was a mixed blessing because, while its silt assisted in preserving the building, the flood waters eroded the First Pylon and Forecourt. In front of the temple to the left is the **Mamissi of Ptolemy VII**, which has been virtually destroyed by flooding, and to the east is the **Gate of Neos Dionysus**, who was the father of Cleopatra, and the **Chapel of Hathor**, which is impressively carved and has a central panel covered by the key of life.

With the Pylon and much of the **Forecourt** now destroyed by water erosion, only the stumps of the colourful columns, with a high-water mark clearly visible at about 2.5 m, and a few pieces of its walls now remain. Continuing the theme from the rest of the temple the twin deities are divided so that the left-hand columns are dedicated to Horus the Elder and the right-hand ones to Sobek-Re. In the centre of the forecourt is the base of a huge square

Temple of Sobek & Horus at Kom Ombo

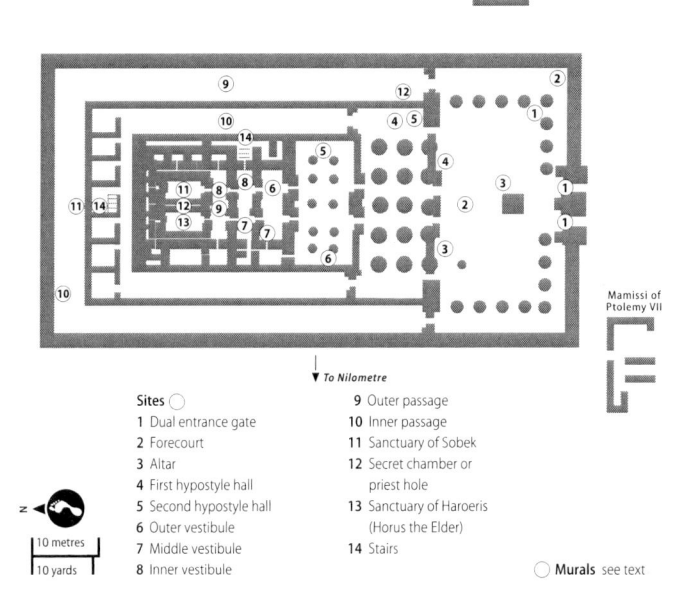

Sites ○
1 Dual entrance gate
2 Forecourt
3 Altar
4 First hypostyle hall
5 Second hypostyle hall
6 Outer vestibule
7 Middle vestibule
8 Inner vestibule
9 Outer passage
10 Inner passage
11 Sanctuary of Sobek
12 Secret chamber or priest hole
13 Sanctuary of Haroeris (Horus the Elder)
14 Stairs

○ **Murals** see text

altar. On the column in the far corner (**1**) note the eye socket in the relief of Horus, which was inlaid for greater decoration. Behind this column, right in the corner (**2**), a staircase rose up to the roof level. At the north end is the double entrance of the **First Hypostyle Hall**, on the left wall of which (**3**) Neos Dionysus undergoes the purification ritual overseen by Horus and on the right (**4**) the same ritual is overseen by Sobek. The capitals are brightly decorated with floral arrays and the bases decorated with lilies. The reliefs on the lintel and door jambs show the Nile gods binding Upper and Lower Egypt together.

The five entrance columns and the 10 columns inside the Hypostyle Hall and its wall reliefs are especially decorative and the curious mixture of the two deities continues. Part of the roof has survived on the east side of the Hall and flying vultures are clearly depicted on the ceiling (**5**). The rear walls leading to the older **Inner Hypostyle Hall**, which has two entrances and 15 columns, show Ptolemy VII holding hymnal texts before the Nile gods. The most striking relief is adjacent on the left of the north wall where Horus the Elder presents the *Hps*, the curved sword of victory to Ptolemy VII, while Cleopatra II and Cleopatra III, his wife and sister respectively, stand behind him (**6**).

This is followed by three double **Entrance Vestibules**, each progressively smaller and higher than the last, also built by Ptolemy VII. The outer vestibule shows the goddess of writing Sheshat measuring the layout of the temple's foundations (**7**), while the middle chamber served as an **Offering Hall** to which only priests were allowed entrance. Look for the long list or calendar detailing the temple gods' various festivals, one for each day (**8**). Two small side rooms served as the library for the sacred texts and the other as a vestry for the altar clothes and the priests' robes. As in Edfu, a staircase originally led to the now-destroyed Chapel of the Disk on the roof.

The inner vestibule has two doors leading to the two separate **Sanctuaries of Horus and Sobek** and between the doors the gods give a Macedonian-cloaked Ptolemy a notched palm branch from which the Heb Sed, or jubilee sign displaying the number of years of his reign, is suspended (**9**). Khonsu, who is wearing a blue crescent around a red disk, is followed by Horus in blue symbolizing the air, and Sobek in green representing the water. Beneath the sanctuary are the crypts, which are empty and usually closed to the public. Visible is a small **secret chamber**, from where the priests spoke to the gods. It lies between the two sanctuaries, in what would have appeared as a very thick wall.

On the inner wall of the **outer corridor** (**10**) is the first known illustration of medical instruments, including bone-saws, scalpels, suction caps and dental tools, which date from the second century AD. While your guide may tell you that complicated operations were carried out 1800 years ago, it is most probable that these were instruments used in the mummification process. Adjacent to the left is a repeated relief of Isis on a birthing stool. Nearby the temple corridor floor is marked with graffiti, drawn by patients and pilgrims who spent the night there before the next day's healing ceremonies. Also in the outer corridor, at the back of the temple (**11**), Horus and Sebek stand either side of a small panel surrounded by mystic symbols of eyes, ears and animals and birds each sporting four pairs of wings. Continue round the corridor to (**12**) where the traditional killing of the enemies scene, much eroded, this time includes a lion.

In the northwest corner of the temple complex is a large circular well that has a stairway, cistern and rectangular basin that are believed to be connected in some ways with the worship of the crocodile god Sobek.

What colour is a camel?

With some imagination it is possible to distinguish five different colours of camel. The white camel is the most beautiful and the most expensive as it is claimed to be the fastest runner. The yellow version is second best – and slightly cheaper. Looking for a solid, dependable beast to carry the baggage? Choose red. A blue camel, which is really black but is called blue to avoid the problems of the evil eye, is not high in the popularity stakes. And a creature that is a mixture of white, red, yellow and black is just another unfortunate beast of burden.

Daraw Camel Market (Souk El-Jamaal)

ⓘ *8 km south of Kom Ombo. The camel market is on Tue from 0700-1400, and occasionally on Sun or Mon in winter. It's most lively in the early morning. The livestock market is also on Tue, where hundreds of cows, chickens, sheep, and goats mill about as their proud owners try to strike up a good deal (there's another one in Kom Ombo on Thu, same hours). To get there, take a train (45 mins, buy ticket on board, all trains stop at Daraw) or bus (hourly) from Aswan, they will drop you on the main road, from there, walk north across the tracks (take a right as you exit the train station, walk 200 m, and take another right to cross the tracks), follow the road for about 3 km, after you pass the open fields and see houses, turn right and follow the sounds and scents, if you want to take a private taxi from Aswan the trip should cost around E£200 return. If you're on a felucca, ask the captain to drop you in Daraw and hire a pickup to take you to the market and back (about E£20-25 per group).*

An easy stop if you're sailing a *felucca* up the Nile is the village of Daraw. Except for one of the most interesting and unforgettable camel markets in the world, there's not much to see in the dusty little town. Sudanese merchants and Bishari tribesmen wrangle and haggle with Nubian farmers and Egyptian peasants (*fellaheen*) over camels that have walked for weeks by caravan along the Forty Days Road to be showcased. When they reach Abu Simbel, trucks usually bring the camels to the veterinarian in Daraw where they receive the necessary inoculations to ensure good health before heading to the market. Once in the market, camels go for over E£5000 depending on their age, sex, and general well being. Strong healthy females tend to be worth the most, for their reproductive capabilities. Only the males are killed for their meat. After being sold in Daraw, many camels end up at the camel market in Birqash, about an hour north of Cairo. In addition to milk and meat, camels are used for working the fields and carrying tourists around.

◉ South of Luxor to Aswan listings

For sleeping and eating price codes and other relevant information, see pages 11-15.

Where to stay

Esna *p106*

Esna is so close to Luxor, that most visit it on a day trip or on a cruise.

€ Haramin, about 1 km south of the ticket kiosk along the Corniche. It's very basic but probably the best of 3 not very nice options.

There's also **€ Al Medina** in the central square and **€ Dar as Salaam** closer to the temple.

Edfu *p107*

There are no good hotels in town and most tourists are either only passing through or staying on cruise ships. You could try:

€ El-Medina, just off the main roundabout on Sharia El-Gumhoriyya, T097-471 1326, friendly but shabby.

Kom Ombo *p110*

Kom Ombo is so close to Aswan, it is not worth staying there.

€ Cleopatra Hotel, near the service taxi depot on Sharia 26th July. Probably the best bet if you're desperate.

Restaurants

Esna *p106*

There are a few cafés and stalls sprinkled around the central square.

Edfu *p107*

In addition to the standard food stalls, there is a pricey café by the temple.

€ Zahrat El-Medina Restaurant, on the Corniche across from El-Medina. Cheaper place to sit down for a bite.

Kom Ombo *p110*

Besides the small stalls that serve *fuul*, *taamiyya* and *kebab*, there are a couple of cafés by the Nile serving meat standards.

Shopping

Esna *p106*

When the cruise ships reach the locks here the traders appear in a flotilla of small rowing boats and attempt to sell a wide variety of clothing, etc. Goods are hurled from the boats in a polythene bag onto the top deck of the ship for the purchaser to examine and then barter over the price. Rejected goods are thrown back (although these are not always dispatched with the same accuracy as they were received!). If a price is agreed and a purchase made, a small garment to act as ballast, again in a bag, is then thrown up on deck with the expectation that payment will be placed inside the package and returned to the sender.

Edfu *p107*

The main tourist bazaar is next to the Edfu temple complex and offers a colourful selection of cheap goods, particularly *gallabiyas*, scarves and other local souvenirs. However, as t is impossible to enter the temple without walking past the stalls, here you find some of the most aggressive sales techniques in the country.

Transport

Esna *p106*

Bus

From **Luxor** to Esna and further south buses are cheap and frequent but crowded in the morning, and they stop a lot, which makes service taxis a quicker option.

Service taxi

Service taxis to **Luxor** (1 hr, E£3), **Edfu** (1 hr) and **Aswan** (2-3 hrs). From the service taxi drop-off point in Esna, you can either walk the 1 km to the temple, take a pick up or hire a carriage.

Train

Virtually all trains heading south from **Alexandria** and **Cairo** to **Aswan** stop at Esna, as do northbound trains from Aswan. The station is an awkward 5 km out of town on the opposite bank of the Nile.

Edfu *p107*

Bus

Buses arriving in Edfu sometimes stop on the east bank opposite town, which requires further transport into town with pickups. You can catch a bus out of town north to **Luxor** through **Esna** (2 hrs) or south to **Aswan** via **Kom Ombo** (1 hr) from Sharia Tahrir halfway between the bridge and the temple. There

Felucca trips

Due to the direction of the river's flow, wind conditions and the problematic locks at Esna, extended *felucca* trips start in Aswan and go north towards Luxor. Most common are the one-day/one-night trips to nearby Kom Ombo (where the *felucca* stops immediately in front of the temple) and the three-day/two-night trips to Edfu. From there, it's possible to carry on overland to other significant sights between Aswan and Luxor.

Feluccas don't go all the way to Luxor and you will have to take a microbus or taxi the final leg of the journey. It's easy to hire a taxi back to Aswan or north to Luxor from your destination and captains will be keen to arrange it for you (it will be more expensive than what you could find on your own). This is where you are often at the mercy of unscrupulous drivers who insist that there is no way of travelling on by public transport. In fact, a very common problem are captains who make the final stop before the actual town of Edfu and force passengers to take a taxi onwards, refusing to sail any further. Be assured that from both Kom Ombo and Edfu there are microbuses going north and south, though you might have to take a taxi to the microbus station and wait a while for the vehicle to fill up.

The standard number of passengers is between six and eight. It's better to aim for six if you want a bit of space to move about. The government has established fixed prices for *felucca* trips. If there are at least six passengers, it should cost about E£50 per person for one night (to Kom Ombo), E£75 for two nights and E£95 for three nights (to Edfu town itself). The tourist office in Aswan can advise you on the latest figures. The price does not include the cost of the necessary 'permission' (an additional E£5), or the cost of food and bottled water (an additional E£35-45 per day for three meals). If you want beer or other extras, plan to bring it yourself, or ask for it and pay extra. Whether or not demand for *felucca* cruises is high, captains will ask for more; bargaining is the norm. Beware of a captain who accepts a price lower than the ones cited, chances are the money you save is coming out of the amount allotted for your food or you run the risk of being deposited somewhere south of your desired destination. If there are fewer than six people in your group, you can pay more to accommodate for the captain's loss.

With more than 500 *feluccas* based in Aswan, it can be a stressful experience choosing a captain, but it's time well spent once you're lazily meandering down the Nile. Find a captain who speaks English and has a few years' experience behind him. It is strongly recommended you ask the tourist office for a list of recommended captains, and you can leave a note with them if you're looking for other passengers to share a boat with. If you're only opting for a *felucca* because you're on a budget and would rather be cruising down the Nile in more luxurious style, bear in mind that it's possible to get a four-star cruise ship for US$40-50/night – even less in summer. Ask at the tourist information office if they have any leads or take a wander down the Corniche and speak to the managers of the boats. If there are spare berths it is possible to negotiate a decent rate and bypass the travel agents.

Note As well as regular Nile cruises you can also start *dahabiya* trips from Aswan, for more information on these options see pages 54 and 57.

is also a daily morning bus to **Marsa Alam** that is supposed to leave at 0800 (3 hrs). **Aswan** to **Luxor** at 0800 and stop at Kom Ombo and Edfu for about 1 hr. The 1100 convoy goes directly to Luxor.

Service taxi
If foreigners are permitted to ride in them, service taxis are the quickest option. Find them at the west end of the bridge. Prices are comparable to the public buses. North to **Esna** (1 hr) and **Luxor** (2 hrs), or south to **Kom Ombo** (45 mins) and **Aswan** (1 hr).

Train
Trains to and from **Luxor** and **Aswan** stop at Edfu, but the station is 4 km from town on the other side of the Nile.

Kom Ombo *p110*

Bus
Buses running between **Aswan** and **Luxor** usually stop in town on Sharia 26th July about 350 m south of Sharia El-Gumhoriyya.

Service taxi
Service taxis north to **Edfu** (1 hr) and Luxor (2 ½ hrs, E£11) or south to **Aswan** (45 mins) are at the terminal on Sharia 26 July just south of Sharia El-Gumhoriyya.

Train
To/from **Luxor** and **Aswan** stop at Kom Ombo station just across the highway.

Aswan

Aswan, Egypt's southern frontier town, in its delightful river setting, is a highlight of any Nile cruise. It is stunningly beautiful, charmingly romantic, and the sunniest city in Egypt, hence its popularity. However, the city's undoubted attractions are helping to send it the same way as Luxor and the ever-growing tourist scene has all the accompanying downsides of increased hassle, clean-ups of the *souk*, *felucca* captains waiting on every corner and hideous buildings springing up. But though the sense of ancient enchantment that used to pervade the very air of Aswan is hard to find now, it is still here – you just might have to look on the west bank or in one of the villages to find it. The city itself is not too large to walk around in the cooler part of the day and the pace of life is slow and relaxing. From the cool and inviting Corniche you can watch tall-masted *feluccas* handled masterfully by a tiny crew and listen to Nubian musicians. Across the river, dramatic desert cliffs merge with palm-lined Nile waters, and huge apricot-coloured sandbanks appear startling against the cloudless blue sky. In the late evening you can watch the flocks of egrets skimming the surface of the Nile as they go to roost before you feast on freshly caught Nile fish. In the early morning you can watch the sun rise behind the city and hear the call of the *muezzin*. With the outstanding Nubian museum, colourful west bank villages and islands to explore, as well as proximity to several notable temples and the nearby High Dam, the city is much more than a stopover en route to Abu Simbel.

Arriving in Aswan

Getting there and around The railway station is at the north end of the town, about two minutes' walk from the Corniche, or 10 minutes' walk from the heart of the *souk* heading south. Most mid-range and higher-end hotels are by the Nile. Budget hotels are scattered around the railway station and in the *souk*. The inter-city bus station and service taxi station are about 4 km out of town. To get to town from the bus station, take a microbus (50 pt) or a private taxi (E£5-10). *Feluccas* and cruise boats moor along the Corniche. Aswan's desert airport is 24 km south of town. There is no bus service connecting the airport and town. A taxi costs about E£40-50 for a hard bargainer. Bicycles are becoming very popular for covering short distances. There are several hire shops around the *souk* and Corniche and an especially reliable one behind the train station. Cross the railway station via the bridge, walk ahead and you'll find the bike shop on the first corner to the right, near the mosque. The going rate is E£15 per day. ▸▸ *See Transport, page 138.*

Note If arriving at the station on one of the official tourist trains, you will be met by hotel touts, taxi drivers and *felucca* men keen to push tours and misinformation upon you. It's best to politely ignore them, and either head straight to the tourist information centre next door for help and advice, or get a taxi to the hotel of your choice with a driver that isn't loitering in the immediate vicinity of the station (a maximum of E£10 to any hotel in town). Don't be tempted to agree to a tour with any middleman or taxi driver who is touting at the station. For *felucca* trips, it is best to visit the main tourist office who can recommend trustworthy captains. Use your hotel (or a tour operator) to arrange trips to Abu Simbel only, and not for *felucca* voyages. As well as cutting out any middlemen, this allows you to establish exactly what you want and what you are paying for, and means the crew are directly responsible for providing what was agreed in the first place.

Information There are two tourist offices in Aswan, quite close to one another. The primary **tourist office** ① *T097-231 2811, T010-576 7594, daily 0800-1500 and 1800-2000 winter, 1900-2100 summer, Ramadan 1000-1400 and again after* iftar, is next to the train station in a little domed building. It's worth stopping off here immediately on arrival at the station, as manager Hakeem Hussein offers possibly the best and most informative tourist office in the country. He will happily assist you in navigating the area, giving you the most recent of the ever-changing schedules and prices of transport, tours and entertainment. He can be contacted on his mobile (T010-576 7594) outside office hours. They can also help in booking trustworthy and suitable accommodation and advising on *felucca* trips and tours.

Background

Aswan's indigenous inhabitants are the ethnically, linguistically and culturally distinct **Nubians** who are more African than Arab. A robust civilization had flourished on the southern banks of the Nile since the time of the first pharaohs, and despite being frequently invaded and conquered by their northern neighbours who were dependent on their gold mines, the Nubian kings actually controlled all Egypt during the 25th Dynasty (747-656 BC). Many favoured Nubians became noblemen and administrators throughout ancient times, and Cleopatra was from the modern-day Sudanese town of Wadi Halfa. Indeed, the term 'Nubian' today is equally applicable to the Sudanese who live along the Nile as far south as Khartoum. The later Nubian kingdom of Kush, whose capital was the Sudanese town of Merowe and which included Aswan, remained largely independent from Egypt. Having been the last region to adopt the Christian faith, Nubia became a stronghold of the faith and a sanctuary for Coptic Christians fleeing the advance of Islam.

For many centuries a sleepy backwater, Aswan assumed national importance when it became the headquarters for the successful 1898 Anglo-Egyptian re-conquest of Sudan. With the 1902 construction of the first **Aswan Dam** the town became a fashionable winter resort for rich Europeans who relished its dry heat, luxury hotels and stunning views, particularly from the *feluccas* sailing on the Nile at sunset. But the dam also caused many Nubian villages to the south of Aswan to be submerged by the rising waters. With no decent agricultural land left to farm, menfolk headed to the cities leaving the women in charge, and Cairo's population of *bawabs* (doorkeepers) is still predominantly Nubian today. With the building of the Aswan High Dam in 1970, the swamping of Nubia was complete and many of those who were displaced joined in swelling the populations of Aswan and Kom Ombo. Despite the subsequent construction of a number of heavy industries in Aswan, to take advantage of the cheap hydroelectric power generated at the dam, the town has retained its attractive charm and relaxed atmosphere.

Places in Aswan

The **Nubia Museum** ① *T097-231 9111, 0900-2100 summer, E£50, students E£25*, stands on a granite hill to the south of the town on the road past the Old Cataract Hotel.

The UNESCO-sponsored Nubia Museum is regarded as a great success, and most visitors to Aswan feel that an hour or so here is well spent. The building incorporates features of Nubian architecture and showcases some 5000 artefacts tracing the area's culture from prehistoric to modern times. The colossal statue of Ramses, the remaining

The souk

The *souk* or bazaar economy of North Africa has distinctive characteristics. In Egypt a series of large *souks* continues successfully to exist while bazaar economies elsewhere are faltering. In Egyptian cities as a whole, such as Aswan, Islamic ideas and traditional trading habits have remained strong.

The bazaar originally functioned as an integral part of the economic and political system. Traditional activities in financing trade and social organizations were reinforced by the bazaar's successful role in running international commodity trade. The bazaar merchants' long-term raising of credits for funding property, agricultural and manufacturing activities was strengthened by this same trend.

There is a view among orientalists that Egyptian/Islamic cities have a specific social structure and physical shape. The crafts, trades and goods were located in accordance with their 'clean' or 'unclean' status, and whether or not these goods could be sold close to the mosque or *madresa*. Valuable objects were on sale near to the main thoroughfares, the lesser trades, needing more and cheaper land, were pushed to the edge of the bazaar. There was a concentration of similar crafts in specific locations within the bazaar so that all shoe-sellers, for example, were in the same street. These ground rules do not apply in all Egyptian bazaars but in many cases they are relevant in different combinations. Thus, there is a hierarchy of crafts, modified at times by social custom and Islamic practice, which gives highest priority to book-making, perfumes, gold and silver jewellery, over carpet-selling, and thence through a graded scale of commodities through metal-work, ceramics, sale of agricultural goods and ultimately low-grade crafts such as tanning and dyeing.

---

part of a temple at Gerf Hussein, dominates the entrance, a reminder of his positive presence in Nubia. The prehistoric cave depicts the first attempts at rock carvings and the use of tools. The pharaonic period demonstrates the importance of this region to the rulers of Egypt as a gateway to the south. There are sections devoted to Graeco-Roman, Coptic and Islamic influences in Nubia, and of course a section about the UNESCO project to save the monuments threatened by the creation of Lake Nasser. The colourful exhibition of folk heritage emphasizes the individuality of Nubian culture. The most common crafts are pottery and the weaving of baskets and mats from palm fronds.

On the hill on the way to the Nubia Museum are the **Fryal Gardens** ① *daily 0900-2200, E£5*, popular with courting couples, and a good place to stop off for a *haga saah* (something cold) under the shady trees and enjoy views down onto the first cataract.

On the outskirts of Aswan about 2 km along the highway south, is the **Unfinished Obelisk** ① *daily 0600-1600 winter, 0600-1700 summer, E£25, students E£15*, in the quarries that provided red granite for the ancient temples. You can walk the 2 km, hire a bike, or take a taxi for E£25 return. The huge obelisk, which would have weighed 1168 tonnes and stood over 41 m high, was abandoned before any designs were carved when a major flaw was discovered in the granite. It was originally intended to form a pair with the **Lateran Obelisk**, the world's tallest obelisk that once stood in the Temple of Tuthmosis III at Karnak but is now in Rome. When it was discovered in the quarry by Rex Engelbach in

1922 the unfinished obelisk shed light on pharaonic quarrying methods, including the soaking of wooden wedges to open fissures, but shaping and transporting them remains an astounding feat.

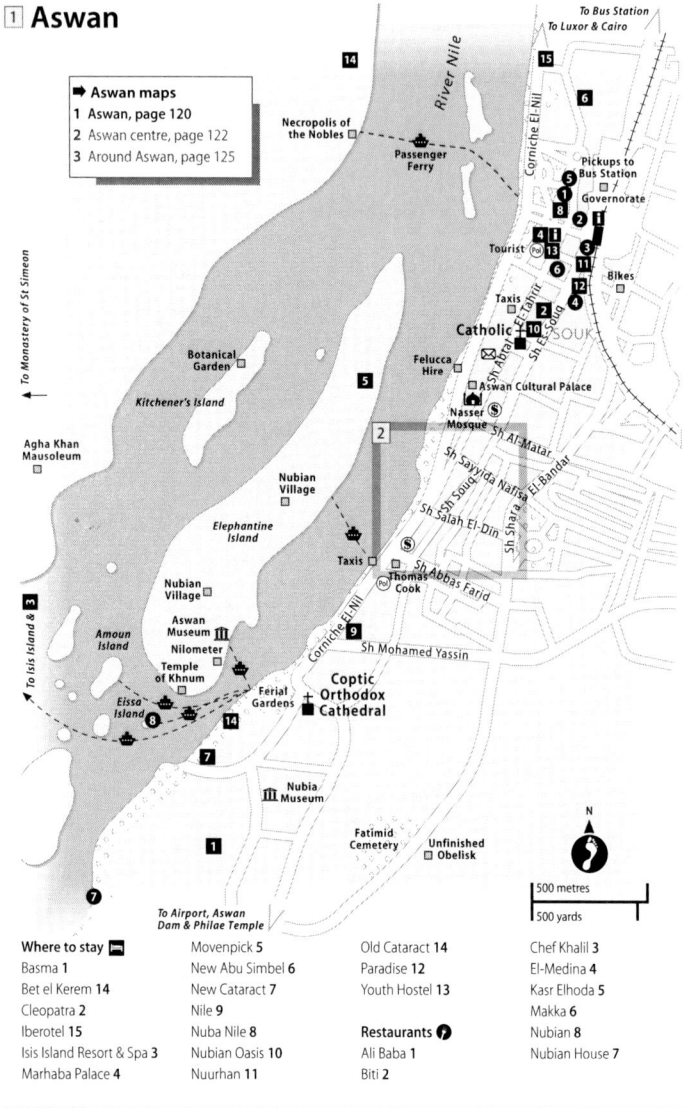

Aswan

➡ **Aswan maps**
1 Aswan, page 120
2 Aswan centre, page 122
3 Around Aswan, page 125

Where to stay
Basma **1**
Bet el Kerem **14**
Cleopatra **2**
Iberotel **15**
Isis Island Resort & Spa **3**
Marhaba Palace **4**
Movenpick **5**
New Abu Simbel **6**
New Cataract **7**
Nile **9**
Nuba Nile **8**
Nubian Oasis **10**
Nuurhan **11**

Old Cataract **14**
Paradise **12**
Youth Hostel **13**

Restaurants
Ali Baba **1**
Biti **2**

Chef Khalil **3**
El-Medina **4**
Kasr Elhoda **5**
Makka **6**
Nubian **8**
Nubian House **7**

120 • **South of Luxor** Aswan

Note It's easy to combine a visit to the Unfinished Obelisk with a trip to the High Dam or the Philae Temples, see pages 126.

Elephantine Island
ⓘ *Felucca to Elephantine Island E£25 per hr as your captain waits; E£30 per hr to sail around; or a local ferry (E£1) runs from 0600 until 2400, leaving from in front of the EgyptAir office and landing in front of the Aswan Museum.*

Opposite the Corniche and only a short ferry ride away in the middle of the Nile is sultry Elephantine Island. Measuring 2 km long and 500 m at its widest point, the island gets its name from the bulbous grey rocks off its south tip that resemble bathing elephants. There are a couple of Nubian villages and some interesting ruins that are well worth a visit, and meandering to the far side for an unimpeded vista of the the Aga Khan Mausoleum (see page 123) and the amber sands of the west bank is a timeless interlude from life. Also, the hideous tower of the Movenpick Hotel on the island is somehow less noticeable close up than it is from the Corniche, from where it impedes every view.

The **Aswan Museum** ⓘ *daily 0800-1600 winter, 0800-1700 summer, E£30, students E£15 and E£10 for camera, price includes entrance to the museum, the ruins of the Yebu and the Nilometer,* was closed for restoration at the time of writing; the Nilometer and ruins can still be visited, although there is no reduction in the ticket price. Established in order to display relics salvaged from the flooded areas behind the Aswan dams, which is ironic because the villa and its sub-tropical gardens originally belonged to Sir William Willcocks, designer of the first Aswan Dam. It offers a spread of pharaonic material, Roman and Islamic pottery, jewellery, and funerary artefacts. The ground floor is arranged in chronological order with items from the Middle and New Kingdoms, including pottery, combs and some jewellery, while the basement displays a series of human and animal mummies and an impressive gold-sheathed statue of Khnum.

You can see the **Roman Nilometer** if you take the pathway southwards to the left of the museum entrance. This fascinating device, rediscovered on the southeast tip of Elephantine Island in 1822, was designed to measure the height of the annual Nile flood. This enabled the coming season's potential crop yield to be estimated and the level of crop taxation to be fixed. Besides Roman and very faint pharaonic numerals, there are also more recent tablets inscribed in both French and Arabic on the 90 walled stairs that lead down to a riverside shaft.

Long before Aswan itself was occupied, Elephantine Island's fortress town of **Yebu** (the word for both elephant and ivory in ancient Egyptian) was the main trade and security border post between the Old Kingdom and Nubia. It was reputed to be the home of Hapy, the god of the Nile flood, and the goddess of fertility, Satet, both of whom were locally revered, and the regional god Khnum, who was represented by a ram's head. The ruined **Temple of Khnum** (30th Dynasty), at the south end of the island, boasts a gateway portraying Alexander II worshipping Khnum, which suggests that the Greeks added to this temple complex. The island has a number of less impressive ruins, and temples have been built here for four millennia. Make time when visiting to take advantage of an outstanding high viewpoint to enjoy the beautiful panorama of the Aswan Corniche to the east, including the picturesque Old Cataract Hotel, the islands and the Nile itself.

In addition to the museum, Nilometer and temple ruins, there are two small Nubian villages on Elephantine Island. A wander here gives a taste of contemporary life, albeit not much changed in centuries. You will almost certainly be invited into someone's home, most likely by Mohammed who has a beautiful Nubian House (aka the crocodile house) next to the museum (signed). Decorated with traditional Nubian handicrafts, you can enjoy a cup of tea or a cold drink on his colourful roof. Be forewarned that this rooftop operates as a commercial café/bazaar so that a wrangle over the price of your drink doesn't spoil your experience.

Kitchener's Island
① *Daily from 0800 until sunset, E£10, accessible by* felucca.

Kitchener's Island lies north of the larger Elephantine Island and, originally known as the 'Island of Plants', it has a magnificent **Botanical Garden**. The beautiful island was presented to Lord Kitchener, who had a passion for exotic plants and flowers from around the world, in gratitude for his successful Sudan campaign and the gardens have

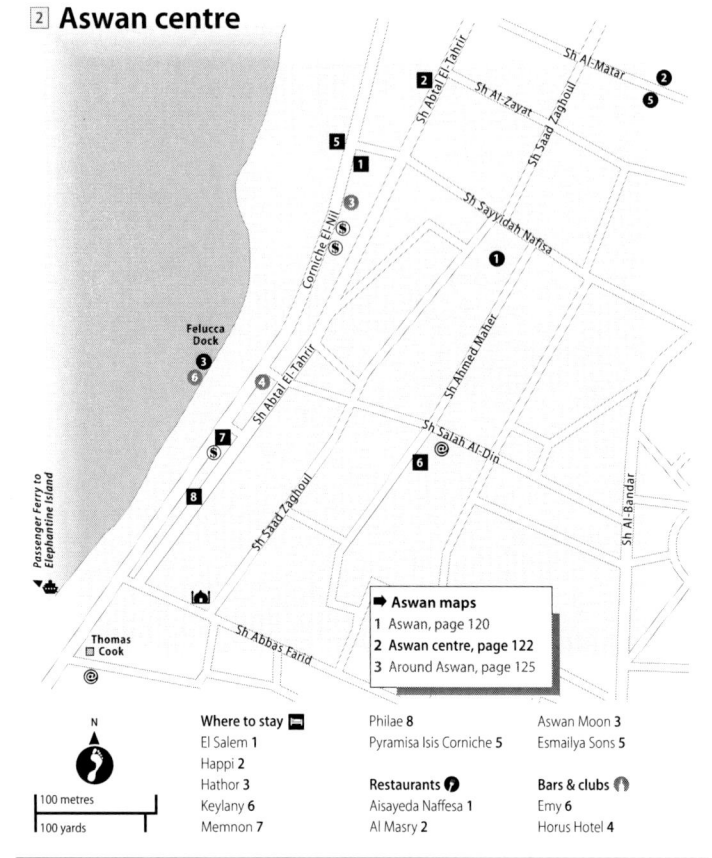

2 Aswan centre

➡ **Aswan maps**
1 Aswan, page 120
2 Aswan centre, page 122
3 Around Aswan, page 125

Where to stay
El Salem 1
Happi 2
Hathor 3
Keylany 6
Memnon 7
Philae 8
Pyramisa Isis Corniche 5

Restaurants
Aisayeda Naffesa 1
Al Masry 2
Aswan Moon 3
Esmailya Sons 5

Bars & clubs
Emy 6
Horus Hotel 4

been maintained in their original style. The atmosphere on the island, which is almost completely shielded from the bustle of Aswan by Elephantine Island, is very relaxed and its lush vegetation, animals and birds make it an ideal place to watch the sunset. There is an expensive café at the south end of the island.

The west bank

Aga Khan Mausoleum

The beautiful **Aga Khan Mausoleum** ⓘ *closed to the public*, on a hill on the west bank of the Nile opposite the town, was built of solid marble for the third Aga Khan (1877-1957) who was the 48th Imam of the Ismaili sect of Shi'a Muslims. He was renowned for his wealth and was given his body weight in jewels by his followers for his 1945 diamond jubilee. As an adult he visited Aswan every winter for its therapeutic climate, having fallen in love with its beauty and built a villa on the west bank. Until her death, his widow lived in the villa every winter, and erected the mausoleum on the barren hill above the villa. It is a brilliant white marble building, closely resembling a miniature version of the Fatimids' mausoleums in Cairo, the only hint of colour being the fresh red rose that was placed daily on the sarcophagus by his wife.

Necropolis of the Nobles

ⓘ *The tombs are open from 0700-1600 winter, 0700-1700 summer, E£25, students E£15, access by* felucca *or ferry (E£1-E£5) from the dock slightly to the south of the Governorate building in the northern part of town. Go down the only steps with no cruise ship sign above them, the ticket office is above the ferry landing. Wear a strong pair of shoes and take a torch. There is a guide on duty to show the way, unlock the tombs and turn on the electric lights, his services are part of the entry fee but a small tip is also a good idea.*

The Necropolis of the Nobles at Qubbet Al-Hawwa (Dome of the Wind) is further north along the west bank of the Nile (west being the world of the dead and east the world of the living). The riverside cliff is lined with tombs from various periods that have been discovered during the last century. Just above the waterline are the Roman tombs, and higher up in the more durable rock are those of the Old and Middle Kingdoms. The majority of the dead are believed to have been priests or officials responsible for water transport between Egypt and Nubia. Most tours begin at the southern end with the tombs of Mekhu and Sabni. Most of the tombs are numbered in ascending order from south to north. Only the more interesting ones are mentioned here.

Tomb of Mekhu (No 25) Mekhu was a chief overseer in Upper Egypt at the time of the Sixth Dynasty and was killed while on official duties. His son Sabni mounted an expedition to reclaim his father's body and successfully returned to Aswan to give Mekhu a ceremonial burial. The main chamber is cut out of solid rock leaving 18 slightly tapering columns, decorated with reliefs of the family and fragments of other funeral scenes. The inner wall to the left carries a series of false doors inscribed to Mekhu. Also accessed from here (the original entry is blocked) is a memorial to Mekhu's son **Sabni (No 26)**. To the right of the main chamber is a large false door and a depiction of fishing and fowling from river craft.

Tomb of Sarenput II (No 31) Sarenput, who was governor or Guardian of the South at the height of the Middle Kingdom, has the largest, most elaborate and best preserved tomb in this necropolis. The first hall, containing a small granite offering table, has a decorated ceiling and distinctive striped door lintel. Steps lead to a narrow connecting corridor that has six niches with statues of Sarenput II. In the inner chamber, four pillars represent the deceased on their inward-facing sides. In a small recess at the rear of the tomb there is an elaborate relief portraying him with his wife, son and mother in a beautiful garden.

Harkhuf (No 34) Harkhuf was Guardian of Southern Egypt and a royal registrar in the Sixth Dynasty. Though he achieved great fame as a noble of Elephantine and leader of diplomatic and military expeditions, his tomb-temple is modest. On the right side of the entrance wall to the main chamber are the remains of a verbatim copy of a letter from Pepi II commending Harkhuf and, around the doorway, offering scenes. Inside the small rock-cut chamber, the four columns carry pictures of the deceased and biographical texts. On the inner wall there are two niches, the left-hand one with a false door bearing offering scenes and the right-hand one with a small offering table below a painted stela. An inclined shaft leads to the burial chamber. Adjacent, lies the tomb-temple of **Pepinakht (No 35)**, who led military campaigns to Asia and the south which are described by wall texts inside.

Tomb of Sarenput I (No 36) The grandfather of Sarenput II was both Guardian of the South and also the overseer of the priests of Khnum and Satet during the 12th Dynasty (1991-1786 BC). The tomb is one of the largest, but unfortunately many of the reliefs are badly decayed. Those carved on the polished limestone doorway, however, are wonderfully clear, through which you enter into an antechamber with six columns close to the inner wall, which originally carried a finely decorated portico. On the right column there are carvings on all faces of a likeness of Sarenput. The inner wall carries important scenes in good condition. On the left is a scene of the deceased spearing fish, his wife clutching him, lest he should fall, and his son on the adjacent bank. Above are farming scenes with oxen. An inner hall is entered through a narrow doorway, a modest room where the pillar decorations and the paintings on the plaster of the walls have all but disappeared. Fragments show scenes of fowling, boating and women at work. A narrow corridor has been cut into the west wall rising to the small burial chamber with two columns and a niche and shrine for Sarenput.

Tomb of Ka-Gem-Em-Ahu To the north of these tombs is a separate tomb-temple, to Ka-Gem-Em-Ahu, reached by a sandy path. Ka-Gem-Em-Ahu was the high priest of Khnum in the late New Empire. His tomb was discovered by Lady William Cecil in 1902. Most of the plaster work has been lost from the six-pillared outer courtyard but scenes of boats on the Nile can still be made out with one or two residual depictions of funeral scenes, such as the weighing of the heart. Enter the low entrance to the main tomb where the ceiling is quite ornately decorated with flowers, birds and geometric designs. Although the walls are quite plain, the left-hand side inner pillar carries painted plaster with a representation of the deceased and his wife. A sloping passage leads from the main chamber to the burial chamber below, which is difficult to access.

Around Aswan

Map labels:
- Necropolis of the Nobles
- Aswan
- Monastery of St Simeon
- Kitchener's Island & Botanical Gardens
- Agha Khan Mausoleum
- Elephantine Island
- Unfinished Obelisk
- Saluga Island
- Siheil Island
- Boats to Philae Temple
- New Port
- Aswan Dam
- Awad Island
- Agilkia Island (New location of Philae Temple)
- Bigah Island
- Philae Island
- Hisha Island
- Granite Islands
- High Dam Port
- Aswan High Dam
- Kalabsha Temple
- Lake Nasser

➡ Aswan maps
1 Aswan, page 120
2 Aswan centre, page 122
3 Around Aswan, page 125

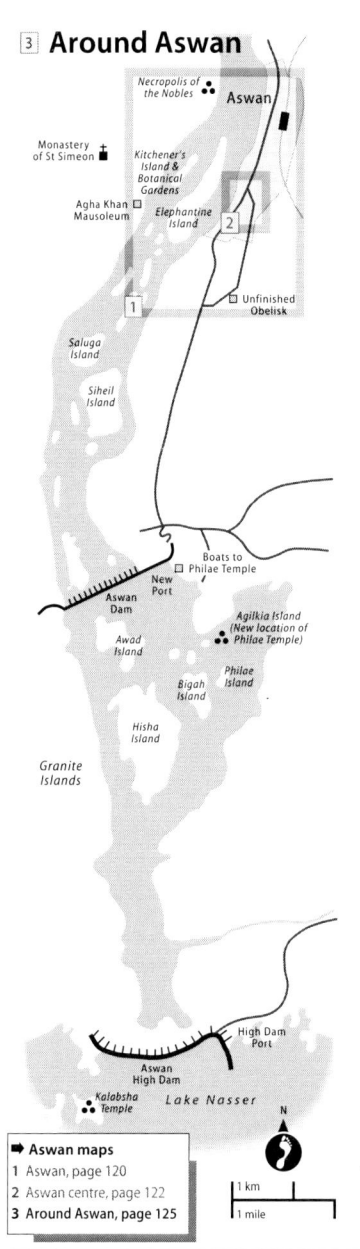

Monastery of St Simeon

ⓘ *Daily from 0700-1600 winter, 0700-1700 in summer, E£25, students E£15, accessible by ferry from just south of the Governorate building (should be E£1 but foreigners may struggle to get it for less than E£5), and then either by a 30-min walk through soft sand or a 10-min camel ride (which can carry 2, aim for E£40) hired near the landing stage, or hire a pick up to take the back road and wait for you (E£30-40).*

This desert monastery, which lies on the west bank inland from the Aga Khan's Mausoleum, was founded and dedicated in the seventh century to a fourth-century monk Anba Hadra, who was later ordained bishop.

Following an encounter with a funeral procession on the day after his own wedding Anba Hadra decided, presumably without consulting his wife, to remain celibate. He became a student of St Balmar, rejected urban life and chose to become a desert hermit living in a cave. The fortress monastery stands at the head of a desert valley looking towards the River Nile and from where the dramatic sunsets appear to turn the sand to flames. Until Salah Al-Din destroyed the building in 1173 it was used by monks, including Saint Simeon about whom little is known, as a base for proselytizing expeditions first south into Nubia and then, after the Muslim conquest, north into Egypt.

Although the monastery is uninhabitable its main feature the surrounding walls, the lower storeys of hewn stone and upper ones of mud-brick, have been preserved and the internal decorations are interesting. At intervals along the walls there are remains of towers. Visitors are admitted through a small gateway in the east tower that leads to a church with a partially collapsed basilica but the nave and aisles are still accessible. There is a painting of the ascended Christ near the domed altar recess and four angels in splendid robes. The walls of a small cave chapel, which can be entered via the church, are richly painted with pictures of the Apostles which were partially defaced by Muslim iconoclasts. The cave chapel leads to the upper enclosure from which the living quarters can be entered. Up to 300 monks lived in simple cells with some hewn into the rock and others in the main building to the north of the enclosure, with kitchens and stables to the south.

Nubian village
One of the most accessible and colourful of Aswan's Nubian villages lies here on the west bank just 200 m north of the ferry landing. Not visited as often as those on Elephantine Island this village remains a peaceful place to wander around either before or after visiting the Monastery of Saint Simeon or the Necropolis of the Nobles.

Aswan Dams
ⓘ *Cross the High Dam between 0700-1600 winter, 0700-1700 summer, E£20, students E£10. A taxi here from Aswan costs E£35 return, if the taxi takes you and waits at the unfinished obelisk and Philae temple (around a 3-hr trip), it should cost around E£70. Note that you will also have to pay for the motorboat to transport you to and from the island of Philae, an additional E£40 for the boat or E£5 per person.*

There are in fact two Aswan Dams but it is the so-called **High Dam**, just upstream from the original 1902 British-built Aswan Dam, that is Egypt's pride and joy and which created Lake Nasser, the world's largest reservoir. In fact the High Dam is so big (111 m high, 3830 m long, 980 m wide at its base and 40 m at its top) that it is almost impossible to realize its scale except from the observation deck of the lotus-shaped Soviet-Egyptian Friendship tower or from the air when landing at nearby Aswan airport. It is claimed that the structure of stones, sand, clay and facing concrete give it a volume 17 times that of the Pyramid of Cheops. To help appreciate the scale and consequences of the dam's construction, the visitors' pavilion, which includes a 15-m-high model of the dam and photographs of the relocation of the Abu Simbel temple, is worth a visit. Occasionally, crossing the dam is prevented for security reasons. The contrast, however, between the view of the narrow river channel looking towards Aswan on the downstream side of the dam and the vast area of Lake Nasser, almost like an open sea, as you look upstream, could not be more marked.

Philae temples
ⓘ *0700-1600 winter, 0700-1700 summer, E£50, students E£25, permit for commercial photography E£10, no charge for video recorders. The easiest way to get to Philae is to join one of the many organized tours from Aswan, although this means you will have to follow a schedule. Or take a taxi to the dock (E£30-35 return) and then a motorboat to the temple. The boats seat 8 people and should cost E£5 per person (although the boat men will demand E£20) or E£40 per private boat for the return journey including a 1-hr wait. Make sure you state a 2-way trip or you will have problems later when they try to charge double.*

Few would dispute that among the most beautiful and romantic monuments in the whole of Egypt are the Philae temples, which were built on Philae Island in the Ptolemaic era (332-30 BC) as an offering to Isis. In fact, the Temple of Isis and the rest of the monuments were moved to the neighbouring **Agilkia Island** by UNESCO in 1972-1980 when the construction of the High Dam threatened to submerge Philae forever. They

The great dams of Aswan

Although it has since become a cliché, the Nile really is 'the lifeblood of Egypt' and the combination of a restricted area of agricultural land and an ever-expanding population has necessitated the very careful management of what limited water is available. The theory behind the construction of the Aswan dams was that, rather than years of low water levels, drought and famine being followed by years when the Nile flooded and washed half the agricultural soil into the Mediterranean, the flow of the Nile could be regulated and thereby provide a much more stable flow of water. Unfortunately, although the two dams did control the Nile waters and thereby boost both hydroelectric power and agricultural production, the mushrooming population outstripped the gains and Egypt now imports almost half of its cereal requirements. At the same time it is now recognized that the High Dam was planned and built when the level of the Nile was particularly high. Whether it is because of climatic change or simply part of an apparent 20- to 30-year cycle the volume of water reaching Aswan is decreasing and if the trend continues it may be necessary to pipe natural gas from the Gulf of Suez to generate the electricity at the giant 2100 mw power station at Aswan.

The original Aswan Dam was built by the British between 1898-1902 and was then raised twice in 20 years to make it the largest dam in the world. Although no longer used for storage or irrigation, the dam, which is crossed by the road to the airport, is now mainly used to provide local power. After the 1952 Revolution, the new leaders recognized that massive population pressure meant that a more radical solution was required both to control the waters of the Nile and generate sufficient electricity for the new industrial sector and bring power to every Egyptian village. To finance the construction of the planned High Dam, following the withdrawal of a World Bank loan under US pressure, Nasser nationalized the Suez Canal and persuaded the USSR to help build the dam. Construction started in 1960 and was completed in 1971 after Nasser's death in September 1970.

Although it took a number of years to fill, the most visible effect of the dam was the creation of Lake Nasser. This has enabled Egypt, unlike Sudan or Ethiopia, to save water during times of plenty and have an adequate strategic reserve for times of shortage. The extra water from the dam significantly increased the area of land under permanent irrigation and allowed over one million feddans (about 400,000 ha) of desert to be reclaimed. In addition, the extra electric power facilitated the expansion of the industrial sector not only around Aswan but throughout the country.

There were, however, major environmental implications of the dam's construction because the rise of Lake Nasser flooded the homeland of the Nubians who were forced to migrate north to other towns and cities (to date they have been offered negligible compensation). Another drawback is that the lake accumulates the Nile's natural silt that used to fertilize the agricultural land downstream from Aswan. Consequently farmers in Lower Egypt are now having to rely heavily on chemical fertilizers, destabilizing the whole food chain. In view of its expanding population, however, Egypt would be in an absolutely hopeless situation without the dams.

were then reconstructed to imitate the original as closely as possible but the new position no longer faces neighbouring Bigah island, one of the burial sites of Osiris and closed to all but the priesthood, which was the raison d'être for the location in the first place.

Temple of Isis Although there are other smaller temples on the island it is dominated by the Temple of Isis. Isis was the consort of her brother Osiris and eventually became the 'Great Mother of All Gods and Nature', 'Goddess of Ten Thousand Names', and represented women, purity and sexuality. Isis is attributed with having reconstructed Osiris' dismembered body and creating his son Horus, who became the model of a man and king. In the third to fifth centuries the worship of Isis became Christianity's greatest rival throughout the Mediterranean. There have even been claims that the early Christians developed the cult of the Virgin Mary to replace Isis in order to attract new converts.

Different parts of the Temple of Isis, which occupies over a quarter of the new island, were constructed over an 800-year period by Ptolemaic (332-30 BC) and Roman (30 BC-AD 395) rulers. At the top of the steps where the motorboats arrive is the **Kiosk of Nectanebo (1)**, from where runs a Roman colonnaded Outer Court leading to the main temple. Its irregular shape gives the impression of greater length. On the west or lake side of the court the **Colonnade of Augustus and Tiberius (3)** is well preserved and contains 31 columns with individual capitals, plant shaped – papyrus in various stages of bud. There are still traces of paint on some of the columns and on the starred ceiling. On the right is the plainer **First Eastern Colonnade (4)** behind which are the foundations of the **Temple of Arensnuphis (5)** (Nubian God), the ruined **Chapel of Mandulis (6)** (Nubian God of Kalabsha), and the **Temple of Imhotep (7)** (the architect of Zoser's step pyramid at Saqqara who was later deified as a healing God).

The irregular plan of the temple is due to the terrain. A huge granite intrusion has been incorporated into the right-hand tower of the First Pylon and steps to this pylon are also to accommodate hard rock. You enter the temple through the **First Pylon of Ptolemy XIII Neos Dionysus (8)** with illustrations showing him slaying his enemies as Isis, Horus and Hathor look on. The pylon was originally flanked by two obelisks, since looted and transported to the UK, but today only two lions at the base guarding the entrance remain. The **Gate of Ptolemy II Philadelphus (11)**, just to the right of the pylon's main **Gate of Nectanebo II (10)**, is from the earlier 30th Dynasty (380-343 BC). On its right is graffiti written by Napoleon's troops after their victory over the Mamluks in 1799.

Arriving in a large forecourt to the left is the colonnaded **Mammisi (14)**, used for mammisi rituals. It was originally built by Ptolemy VII and expanded by the Romans, which explains why images of Isis with Horus as a baby are intermingled with the figures of contemporary Roman emperors. In the inner sanctum of the Mammisi itself are historically important scenes of Isis giving birth to Horus in the marshes and others of her suckling the child-pharaoh. A curiosity to note on the outer western wall of the Birth House is a memorial to men of the Heavy Camel Regiment who lost their lives in the Sudanese Campaign of 1884-1885. The tablet commemorates the nine officers and 92 men who were killed in action or died of disease. Look carefully at the Hathor-headed columns facing into the Inner Court from the walls of the Mammisi – at the far end her face is straight but at the near end she is smiling. On the opposite side of the forecourt from the Mammisi is the late Ptolemaic **Second Eastern Colonnade (13)** behind which are a number of attractive reliefs and six small function rooms including a library.

Philae temples

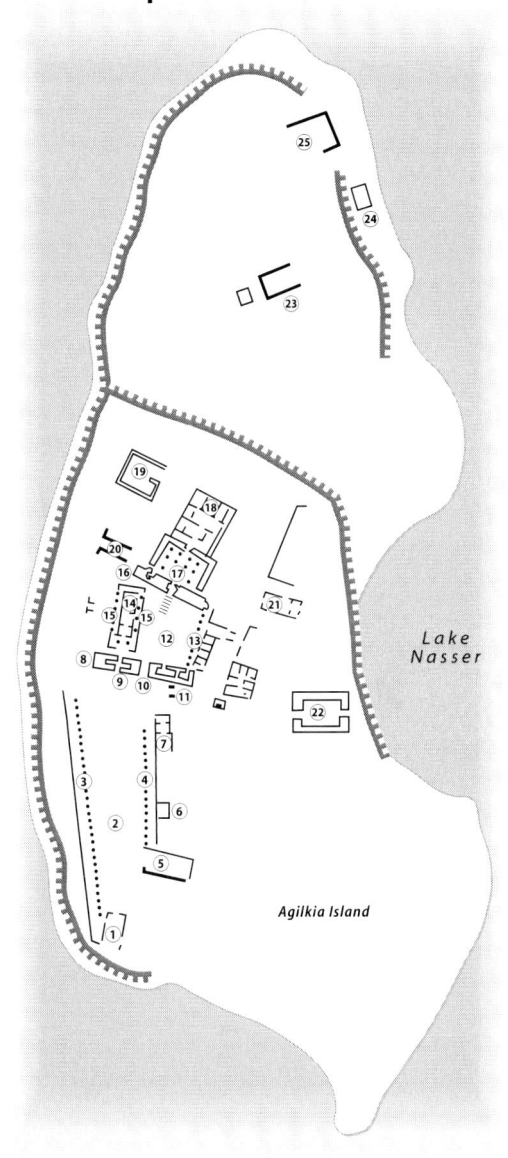

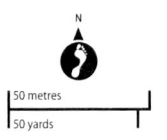

Kiosk of Nectanebo **1**
Outer court **2**
Western colonnade
 of Augustus Tiberius **3**
First eastern colonnade **4**
Temple of Arensnuphis **5**
Chapel of Mandulis **6**
Temple of Imhotep **7**

Temple of Isis

First pylon (Ptolemy XIII
 Neos Dionysus) **8**
Entrance to mammisi **9**
Gate of Nectanebo II **10**
Gate of Ptolemy II
 Philadelphus **11**
Inner court **12**
Second eastern colonnade **13**
Mammisi (birth house) **14**
Composite columns
 with Hathor's heads **15**
Second pylon **16**
Hypostyle hall **17**
Sanctuary **18**

Temple of Harendotes **19**
Hadrian's Gate **20**
Temple of Hathor **21**
Kiosk of Trajan **22**
Temple of Augustus **23**
Roman arch **24**
Gate of Diocletian **25**

Lake Nasser

Agilkia Island

South of Luxor Aswan • 129

The axis of the temple is changed by the **Second Pylon (16)**, set at an angle to the first, which was built by Ptolemy XIII Neos Dionysos and shows him presenting offerings to Horus and Hathor on the right tower (some of the scenes on the left tower were defaced by the early Christians). Beyond the Pylon a court containing 10 columns opens onto the **Hypostyle Hall (17)**, much reduced in size due to lack of space. These columns have retained few traces of their original colour although the capitals are better preserved. The ceiling in the central aisle has representations of vultures that were symbolic of the union of Lower and Upper Egypt. The rest of the ceilings have astronomical motifs and two representations of the goddess Nut. On either side of the wall, backing onto the Second Pylon, Ptolemy VII and Cleopatra II can be seen presenting offerings to Hathor and Khnum. The crosses carved on pillars and walls here provide evidence of the Coptic occupation. From the entrance at the far end of the Hypostyle Hall is a chamber that gives access to the roof. The interconnecting roof chambers are all dedicated to Osiris and lead to his shrine. Vivid reliefs portray the reconstruction of his body.

Continuing upwards and north from the chamber, linked to the Hypostyle Hall, are three rooms decorated with sacrificial reliefs representing the deities. The central room leads to a further three rooms linked to the **Sanctuary (18)** in which is a stone pedestal dedicated by Ptolemy III, which formerly supported the holy barque of Isis. Reliefs portray Isis and her son surrounded by Nubian deities. The temple's exterior was decorated at the direction of the Emperor Augustus.

Hadrian's Gate (20) has some very interesting reliefs on the north wall depicting Isis, Nephthys, Horus and Amun in adoration before Osiris in the form of a bird. Behind is the source of the Nile emerging from a cavern while Hapy, a Nile god in human form with a headdress of papyrus, is shown pouring water from two jars, indicating the Egyptians' knowledge that the Nile had more than one source. The south wall depicts a mummified Osiris lying on a crocodile together with another image of the reconstructed Osiris seated on his throne with his son Horus.

Smaller shrines can be seen throughout the island dedicated to both Nubian and local deities. East of the temple of Isis is the small **Temple of Hathor (21)**. Two columns have Hathor-capitals while, in a famous relief, the local deities play musical instruments. Much of the later additions to the buildings on Philae were Roman due to its position as a border post (such as extension of walls, huge gates and kiosks). **The Kiosk of Trajan (22)**, built in AD 167 has 14 columns with floral motifs and stone plaques on the lintels that were intended to hold sun discs, though these were never completed. Only two walls have been decorated and these depict Osiris, Horus and Isis receiving offerings from the Emperor Trajan. It is thought that the Kiosk originally had a wooden roof. From here, looking southeast towards the original Philae Island, it is possible to see the remains of the coffer dam that was built around it to reduce the water level and protect the temple ruins before they were moved to Agilkia. At the northeast end of the island is the ruined **Temple of Augustus (23)** and the **Gate of Diocletian (25)**. These were next to a mud-brick Roman village that had to be abandoned by the archaeologists when Philae was moved because the water had already caused such severe erosion.

Sound and Light show ⓘ *Usually there are shows daily at 1830, 1945 and 2100 in winter and 2000, 2115 and 2230 in summer. These change during Ramadan and the show can be totally booked out by private tour companies, so check with the tourist office, call*

David Roberts – painter of Egypt

David Roberts was a remarkable man whose oriental paintings brought to life Egypt and its heritage for many people in the Western world. His pictures are full of atmosphere and wonderful colour. Among the most famous are the *Temple of Dendara*, *Island of Philae*, *Nubia* and *A Street in Cairo* together with his paintings of the Temple of Ramses II at Abu Simbel.

Roberts, born in 1796, had a difficult childhood as the son of an impecunious Edinburgh cobbler. He eventually became known as a painter of theatrical scenery at the Old Vic and Covent Garden before making his name as a picture painter with items such as *The Israelites leaving Egypt* and scenes of his travels in Spain.

David Roberts arrived in Egypt in 1838 and spent 11 months travelling through the Nile Valley and visiting the Holy Land. He was a prolific sketcher of sites and left six volumes of lithographs of this visit, including several scenes of Cairo. Many of these and other scenes were later translated into oil paintings.

Roberts returned to Great Britain where, in his absence, he had been made an associate of the Royal Academy. He lived to 69 years and produced many masterpieces based on his travels in Egypt, incidentally providing a wonderful record of the state of Egyptian monuments of the time.

There are many inexpensive cards and books with copies of his illustrations. It is useful to have one with you when visiting the major sites. They show very clearly parts that have disappeared, parts that are now too high to view and give an excellent idea of the coloured decorations.

T097-230 5376 or see www.soundandlight.com.eg for the latest schedule. Mon English/French; Tue French/English; Wed French/English; Thu French/Spanish/English; Fri English/French/Italian; Sat English/Arabic; Sun German/French/ English. 'Cheap tours from Aswan abound, but if you want to go alone tickets cost E£75 (no student discount), you'll have to pay for a taxi (E£30-35 return) and the motorboat (E£5 if you share with a group, E£40 on your own). Give yourself at least 45 mins to get there from Aswan.

Like most big temples in Egypt, Philae has its own Sound and Light Show. This one is an informative and melodramatic hour-long floodlit tour through the ruins. Some find it kitchy, and others majestic. Arriving before sunset in time for the first show can be especially memorable. Travelling out from the harbour in a small flotilla of boats, watching the stars come out and tracing the dark shapes of the islands in the river silhouetted against the orange sunset sky is a stunning prelude to the beauty of the ancient floodlit ruins.

Soheel Island and West Soheel village.

Soheel Island is near the First Cataract, about 4 km upriver from Aswan. It is reachable by *felucca* (haggle to get it for E£50-60) or you can take a micro or taxi from the Corniche and ask to go to the stadium area ('stad'). When you get there ask for the Tameem Il Sahi (a clinic), and on the riverbank near the clinic there are boats with which you can negotiate to go across to Soheel Island. It's a very short distance so you should get it for E£10-20. From the ferry landing you can visit the Nubian village (free) and the **Famine Stela** ⓘ *E£25, student E£15. The stela area is a little overpriced and you may be able to get in just for* *a donation*. The granite boulders of the hill here are decorated with Ptolemaic designs. Following the scratchings to the summit, you get a wonderful view over the First Cataract area and see the Famine Stela itself. This dates to Zoser's reign and describes how a lengthy period of famine was ended by the building of a new temple on Soheel Island.

To see a slightly different style of Nubian village, an interesting trip can be made to West Soheel. This is close to the Old Dam and can be easily reached by taxi and perhaps incorporated into a trip to the Unfinished Obelisk and Philae. By public transport, take a micro from the Corniche going south. Ask for the 'khazan' and get off after you have crossed the dam. There is a traffic circle with an obelisk in the centre. A sign clearly points north along the bank to 'Gharb Sohail' (West Soheel), wait by the sign to get a pickup to the village. There are numerous houses vividly decorated with colourful Nubian designs, dead crocodiles nailed over the doorways and some live (caged) crocs too. From the village you can see over to Soheel Island where the Famine Stela is. It is possible to get a boat to row you over and wait for you for an hour, but from this side of the island you need to ford a stream and scramble through acacia thicket to reach the site. Much easier to access from the other bank. Going back to Aswan you may be lucky enough to get one micro all the way from West Soheel to the Corniche.

⊙ Aswan listings

For sleeping and eating price codes and other relevant information, see pages 11-15.

Where to stay

Aswan *p117, maps p120, p122 and p125*

Although it's a primary destination for visitors to Egypt, the hotel scene in and around Aswan is rather stagnant as increasing numbers of tourists stay on cruise boats or *dahabiyas*. Some classic budget options are dotted around the *souk* and you can also find surprisingly cheap rooms on the Corniche with stunning views of the Nile. It is possible to stay in houses on Elephantine Island – spend a few hours there and someone is sure to suggest it to you – but it will be very basic accommodation.

Note that the prices for accommodation fluctuate significantly. In the summer, prices can decrease up to 50%. Use the following price codes to get a general idea, but definitely enquire further. Plan to bargain. Even in mid-range and more expensive hotels, you can strike a deal. Note that when booking online it is vital to be clear about what exactly you expect to be included in the price. For example, get in writing that you have a Nile view, that breakfast and taxes are included, etc, to ensure there are no arguments when it comes to paying your bill.

€€€€ Iberotel, Corniche El-Nil, T097-232 8824, aswan@jaz.travel, www.iberotel.com. Formerly the **Army Hotel**, this spotless 151-room hotel has undergone a major refit. The main building east of the Corniche has an imposing lobby decorated with pharaonic-style lotus columns and Orientalist paintings. There are all the usual amenities as well as a small shopping mall and adjacent bowling complex. The views from the 7th-floor **Panorama** restaurant are so good that bookings must be made before 1500 if non-residents want to dine there. A gleaming tiled tunnel runs under the Corniche to the pool area where there are 44 tastefully appointed Nile-side chalets. Inside the rooms is non-smoking, but smokers can request a room with a terrace to indulge their habit.
€€€€ Isis Island Resort and Spa, T097-231 7400. Presumably designed to

blend in with the surroundings (which it almost does at sunset) this pink monstrosity is spread over its own island to the south of town at the first cataract, it's a picturesque setting and relaxing atmosphere. Rooms are constantly being refurbished and many cannot be called truly 5-star. But the pool is great, their terrace is a marvellous place to watch the sun go down and it's still an excellent place to get away from it all. Frequent free boats shuttle residents back and forth.

€€€€ Movenpick, Elephantine Island, T097-230 3455, www.moevenpick-hotels.com. Fabulous balconied rooms, excellent location in middle of river, reached by a free ferry, the hideous tower that spoils most views in Aswan is less of an obstruction from the confines of the hotel. Stunning views particularly at sunset, **Orangerie Restaurant** and the **Lounge Bar** are chic, and the pool and grounds are superb. Recommended as the only place for pure luxury in Aswan.

€€€€ Old Cataract Hotel, Sharia Abtal El-Tahrir, T097-231 6000, www.sofitel.com. An Edwardian Moorish-style hotel, probably Egypt's most famous, the **Old Cataract** featured in Agatha Christie's *Death on the Nile* and has been *the* place to stay in Aswan since it opened in 1899. Unfortunately, it has been closed for renovation but is due to reopen soon, so check the website for the current status. Connected by a series of gardens is the cheaper, modern **New Cataract**, in an unfortunate slab of a building (also closed for refurbishment).

€€€€-€€€ Philae Hotel, 79 Corniche El-Nil, T097-231 2090, T010-222 9628, hanan-attiatallah@web.de. Newly refurbished to a very high standard, this Egyptian-German enterprise offers pristine en suite rooms with double glazing so you can enjoy your Nile view without the accompanying noise. Chic locally sourced ornaments and lamps blend harmoniously with ultra-clean comfortable modern fittings. An excellent choice.

€€€ Basma Hotel, Sharia El-Fanadek, T097-231 0900/1, www.basmahotel.com. Perched on Aswan's highest hill, commanding breathtaking views of the west bank and Aga Khan's mausoleum, the **Basma** is a generic 4-star hotel with all the usual amenities. However, the large pool is welcoming, staff are friendly and the terrace good for a sunset beer until the **Old Cataract** reopens. It is handily located for the Nubian Museum.

€€€ Cleopatra, Sharia Saad Zaghloul, Aswan, T097-231 4001-4. Located in the heart of the *souk*, the lobby is quite chic in a modern-Orientalist kind of way but carpeted rooms are decidedly retro and could do with a lick of paint. Balconies overlook town and there are all the usual 3-star facilities though bathrooms are nothing special. Pool on top floor is clean but small.

€€€ Marhaba Palace Hotel, Corniche El-Nil, T097-233 0102-4, www.marhaba-aswan.com. Rooms are spotless and well furnished, some have huge terraces, but bathrooms are a bit squashed. The roof cafeteria has a great view across the river thick with *feluccas* to the Tombs of the Nobles, unblemished by the Movenpick tower. There's a decent pool and restaurant, but it's pricey; try to negotiate a discount.

€€€ Nile Hotel, 15 Corniche El-Nil, T097-231 4222, www.nilehotel-aswan.com. A pleasant, bright hotel that is deservedly popular. Rooms all have Nile views, side-view rooms have balconies while front-facing don't (though they are bigger). Subtle decor, rag rugs, TV, fridge, minibar, a/c, safety boxes and the dining room is more attractive than most. There is also a suite, more expensive, but very spacious with an immense terrace.

€€€ Pyramisa Isis Corniche Hotel, Corniche El-Nil, T097-231 5200, www.pyramisaegypt.com. Chalet rooms are a bit overpriced for the quality, but this is the only hotel actually on the riverbank facing Elephantine Island. Offers a/c bungalows in a small garden with a pool and all the usual 4-star amenities, riverside terrace and restaurant with superb sunset views. Don't expect anything very grand, and look for a good deal online.

€€ Bet El-Kerem, Nagh El-Kuba, west bank, T012-384 2218, www.betelkerem.com, on the west bank 200 m north of the ferry landing for the Necroplois of the Nobles. This tranquil hotel offers a chance to get away from the bustle of Aswan. 9 double rooms are simply furnished and decorated with bright Nubian artwork. The rooftop cafeteria with its comfy benches, rag-rugs and outstanding views across the Tombs of the Nobles and the Nile is the undoubted highlight. Soft drinks are free and the (slightly overpriced) food is freshly cooked and tasty. Very friendly, welcoming staff.

€€ Cleopatra, Sharia Saad Zaghloul, Aswan, T097-231 4001-4. Located in the heart of the *souk*, the lobby is quite chic in a modern-Orientalist kind of way but carpeted rooms are decidedly retro and could do with a lick of paint. Balconies overlook town and there are all the usual 3-star facilities though bathrooms are nothing special. Pool on top floor is clean but small.

€€-€ Paradise Hotel, Saad Zaghoul, 2 mins from the railway station, T097-232 9690/1. Opened in 2008, this is a good-value choice if you can rise above some bad-taste fixtures and fittings. New mattresses, large beds, breakfast included, and the staff make every effort to please. Rooftop coffee shop has a panoramic view of the Nile and there's an Italian restaurant. Front-facing rooms are the more spacious pool at Cleopatra Hotel.

€ El Salam Hotel, 101 Corniche El-Nil, T097-230 2651. Slightly cheaper than the **Hathor** next door, rooms are pristine, linens fresh, those at the front have huge balconies (but shared bath) while side-view rooms have private bath. If you ignore the gloomy corridors and faded prints of England circa 1970, this is a fine hotel in a good location.

The rooftop's a bit shabby but the view more than makes up for this. Staff are friendly and there's no hassle.

€ Happi Hotel, Sharia Abtal El-Tahrir, T097-231 4115/6. Closed for refitting at the time of writing, but has Nile views from rather cramped singles and more spacious double rooms. Bathrooms are notably clean, beer and decent food are available, the Happi is perennially popular.

€ Hathor, Corniche El-Nil, T097-231 4580. Has an excellent location and great rooftop with loungers, though the pool is very small. Decent rooms have a/c (controlled from downstairs) and baths are clean and tiled, if a bit cramped. Soft pillows rather than bolsters, bigger than average beds and a nice atmosphere make it the best choice in this price bracket (doubles E£100, including breakfast). Wi-Fi is E£10 for your whole stay.

€ Keylany Hotel, 25 Sharia Keylany, (known by locals as Sharia Gedid) at the southern end of the *souk*, T097-231 7332, www.keylanyhotel.com. Spotless white painted rooms, attractive tiled floors and a lovely rag-rug-and-reeds chill-out café on the roof make the Keylany a nice place to be. There are also older, slightly scruffier rooms with shared bath that are more backpacker affordable. A/c, fridge, safety box, and plans for a pool on the roof. The internet café in the basement is effective but expensive, though Wi-Fi is free for hotel residents.

€ Memnon Hotel, Corniche El-Nil (entrance is from the back street), T097-230 0483, www.memnonhotel-aswan.com. The a/c rooms are clean, if a bit tatty, some have superior bathrooms, others better views – look at a few. Rooms at the back (no view) or those on the 1st floor (carpeted) are marginally cheaper. Again, the rooftop pool doesn't beckon but the view is panoramic. There are plans for a rooftop restaurant. The lift is only for the fearless – watch out for the gap in the floorboards.

€ New Abu Simbel Hotel, Sharia Abtal El-Tahrir, T097-230 6096. On the northern side of town, the hotel's selling point is its pleasant garden where breakfast is served and the staff are mellow. Rooms are clean but getting jaded with a/c, private bath, and balcony views (over a school yard) to the Tombs of the Nobles. Across the street from a few local *ahwas*, it's still a good place to escape any bustle and hassle.

€ Nuba Nile Hotel, Sharia Abtal El-Tahrir, T097-231 3267, info@nubanile.com. This is a good deal (doubles E£180) and can get pretty busy; it's wise to book ahead. Rooms have large comfortable beds, some touches of *mashrabiya*, a/c (2 installations in some rooms), though vary in size – look at a few if you have the chance. The teeny pool on the roof is more for dangling your feet than swimming, internet in the foyer café is E£4 per hr, no seasonal discounts. Breakfast included.

€ Nubian Oasis Hotel, 234 Sharia Saad Zaghloul, T097-231 2123/6. A budget hotel located in the middle of the *souk*, fairly basic rooms have grubby paintwork but clean linen and a/c. Some rooms on higher floors have good views of town and beer is available on the rooftop terrace with impressive vistas for E£10. Free internet for 30 mins then E£5 per hr after that. Breakfast served from 0300 onwards – handy for early starts to Abu Simbel. Doubles E£50, singles E£30. Hassle from touts has been reported.

€ Nuurhan, Sharia Saad Zaghloul, T097-231 6069. Another cheap option in the middle of the *souk*. Reasonably clean and comfy rooms with drab furniture (some don't have curtains), price varies depending on whether you have a/c and private bath (doubles E£45), although shared baths are actually newer and preferable. Expect *felucca* tours to be pushed on you.

€ Youth Hostel, 96 Sharia Abtal El-Tahrir, entrance from the alley on the right of the **October Hotel**, T097-230 2313. Dorms with fans, 8 beds (bunks) and nothing else cost E£12 or triples are E£17 per bed. Usually empty, except when universities let out and then it becomes a popular spot for Egyptian college students. Open all year, midnight curfew casually imposed. It's only really worth staying here if you're on the tightest of budgets, but the sheets are clean, staff welcoming and you won't be pestered to go on a tour.

Restaurants

Aswan *p117, maps p120, p122 and p125*
For expensive and exceptionally chic dining options, there's nothing outside the resort hotels. There are, however, a number of mid-range and cheap restaurants that serve good food. There are also a couple of notable *fatir* pizza joints, and of course the sit-down cafeterias, some floating on the Nile where the setting can be better than the food. Tourists often get charged double local prices in smaller places, so it might be worth brushing up on Arabic numerals so you can read the menu and get a better price.

€€€ 1902 Restaurant, in the **Old Cataract Hotel**. If the **Cataract** has opened again after refurbishments, the 1902 will be serving international food spiced with Nubian dancers in classic decor. Even budget-conscious visitors may want to indulge in a cup of tea or a glass of wine at sunset on the terrace. It really is an institution.

€€€ Darna Restaurant, New Cataract Hotel. Impressive buffet in a restaurant resembling an Egyptian house.

€€€-€€ Nubian Restaurant, on Issa Island south of Elephantine, T097-230 0307, T012-216 2379. Set Nubian meals for about E£75. Wine and beer are available, but pricey. The restaurant offers a free boat that leaves from the dock in front of EgyptAir. The setting is romantic, but the folkloric show is clichéd and doesn't happen if tour groups aren't around.

€€ **Al Masry Restaurant**, Sharia Al-Matar. Spotless a/c restaurant popular with locals and tourists alike. Offers standard meals of fish, chicken, kebab and pigeon.

€€ **Aswan Moon**, on the Corniche, T097-231 6108. The most acclaimed of the floating restaurants, the food is OK, but it's better to come here for the Nile-side setting and colourful atmosphere plus it's 10° cooler by the river than on the street. More lively at night, sometimes there's entertainment in the summer and it's a good place to meet other travellers and/or *felucca* captains.

€€ **Biti**, in the main Midan in front of the train station, T097-230 0949. Cute pizza restaurant on 3 levels, the 2nd floor has a/c, the 3rd is on the roof. Excellent *fatir* costs E£35 for 5 toppings, good service and they also home deliver between 1900-0100; most delightful is the view over the square. Open 1000-0330, good place to people watch once the sun sets.

€€ **Chef Khalil**, in the *souk*. Serves tasty seafood by the weight. Choices include lobster, prawns and sole, and various fillet of other locally caught fish. All meals accompanied by *tahina*, salad and chips or rice. Entrées are E£45-60. If this tiny restaurant is full, hang out, it's worth the wait.

€€ **El-Medina**, in the heart of the *souk*. Clean, renowned local joint that serves up good home-made cooking. Mostly meat dishes, but they will prepare you a veggie plate.

€€ **Makka**, Sharia Abtal al Tahrir, T097-230 3232. Open 1200-0100. On the tour group circuit, but therefore clean and comfortable with good food. Stuffed pigeon and a wealth of kebabs all come with salads, rice and veg.

€€ **Nubian House**, on the hill behind the Basma Hotel, T097-232 6226. A popular intimate restaurant serving authentic and delicious Nubian food for E£20-30 per entrée. *Sheesha* also on offer, but no alcohol. Outdoor seating with stunning panoramic views over all of Aswan make it worth the trek from the centre of town, especially around sunset. When there are groups in for dinner a Nubian troupe provides music, so call ahead if you wish to join or avoid this.

€€ **Panorama**, on the Corniche, T097-230 6169, an old-timer on the Aswan restaurant scene. Known for good-quality, traditional Egyptian food and an eclectic collection of Nubian artefacts. Serves reliable tasty tagines, has an extensive menu of herbal teas and non-alcoholic cocktails and delicious Nubian coffee to finish. Service can be slow but food is cooked to order and is worth the wait.

€€ **Pharaohs**, on the west bank south of the Aga Khan's Mausoleum, T012-791 9895. Accessible only by boat, good Nubian home cooking for E£50-60 per person, something a bit different and beautiful boat trip to get there. Call ahead, don't just turn up.

€€-€ **Aisayeda Naffesa**, Sharia Ahmed Maher, T097-231 7152. This place has been around for years and serves up tasty Egyptian dishes, however their juices are a let down. They have a few tables under the awning outside and, though you will typically be charged more than locals, it is still cheap and recommended for ambiance and flavour.

€€-€ **Esmailya Sons Restaurant**, Sharia Al-Matar, has standard meat, soup, rice, salad and veg meals, though the fish option is most popular. It's opposite **Al Masry** restaurant and is significantly cheaper, there's a menu displayed outside in Arabic and English.

€ **Ali Baba**, Sharia Abtal al Tahrir, has the best *koshari* in town but at annoyingly inflated tourist prices. The right-hand half of the building has takeaway Egyptian staples.

€ **Kasr Elhoda**, Sharia Abtal al Tahrir, north of the station. Open 1000-0200. Has cheap (E£15-40) *fatir* and is always packed with Egyptians. It's a typical marble interior with a/c and no English menu. There's also a good bakery next door.

Entertainment

Aswan *p117, maps p120, p122 and p125*

There are nightclubs in the big hotels that offer Nubian and Western floorshows when enough tourists are in town. During the winter, except on Fri, there are nightly performances (from 2130-2300) by the Nubian Folk Troupe at the **Cultural Palace**, T097-232 3344, at the north end of the Corniche. The **Horus Hotel**, 89 Corniche El-Nil, T097-230 3323 has female singers accompanied by *oud* and *tabla* on the rooftop every night from 2200, which can make for a surreal Aswan experience. Beer is E£20 and *sheesha* E£5, the distant west bank lights glowing orange while city minarets glow green sets the atmosphere.

Emy, next to **Aswan Moon**, the best place for an evening drink. The top floor of the floating restaurant picks up a nice breeze and most of the clientele wear *galabiyas* and turbans.

Oscar Hotel on Sharia El Baraka. The basic basement bar is actually open-air and quite friendly to tourists, although other drinkers invariably start arguing amongst themselves later on.

An evening in Aswan is also well spent wandering through the ever-thriving *souk*, puffing on a *sheesha* in a local *ahwa*, or strolling by the Nile. Families tend to congregate in the midan across from the train station, where there are plenty of cafés.

A night time *felucca* sail is always a romantic way to spend an evening, especially in Aswan where the riverbanks are among the most beautiful. Keep your ears open for celebratory sounds as you may well run into a wedding party – which you will very likely be invited to join.

Shopping

Aswan *p117, maps p120, p122 and p125*

Aswan used to have perhaps the most colourful and exotic *souk* in all of Egypt outside of Cairo. Sadly, the huge patchwork of umbrellas and narrow alleys that made up the maze of the *souk* have been swept away during a misguided beautification initiative and what is left is a sterile pedestrianized thoroughfare that lacks any soul. However, though locals buying and selling fresh produce and doing their daily shopping all seem to have migrated to the laneways radiating from the main *souk* street, there is still good tourist shopping to be done while the odd traditional *ahwa* or butchers shop remain lodged in between the alabaster and papyrus. Musical instruments, spices and nuts from the depths of Sudan, tempting baked goods moved along by eager boys on carts, shimmering scarves and embroidered *gallabiyyas*, ancient stereos and local music to play in them – all of it can be found along the endless Sharia Souk. Aswan is a good place to look for acclaimed Nubian music, most music merchants blare tunes from their humble sound systems at all hours. If you want to listen to a particular album, just ask. CDs should cost E£30. There is also a duty-free shop on the Corniche (near the EgyptAir office), as well as a large departmental store on Sharia Abtal El-Tahrir. The best bookshop is **Nubia Tourist Book Center** in the rowing club building (El Nadi el-Tagdeef) on the Corniche, T097-231 9777, open 0800-2300, which stocks AUC titles and books in different European languages, as well as good postcards and Lehnert & Landrock prints. There is also another branch on Sharia Saad Zaghloul, near the Paradise Hotel.

What to do

Aswan *p117, maps p120, p122 and p125*

The major hotels have good sports facilities but remember that with temperatures as high as 50°C (122°F) in summer this is not the place to be engaging in a lot of movement.

Felucca trips

Official prices, regulated by the government, are E£35 per hr though you may struggle to get this. For example, if you sail to Kitchener's Island, Aga Khan Mausoleum and Elephantine Island, and spend a couple of hours wandering around, a 3-hr trip with 1 hr of sailing time should cost around E£90. If there are more passengers, prices usually go up. Haggle hard. For longer *felucca* trips along the Nile, see box, page 115. *Feluccas* can be found on Corniche El-Nil, although the men with the *feluccas* will probably find you first.

Public ferries run to Elephantine Island (E£1, from 0600-2200) from the dock by the EgyptAir office, and another from near the station to the Tombs of the Nobles. Foreigners aren't supposed to use them after sunset, although if you're staying on Elephantine or at Bet El Kerem it shouldn't be a problem to head home late.

Hiking
Plenty of good walks. A walk around Elephantine Island is a good place to start (about 2 hrs depending on your pace).

Swimming
The best and biggest pool in town available to outside guests is at the **Basma Hotel**, where day use costs US$10. More conveniently located (and right on the Nile) but more expensive is the pool at the **Isis Pyramisa** where a day-use room will set you back US$50 but can be used by up to 3 people. The pool at the **Iberotel** is also US$50 for day use, or there's the very affordable **Cleopatra** rooftop pool, for E£20.

Tour operators
All hotels organize transport to Abu Simbel and other sites. Be aware that most hotels pool their guests. What that means is 1 person may pay E£60 for a ride to Abu Simbel in 1 hotel and someone else may pay E£80 in another to wind up on the exact same bus. Shop around a bit and bargain hard, especially when the season is low. However, some hotels will only book their guests on their tours. Cheaper places tend to book cheaper trips and are more open to haggling.

For people with more money, there are numerous travel agencies and guide companies around town who are all touting for your booking. Tours and treatment don't differ much. Half-day tours usually include a trip to the **Unfinished Obelisk**, the **High Dam** and the **Temple of Philae**. Expect to pay around E£180. Travel agencies can also organize *felucca* trips to the nearby islands if you have a group of at least 3 (about E£50-80 per person). Try **Eastmar Travel**, Corniche El-Nil, T097-232 3787; **Misr Travel**, 1 block behind Corniche on way to railway station, adjacent to tourist information; or **Thomas Cook**, Corniche El-Nil, T097-230 4011, daily 0800-1400 and 1700-2000.

Transport

Aswan *p117, maps p120, p122 and p125*

Air
EgyptAir, southern end of the Corniche, T097-231 5000-5, www.egyptair.com, open 0800-2000. There are 4-5 regular daily flights to **Luxor** (30 mins) and **Cairo** (1 hr). There are 1-3 daily flights to **Abu Simbel** – often booked out by tour groups (see Transport, Abu Simbel, page 155). Taxis to the airport cost around E£50.

Bus
The bus station is 3.5 km north of the town centre, **Upper Egypt**, T097-230 0454, office open 0700-1600. A taxi there will cost you E£5-10, or you can grab a covered pickup by the train station or on the Corniche for 35 pt. If heading to Abu Simbel by bus, rules stipulate that only 4 foreigners are permitted per bus, or else they have to join a convoy, although this isn't strictly enforced. Add to that the fact that bus tickets can only be purchased 1 hr in advance necessitating an early start. Currently, there are 3 buses a day

to **Abu Simbel** at 0800, 1100 (less reliable) and 1600 (4 hrs, E£25). 2 buses go to **Cairo**, the 1530 takes 12-14 hrs, and stops at **Hurghada** (6-7 hrs, E£50) while the other leaves at 1700, is a bit cheaper, and stops in **Suez**; both should have a/c and TV. If the 1530 bus to **Hurghada** is leaving too late for you, take an early train to Luxor where you can change to a bus (0815, 1030, 1430, 4 hrs, E£25-32). There's a bus to **Marsa Alam** at 0630 every day, 4-5 hrs, E£25, which you should have no problems boarding. There are frequent buses heading north to **Kom Ombo** (1 hr, E£2), **Edfu** (2 hrs, E£4) and **Esna** (3 hrs, E£6), arriving in **Luxor** (4 hrs, E£10). You can also reach **Sohag** and **Assiut** by bus. Hours, prices and even routes change constantly. For the most current bus schedule, check with the tourist office or your hotel. Be prepared for stops at several checkpoints when travelling by bus. Have your passport ready and don't worry, it's standard procedure.

Ferry

There is 1 ferry per week to Wadi Halfa in **Sudan** run by the **Nile Valley Company**, T018-3160 926, www.takourny.free-boards.net, beside the Marhaba Hotel. Currently these are scheduled to leave on Mon from Aswan at 1200 (though expect delays, and turn up at least 2 hrs early), returning from Wadi Halfa on Wed. The journey takes between 18-24 hrs (1st class E£500, 2nd class E£322, children aged 4-10 E£193).

Taxi

Service taxis now have no security restrictions and are permitted to carry foreigners from Aswan. They will get stopped at police checkpoints on the way out. Some drivers remember the problems of the past and are reluctant to take foreign passengers. Remain calm and persist and they should take you. It's also possible to hire a private taxi for long-distance journeys. For a trip to **Luxor**, stopping at all the major sights along the way, expect to pay E£400.

Train

Trains are definitely the easiest, most comfortable option, though there are some restrictions. Technically, foreigners are only permitted to travel on 3 'secure' trains bound for **Cairo** (0600, 1800, 2000, 12-14 hrs). 1st class E£165. All have a/c and a restaurant on board. There is also a private company that runs sleeper cars to **Cairo** (1600, 1900; US$60, payable in US$ or euro only). For all trains to Cairo, it's wise to book your tickets at least 1 day in advance. 2nd-class trains to Cairo (13 hrs; E£55) via Luxor (3 hrs; E£18) leave at 0730, 1600, 1900, 2100. They usually stop in **Kom Ombo**, **Daraw**, **Edfu**, and **Esna**. As these trains are not supposed to carry foreigners, plan to buy your ticket on the train. Check with the tourist office or train station for the most current schedule.

Directory

Aswan *p117, maps p120, p122 and p125*
Embassies and consulates Passport Office: T097-231 2238, Sat-Thu 0830-1300.
Internet The going rate is E£6 per hr. It's much cheaper to get CDs and DVDs burnt in Luxor than Aswan. **Medical services** Hospitals: German Hospital, on the Corniche, T097-302176.

Lower Nubia

Upon seeing the mighty statues of Abu Simbel, it's difficult to believe that they were buried for centuries by desert sands. Johann Burckhardt (see box, page 148) finally happened upon them in 1813. Their grandiosity is surely the ultimate testimony to Ramses II's sense of self. The giant pharaonic statues are absolutely spectacular and well worth the detour south to the largest man-made lake in the world, that surrounds Abu Simbel. The juxtaposition of crystalline blue water teeming with life and the harsh dry desert outlining it is striking and makes Lake Nasser a treat to explore. Besides the wide variety of migrating birds, there are fox, gazelle and huge crocodiles that live off the shallows and shores of the lake. Fishermen travel from afar to partake in extraordinary fishing (the rich silt that once nourished the riverbank of the Nile now nourishes the bellies of the lake's inhabitants). There is also a magnificent collection of Nubian temples scattered around Lake Nasser's shores and the Lake Nasser cruise, while expensive, is incredibly rewarding.

Lake Nasser Temples

ⓘ *These monuments were previously almost inaccessible to most tourists, but some new roads now allowed overland access via private convoy to the majority of sites.*

Originally spread along the length of the Nile, the important Nubian antiquities saved by UNESCO from the rising waters of Lake Nasser were clustered in groups of three to make for easier visiting. Many of the Nubian monuments do not have the magnificence of those north of the High Dam though their new sites are more attractive. A number were erected in haste in ancient times, with little concern for artistic merit, but for the sole reason of inspiring awe in the conquered people of Nubia.

Kalabsha

ⓘ *Daily 0800-1600 winter, 0800-1700 summer, tickets E£35, students E£20. The easiest way to reach it is by taxi (E£40 round trip) from Aswan or possibly as part of a half-day tour including the Unfinished Obelisk, the Aswan Dams and Philae. You'll need to be firm in negotiations with the boatmen at the west end of the High Dam to get them to take you for E£60. Pay at the end of the return trip after about an hour on the site.*

The Temple of Mandulis The original site of the temple, built in the 18th Dynasty (1567-1320 BC) in honour of Marul (Greek *Mandulis*), was about 50 km south of Aswan at Talmis, which was subsequently renamed Kalabsha. Mandulis was a Lower Nubian sun god of fertility equated with Horus/Isis/Osiris and usually shown in human form with an elaborate headdress of horns, cobras and plumes all topped off with a sun disc. Over the centuries the later Temple of Mandulis, a Ptolemaic-Roman version of the earlier one, developed a healing cult as did those of Edfu and Dendara. It is the largest free-standing Nubian temple and was relocated by West German engineers in 1970 to now stand semi-marooned on an island or promontory (depending on the water level). It is rarely visited by tourists, although so easily accessible from Aswan, and the lake setting and harsh surrounds provide a good backdrop to the remains.

Leading up to the First Pylon is an impressive 30-m causeway used by pilgrims arriving by boat. It is not known why the causeway and first pylon are set at a slight angle to the temple, but in order to align the structure the first court is in the shape of a trapezium, with the pillars on the south side grouped closer together. At either end of the pylon a staircase leads up to the roof and the thickwalls contain four storage rooms, two at each side.

The left portico, beside the entrance to the Hypostyle Hall, portrays the pharaoh being purified and anointed with holy water by Thoth and Horus, while on the right is inscribed a decree ordering the expulsion of pigs from the temple precincts. The column capitals are ornate and flowered, the paintings having been preserved with their original colours. On either side of the doorway leading to the vestibule is a relief of Trajan making offerings to Isis, Osiris and Mandulis on the left and Horus, Mandulis and Wadjet on the right.

Beyond the hall are the vestibules, each with two columns and south access to the roof (now locked). Most of the decoration has survived and on the entrance wall the pharaoh can be seen offering incense to Mandulis and Wadjet, and milk to Isis and

Lake Nasser temples

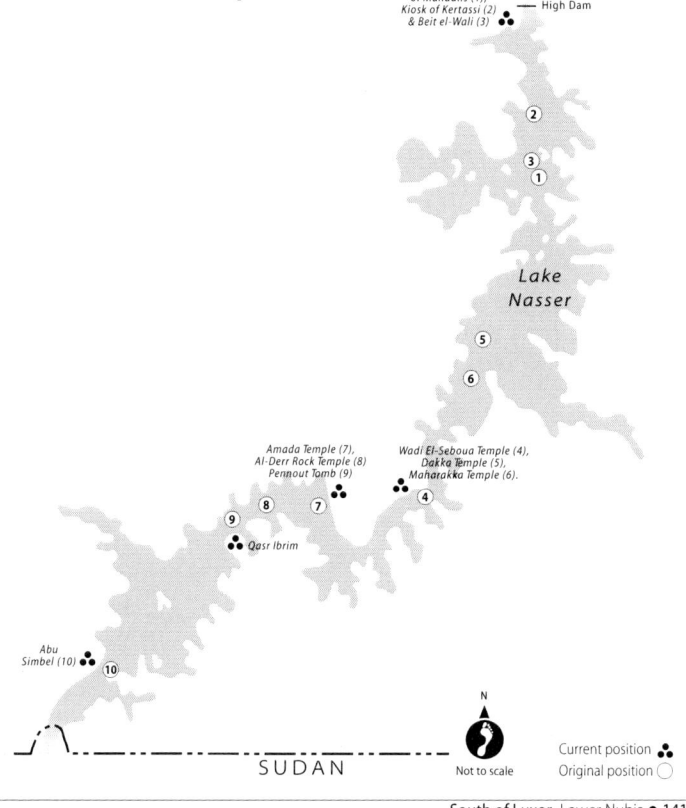

Osiris. The south wall depicts the emperor making libations to Osiris, Isis, Horus, Wadjet and Mandulis. The statue of Mandulis has long since vanished, though he is pictured on the walls among the other deities.

The Kiosk of Kertassi Near the lakeside just south of the Temple of Mandulis is the Ptolemaic-Roman Kiosk of Kertassi rescued by UNESCO from its original site 40 km south of Aswan. Described by the photographer Francis Frith in 1857 as a "bonnie little ruin", the single chamber has two Hathor-headed columns and other lotus-topped columns sharply decorated with foliage and flowers. Dedicated to Isis, the temple is undecorated except for one column in the northwest whose reliefs on the upper part depict the pharaoh standing before Isis and Horus the child.

Beit El-Wali In the hillside behind stands a small rock temple, Beit El-Wali (House of the Governor), again part of the UNESCO rescue mission. It was originally situated northwest of Kalabsha when it possessed a long causeway to the river. The reliefs and residual colours are well preserved and bright, making it worth the short walk. Built during Ramses II's youth by the Viceroy of Kush, it is believed to have been erected in honour of Amun-Re as he is depicted most frequently. The reliefs in the temple's narrow forecourt depict Ramses II victorious against the Nubians and Ethiopians (south wall) and defeating the Asiatics, Libyans and Syrians (north wall). In fact a great deal of smiting and defeating is illustrated. In particular the tribute being offered on the east wall of the

Temple of Mandulis

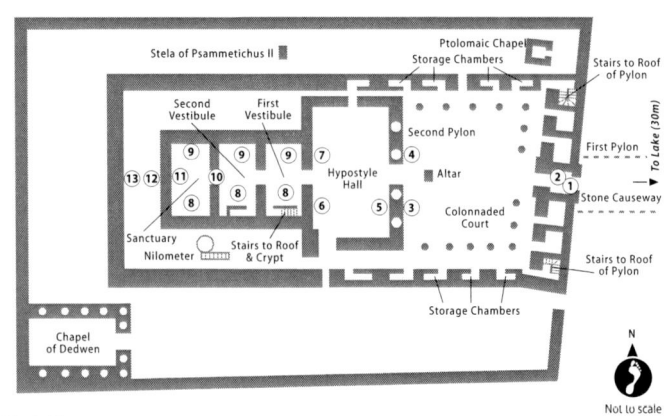

Murals ◯
1 Lintel with sundisc
2 Emperor Augustus with Horus
3 King being purified with sacred water by Horus & Thoth
4 Decree in Greek regarding expulsion of pigs from temple
5 Coptic crosses carved on wall
6 Second register - a pharaoh offers a field to Isis, Mandulis & Horus
7 Second register - Amenophis II offers wine to Mandulis & another
8 Procession of gods, the King in the lead, before Osiris, Isis & Horus
9 Procession of gods, the King in the lead, before Mandulis, a juvenile Mandulis & Wadjet
10 Lintel with sundisc
11 King with various gods
12 King with deities - double picture
13 King before Mandulis

142 • South of Luxor Lower Nubia

Fishing on Lake Nasser

Lake Nasser is the result of flooding 496 km of the Nile Valley with the construction of the Aswan Dam. The extraordinarily rich silt that once coated the valley during the seasonal flood is now at the bottom of the lake, sustaining the marine environment. As a result of the extreme nourishment, the fish have grown to huge sizes and Lake Nasser has become a popular destination for keen fishermen from around the world. There are over 6000 sq km to fish in and 32 species to catch (the two most popular being Nile perch and tiger fish).

Nile perch (*Lates niloticus*) are found in the Nile and other rivers, but grow to their greatest size in large bodies of water such as Lake Nasser. They are large-mouthed fish, greeny-brown above and silver below. They have an elongated body, a protruding jaw, a round tail and two dorsal fins. They are one of the largest freshwater fish in the world and can be over 1.9 m in length and 1.5 m in girth. The record catch in Lake Nasser was a massive 176 kg.

The most common of the tiger fish caught is *Hydrocynus forskaalii*. They have dagger teeth that protrude when their mouths are closed. They resemble a tiger in both appearance (they have several lengthwise stripes) and in habit (they are swift and voracious). They can grow to 5.5 kg.

Catfish are represented by 18 different species in the lake but the two of interest to anglers are *Bagrus* and *Vundu* of which the largest caught in Lake Nasser to date was 34 kg.

The main methods of fishing are trolling – restricted on safari to six hours a day, which covers a wide area and can result in a bigger catch of bigger fish; or spinning or fly fishing from the shore, generally in the cool of the morning, which is a delight and a challenge as it requires more skill as well as a strong line and heavy-duty gloves.

All fishing on Lake Nasser is on a catch and release policy, except those needed for the evening meal.

---

entrance courtyard is well worth examination, while on the wall opposite look out for the dog biting a Libyan's leg. The two columns in the vestibule are unusual in a Nubian monument – being fluted. When this building was used as a Christian church the entrance forecourt was roofed over with brick domes.

Wadi El-Seboua

ⓘ *Daily 0800-1600 winter, 0800-1700 summer, tickets E£25, students E£15. These temples were inaccessible by road until recently, and are not on the programmes of most big tour operators so normal convoy is not an option. But if you want to get there overland it is possible to take a private convoy with a police escort. Enquire at the tourist office in Aswan for help and for up-to-date information about prices. Most people will be visiting as part of a Lake Nasser cruise, during which the boats often moor to see the temples illuminated at night.*

The isolated oasis of Wadi El-Seboua, 135 km from the High Dam, contains the Temple of Wadi El-Seboua, the Temple of Dakka and the Temple of Maharakka. The giant **Temple of Wadi El-Seboua** (Valley of the Lion) is named after the two rows of sphinxes that line its approach. Unfortunately, a number of the sphinxes have been decapitated and the heads illegally sold to treasure hunters. It was constructed between 1279 BC and 1212 BC under

Worship of the Nile crocodile – Crocodylus niloticus

These huge creatures, the largest reptile in Africa, were worshipped as the god Sobek, who was depicted as a man with a crocodile's head. The Ancient Egyptians kept them in lakes by the temples, which were dedicated to crocodile gods, and fed them the best meat, geese and fish and even wine. Special creatures were decked with jewels, earrings, gold bracelets and necklaces. Their bodies were embalmed after death (which for some came after more than 100 years). It is suggested that they were worshipped out of fear, in the hope that offerings and prayers would make them less vicious and reduce the dangers to both man and beast.

The problem was these cold-blooded creatures needed to come out of the river to bask in the sunshine and feed – and they could move at a surprising speed on land. The long muscular tail was used as a rudder and on land could be used to fell large animals at a single blow. Small humans were easy prey.

In other regions they were hunted, eaten and considered a protector as they prevented anyone from swimming across the Nile.

It is fortunate that today these 900-kg creatures can no longer reach the major part of Egypt. They cannot pass the Aswan Dam but they exist to the south of this barrier in large numbers.

Setau, the supervisor of the Viceroy of Kus and is dedicated to Amun, Re-Harakhte and the deified Ramses II. A huge statue of Ramses II and a sphinx stand on either side of the entrance, the base of each decorated with bound prisoners as a reminder of Egyptian supremacy. There are six human-headed sphinxes wearing the double crown in the First Courtyard and four falcon-headed sphinxes in double crown in the Second Courtyard. Again the bases have illustrations of bound prisoners. Steps lead up to the main part of the temple, where the massive statue on the left of the First Pylon is of the wife of Ramses II and behind her leg their daughter Bint-Anath. The corresponding statue from the right of the entrance now lies in the sand outside, damaged when the temple was converted into a church.

The carved reliefs by local artists in poor quality sandstone are crude but much remains of their original colour. Around the court are roughly hewn statues of Ramses II unusually portrayed as a Nubian, holding the crook and flail scepters displayed against the 10 pillars – but most have been damaged. Along the lower register appear a procession of princes and princesses, estimated at a total of over 50 of each, all the offspring of the mighty Ramses. From the far end of the First Pillared Hall the temple is cut into the rock and this inner section has decorations better preserved and with better colours. The Christians who used this as a church covered the reliefs with plaster to permit their own decoration, thus preserving the earlier work. In the Sanctuary a relief on the wall shows Ramses II presenting a bouquet to the godly triad, but early Christians have defaced the figures and Ramses II now appears to be offering lotus flowers to St Peter.

The Temple of Dakka A painful 1500-m walk uphill is the Ptolemaic-Roman Temple of Dakka, reconstructed on the site of an earlier sanctuary. In fact several rulers contributed to its construction and decoration. Started by the Meroitic King Arqamani, it was adapted by the Ptolemies Philopator and Euergetes II and changed yet again by Emperors Augustus and Tiberius.

Like many temples it was used for a time by the Christians as a church and in some places fragments of their decorations remain. This is the only temple in Egypt facing north, an orientation preserved by UNESCO, pointing to the home of Thoth but more probably an error by the foreign-born Ptolemaic builders. The pylon is still in good condition, standing an imposing 13 m in height. The gateway has a curved cornice with a central winged sun disc on either side and a high level niche at each side intended to hold a flag pole, while on the left of the doorway is graffiti in Greek, Roman and Meriotic (ancient Nubian). Stairs in either side of the pylon lead to the roof, from which a fine view is obtained. Look for the deep incisions in the inner pylon wall, probably made by locals convinced that the stone possessed healing properties.

The main temple building is across an open courtyard, but before you enter turn back and admire the vista to the north. There are four interconnecting rooms, many of the decorations being of deities receiving assorted offerings. A staircase leads off the vestibule on the west side up to the roof – again the views are staggering. Off the sanctuary is a small room to the east side leading, it is thought, to a now-choked crypt. Here the decorations are in quite good condition – two seated ibises, two hawks and two lions. The lioness being approached by the baboons needs some interpretation. As an animal could approach a lioness without danger except if she was hungry, if a human was in danger at any time they assumed animal form to worship in safety. The king is seen worshipping gods including Osiris and Isis, and Horus and Hathor. The large pink granite casket in the sanctuary once held the cult statue of Thoth.

The Temple of Maharakka Less impressive is the unfinished Roman Temple of Meharakka, dedicated to Isis and Serapis. This stood on the southern border of Egypt in Ptolemaic and Roman times, but is now a short walk down hill from the Temple of Dakka. Rather plain inside, bar the Roman graffiti from travellers and soldiers fighting Nubian troops in 23 BC, the temple illustrates the union of Egyptian and Roman styles. Isis is depicted full frontal, instead of the more common profile, while her son Horus wears a toga. Other surviving carvings depict Osiris, Thoth and Tefnut. The temple consists of one room – six columns on the north side, three columns on the east and west side and six on the south side joined by screen walls. The capitals of the columns were never completed. For stair access to the roof, from which there are spectacular views, enter the temple and turn right. This is the only known spiral staircase in an Egyptian building. Look east to the pharaohs' gold mines.

Temple of Amada

ⓘ *Daily 0800-1600 winter, 0800-1700 summer, tickets E£45, students E£25. Accessible to cruise boats only, whose passengers are ferried to the site on motor launches.*

Some 40 km further south in the Amada Oasis is the oldest temple in Nubia, the sandstone Temple of Amada, dedicated to Amun-Re and Re-Harakhte. It was built by Tuthmosis III and Amenhotep II, with the roofed pillared court added by Tuthmosis IV, which accounts for the many scenes of Tuthmosis IV with various gods and goddesses on the walls and pillars. At the left of the entrance hieroglyphics detail the victorious campaigns of Meneptah against the Libyans. Before entering the next doorway look up at the Berber

Cobras

The Egyptian cobra occurs on every kingly brow. The *Uraeus*, the cobra's head and the neck with the hood spread, as worn in the head dress of Egyptian divinities and sovereigns, is a sign of supreme power.

Fortunately this is the only place you are likely to see an Egyptian cobra (although Cleopatra conveniently found one in the environs of her palace).

All cobras are potentially dangerous although the venom is used to catch prey rather than eliminate humans. These creatures, though infrequently seen, are not considered in danger of extinction.

There are other cobras in Egypt. The smaller black-necked spitting cobra sprays venom up to the eyes of its attacker – causing temporary blindness and a great deal of agony. The black refers to the distinctive bands round the neck. Sightings are confined to the region south of Aswan. The Innes cobra is exceedingly rare, recorded in particular around St Catherine's Monastery.

---

grafiti of animals high on the wall at both sides. Inside, reliefs on the right show the Pharaoh running the Heb-Sed race, cattle being slaughtered and presented as offerings as heads and haunches. Opposite are the foundation ceremonies, an interesting depiction of the way a site for a building was marked out, foundations dug, bricks manufactured and the construction eventually completed and handed over to the owner. In the central section are more offerings of pomegranates, very realistic ducks and cakes. The stela at the back of the sanctuary tells of the temple's foundation during Amenhotep II's time. The holes in the roof allow light in so one can see, on the back wall, Amenhotep dispensing justice to six Syrian captives: a prisoner is turned upside down and crucified; a grisly reminder to his remote Nubian subjects of the pharaoh's treatment of enemies.

The Rock Temple of Al-Derr Here too is the Rock Temple of Al-Derr, built in honour of Amun-Re, Re-Harakhte and the divine aspect of the pharaoh, notable for the excellent colour and preservation of its reliefs. It is the only temple on the east bank of the Nile in Nubia. In the first Hypostyle Hall the temple's builder Ramses II stands in the Tree of Life and presents libations to Amun. Ibis, the eternal scribe, behind, records the pharaoh's years and achievements. The decorations here are, however, very damaged and only small pieces of these scenes can now be made out. The four large statues of Ramses II as Osiris, incorporated in the last row of columns, are reduced to legs only. The majority of the reliefs on the outer walls boast of the pharaoh's military triumphs and warn the Nubians that his might is unassailable. However, inside the second Hypostyle Hall, the pharaoh, depicted as a high priest, becomes a humble servant of the gods. On the right-hand wall he gives flowers, offers wine, escorts the barque, receives jubilees from Amun-Re and Mut and further along the Heb-Sed emblem is produced nine times. On the opposite wall he has his name recorded on the leaves of a tall acacia tree. Entering the sanctuary, on the left, Ramses is putting in a plea to live forever. In the sanctuary on the back wall there were originally four statues as in the larger temple at Abu Simbel (see page 147), now nothing, but on the wall decorations the king continues to offer perfumes, cake and flowers.

The Tomb of Pennout The rock-cut tomb of the Chief of the Quarry Service, Steward of Horus and viceroy of Wawat (northern Nubia) under Ramses VI, is a rare example of a high official buried south of Aswan. The ancient Egyptians believed that their souls were only secure if their bodies were carried back and buried in Egyptian soil. The tomb's wall paintings rather poignantly reflect this conviction, expressing Pennout's desire to be laid to rest in the hills of Thebes. The walls are decorated with traditional themes, including the deceased and his family. Before entering on the left are the deceased and his wife Takha in adulation, on the main wall is the judgement scene with the weighing of the heart against a feather and below the traditional mourners pouring sand on their heads. On the end wall Horus leads the deceased and wife to Osiris, Isis and Nephthys for a blessing but the lower register has all disappeared. To the left of the inner chamber is a representation of the solar cult. There is no entry into the inner chamber but the three badly mutilated statues of Pennout, and his wife with Hathor between can be viewed. The actual burial chamber lies 3 m below. Above on the lintel is the sun-god barge and howling baboons. What is left of the decoration on the wall to the right shows Pennout with his wife and six sons while on the end wall Pennout in golden colours is in his illustrated biography that continues on toward the exit. It is very disappointing to note that almost all the wall decorations were intact when this temple was moved here and even more disappointing to note that the damage had been caused by illegal removal from the monument.

Qasr Ibrim

ⓘ *Daily 0800-1600 winter, 0800-1700 summer, tickets E£30, students E£15, accessible to cruise boats only.*

The fortress of Qasr Ibrim, 40 km north of Abu Simbel, is the only Nubian monument to inhabit its original site, once a plateau but now an island. It is noted for an exceptional length of continuous occupation, from 1000 BC to AD 1812. The ancient city included seven temples to Isis and a mud-brick temple built by the Nubian king Taharka, ruins of which are visible in the centre of the island. In the pre-Roman period construction of a massive stone temple, similar to the structures at Kalabsha, turned the garrison city into a major religious centre. A healing cult developed and Qasr Ibrim became 'the Philae of the south'. Footprints, carved by pilgrims to commemorate their visit, are still visible in the temple floor. A tavern, 400 BC, on the north side of the island is recognizable by the large piles of pottery shards. The temple was destroyed by early Christians who built an orthodox cathedral on the site in the 10th century AD in honour of the Virgin Mary, the Christian version of Isis, three walls of which remain standing. By the steps to the burial crypt are numerous fragments of red (Roman) and glazed (Ottoman) pottery. Bosnian troops loyal to the Ottoman Sultan invaded the site in 1517 whereupon the cathedral was converted into a mosque, and their descendants inhabited the site for the next 300 years. The fortress was brought under central control in 1812.

Abu Simbel → *For listings, see pages 153-155.*

Abu Simbel, 280 km south of Aswan and only 40 km north of the Sudanese border is the site of the magnificent **Sun Temple of Ramses II** and the smaller **Temple of Queen Nefertari**. With the exception of the temples, hotels and the homes of tourist industry employees, there is almost nothing else here. That is part of its charm, as is the immediate

Burckhardt the explorer

The Anglo-Swiss geographer and explorer, Johann (John) Ludwig Burckhardt was born in Lausanne, Switzerland on 24 November 1784. He studied in London and Cambridge and between 1806 and 1809 lived in Syria, where he learnt Arabic and became a follower of Islam, taking the Muslim name Ibrahim Ibn Abd Allah. He left Syria, en route for Cairo and the Fezzan (Libya) from where he was to attempt to cross the Sahara. Local Bedouin spoke of the ruins of a 'lost city' in the mountains. Knowing that the legendary lost city of Petra was in the vicinity of Aaron's tomb on Jebel Harun he persuaded his guides of a desire to sacrifice a goat in honour of Aaron at his tomb. His scheme succeeded and on 22 August 1812 he was guided through the Siq and into the valley where he saw the Al-Khazneh and the Urn Tomb – enough to recognize the City of Petra. When he arrived in Cairo he could find no immediate transport to Fezzan so instead he journeyed up the Nile and discovered the Temple of Ramses II at Abu Simbel. He next travelled to Saudi Arabia, visiting Mecca. He returned to Cairo where he died on 15 October 1817, before he was able to complete his journey.

---

warmth of the locals that's so refreshing after the cut-and-thrust of Aswan. The village is centred around a couple of little eateries-cum-*ahwas* where the bus drops people off, with a modern *souk* to one side and the cheapest hotels within walking distance. The temples are about a 20-minute walk away, past the banks and post office. It is an attractive sultry little place, utterly sleepy except when the tours are passing through, where swathes of turban are de rigeur for men and you see women wearing traditional Nubian black net dresses decorated with weaving. The setting on the banks of Lake Nasser is beautiful, with heart-shattering rocks meeting the sapphire water, enhanced by the many green gardens dotted around and the single-storey whitewashed dwellings. It's true there are no beds at rock-bottom prices (though if you want to spoil yourself, the Eskaleh could be the place to do it) but you have to accept that you are going be shelling out to see the temples anyway. Altogether, the African atmosphere, dearth of independent travellers, and chance of seeing the temples in total isolation makes Abu Simbel an excellent overnight stop.

Arriving in Abu Simbel
Getting there EgyptAir runs daily flights during the winter high season from Cairo via Luxor to Abu Simbel. Direct from Aswan during the summer when the season slumps there are still at least two flights per day and three during the high season. Book a ticket as early as possible, especially in the peak season. Most tickets are sold on the assumption that you will return the same day but it is possible to include overnight stopovers. Seats on the left-hand side of the aircraft usually offer the best views as it circles the temples before landing at Abu Simbel. There are free buses from Abu Simbel airport to the site of the temples.

It is possible to visit Abu Simbel by road (unaccompanied by a convoy) on the public buses which depart from the main Aswan bus station (3.5 km north of town) supposedly three times per day; you can't buy tickets in advance. Don't take the later buses unless you intend to stay the night.

The Temples of Abu Simbel

ⓘ *T097-3400 766/3400 325/6, daily 0500-1730 winter, 0500-1800 summer, E£95, students E£53.50, photography inside the temples is strictly prohibited. Sound and Light show, E£75 no student discount, lasts 35 mins, first show starts 2000 in summer (1-3 shows, more on Fri), 1800 in winter (1-2 shows), headphones provide commentary in all languages though you have to turn them up very loud to block out the main commentary. If you have come independently, go early to the first Sound and Light show for sunset. You won't be able to go inside the temples, but can marvel at the outside before the show starts. The following morning, head to the temples for dawn. It's pretty much guaranteed that you will be alone, save for Ramses, Nefertari and the custodians, for at least an hour – and as sunrise colours the colossi it takes your breath away. With the waters of Lake Nasser dark, still and silent before them, pink light slowly creeps up over the feet of the great pharaoh and his queen. The majority of tourists come for a couple of hours via plane or as part of the road convoy, and arrive in a stampede which is best avoided.*

The two temples, which were rediscovered in 1813 completely buried by sand, were built by the most egotistical pharaoh of them all, Ramses II (1304-1237 BC) during the 19th Dynasty of the New Kingdom. Although he built a smaller temple for his queen, Nefertari, it is the four gigantic statues of himself carved out of the mountainside that dominate Abu Simbel. It was intended that his magnificent and unblinking stare would be the first thing that travellers, visitors and enemies alike, saw as they entered Egypt from the south. Behind the statues is Ramses II's Temple of the Sun, which was originally built to venerate Amun and Re-Harakhte but really is dominated by, and dedicated to, the pharaoh-god Ramses II himself.

Although it had become the highlight of the trip for the relatively few intrepid travellers who ventured so far south, it was not until the monuments were threatened by the rising waters of Lake Nasser that international attention focused on Abu Simbel. UNESCO financed and organized the ambitious, costly (US$40 million) and ultimately successful 1964-1968 operation, to reassemble the monuments 61 m above and 210 m behind their original site. Despite its magnificence and beauty, for many visitors to Abu Simbel there is a slight tinge of disappointment because of the combined sense of familiarity and artificiality. Yet the sheer audacity of Ramses' egoism and the scale of the feat of saving the temple from the rising waters of the lake make the trip worthwhile.

Ramses II's Temple of the Sun The entrance steps lead up to a terrace, with alternate statuettes of the king and a falcon to mark the edge, where the imposing façade of the main temple (35 m wide by 30 m high) is dominated by the four-seated **Colossi of Ramses II** wearing the double crown. Each figure was originally 21 m high but the second from the left lost its top during an earthquake in 27 BC. There are smaller statues of the members of the royal family standing at Ramses' rather crudely sculptured feet, which contrast with his ornately chiselled and beautiful faces above. Graffiti, written by Greek mercenaries about their expeditions into Nubia, can be seen on the left leg of the damaged statue but it seems everyone who visited in the 1800s left their mark in the tablets of signatures – even his knee-caps haven't escaped.

The sides of the huge thrones at the entrance to the temple are decorated with the Nile gods entwining lotus and papyrus, the plants representing Upper and Lower Egypt around the hieroglyph 'to unite'. Below are reliefs showing Egypt's vanquished foes, the **Nine Bows of Bound Nubians** on the south side **(5)** and **Bound Asiatics** to the north side **(6)**. The colour

Ramses II's Temple of the Sun

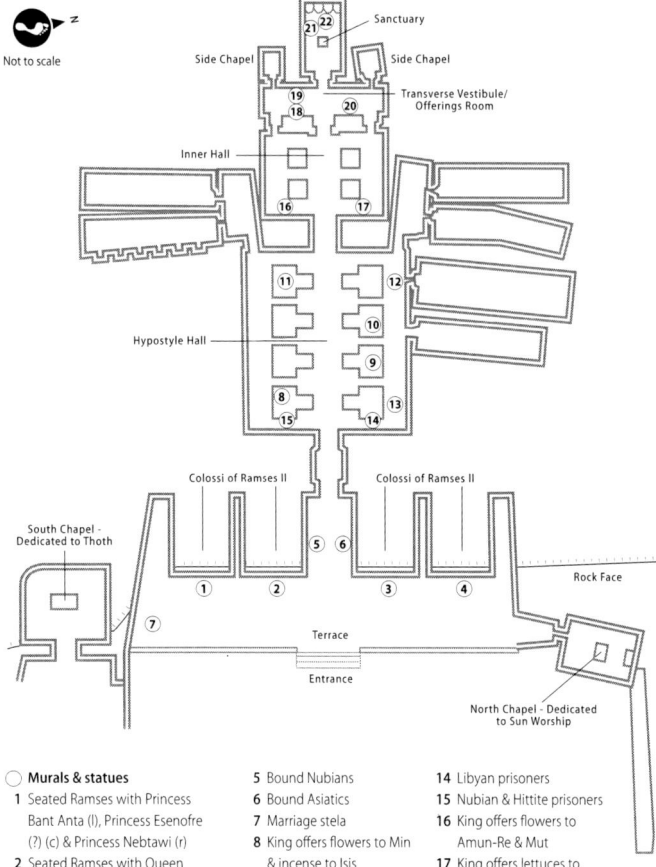

Not to scale

○ **Murals & statues**

1. Seated Ramses with Princess Bant Anta (l), Princess Esenofre (?) (c) & Princess Nebtawi (r)
2. Seated Ramses with Queen Nefertari (l), Prince Amenhirkhopshef (c) & Ramses' mother Queen Muttuya
3. Seated Ramses with Princess Beketmut (l), Prince Ramessesu (c) & Queen Nefertari (r)
4. Seated Ramses with Queen Mother Muttuya (l), Princess Merytamun (c) & Queen Nefertari (r)
5. Bound Nubians
6. Bound Asiatics
7. Marriage stela
8. King offers flowers to Min & incense to Isis
9. King offers wine to Horus & flowers to Mut
10. King offers flowers to Thoth & bread to Anubis
11. King offers wine to Re-Harakhte
12-13. Battle of Kadesh - recruits arriving, encampment, town of Kadesh, enemy chariots
14. Libyan prisoners
15. Nubian & Hittite prisoners
16. King offers flowers to Amun-Re & Mut
17. King offers lettuces to Min & Isis
18. King offers wine to Min
19. King offers incense to a ram-headed Amun-Re
20. King offers bread to Atum
21. King before barque of Amun anoints Min
22. Four (damaged) statues (l-r) of Ptah, Amun-Re, Ramses II & Re-Harakhte

150 • **South of Luxor** Lower Nubia

A bit of Nubian lingo

Hello *Raigri*
How are you? *Er meena bu?*
Good *A denma*
Thank you *Gas si raykum*
Goodbye *Inna fee ya-der*
Hot *Joogri*
Cold *Od*
Come here *In day gerta*
Beautiful *A sheerma*

and clarity of these larger-than-life fettered prisoners is quite confronting, their differing hairstyles and earrings denote their origins. Lining the façade, above the heads of Ramses, is a row of 22 baboons smiling at the sunrise. A **marriage stela (7)** commemorates the union of Ramses II with Ma'at-Her-Neferure, daughter of the Hittite king.

At the entrance into the temple's rock **Hypostyle Hall** is a door bearing Ramses II's cartouche. Entered the temple you are met by eight striking statues of Ramses, 10 m high and clad in a short kilt typical of the Nubian Osiride form, carved into the eight enormous square pillars supporting the roof. The four statues on the right bear the double crown and those on the left the white crown of Upper Egypt, and the first couple of statues have had their beards inscribed with yet more 19th-century graffiti. On the pillars, Ramses presents **flowers to Min and incense to Isis (8), wine to Horus and flowers to Mut (9), flowers to Thoth and bread to Anubis (10)**, while **Re-Harakhte receives wine (11)**. The hall's ceiling is crowded with vultures in the central aisle and star spangled elsewhere. The reliefs on the walls are colourful and well preserved. The north wall is the most dramatic with four different scenes depicting the **Battle of Kadesh** against the Hittites in 1300 BC **(12, 13)** which, despite what these illustrations might imply, was not an unqualified Egyptian success. The depictions of chariots and camps are particularly revealing of ancient battle methods (it seems lions were involved) but, more interestingly, Ramses's double arm lancing a Libyan may have been an ancient attempt at animation. The slaughter of whole bundles of **prisoners**, generally small in size and with their faces shown in supplication, is a common theme **(14, 15)**. The side chambers, branching off from the hall, were probably originally used to store vases, temple linen, cult objects and Nubian gifts. Their walls are lined with reliefs of sacrifices and offerings being made by Ramses to the major gods, including Amun.

The **Inner Hall** has four columns depicting the Pharaoh participating in rituals before the deities. On the far left, Ramses can be seen before Amun **(16)** while on the right he makes an offering of lettuces, considered an aphrodisiac **(17)**. In both these scenes a deified Ramses II has been inserted at a later date. Two sandstone sphinxes, which originally stood at the entrance to the hall, are now in London's British Museum.

Further in and in front of the inner sanctuary is the **Transverse Vestibule** where offerings of wine, fruits and flowers were made. The **Sanctuary** itself, which was originally cased in gold, has an altar to Ramses at its centre, behind which are now statues of Ptah, Amun-Re, Ramses II and Re-Harakhte, unfortunately mutilated. Ramses is deified with his patron gods. Before the temple's relocation the dawn sunrays would shine on all but Ptah (who was linked with death-cults), on 22 February and 22 October. Despite what your guide will say there is no scholastic evidence to connect these two dates with Ramses' birthday and coronation day. A sacred *barque* (boat) would have rested on the altar and the walls beside the door portray the barque of Amun and Ramses. The adjoining side chapels were not decorated.

Temple of Queen Nefertari Although dedicated to the goddess Hathor of Abshek, like that of her husband, the queen's temple virtually deifies the human queen Nefertari. Unsurprisingly it is much smaller than that of Ramses II but is nevertheless both imposing and very, very beautiful. It is cut entirely from the rock and penetrates about 24 m from the rock face. The external façade is 12 m high and lined with three colossi 11.5 m high on either side of the entrance. Nefertari stands with her husband while their children cluster in pairs at their knees. To show the importance of Queen Nefertari her statues are of similar size to those of her husband. Just within the entrance are the cartouches of Ramses and Nefertari. The simple **Hall** has six square pillars, on the aisle side of each is depicted a Hathor head and sistrum sounding box while the other sides have figures of the king and queen making offerings to the gods. Some reliefs in the hall are rather gruesome – the walls backing the entrance show the pharaoh slaying his Nubian and Libyan enemies, who beg for mercy while Nefertari and the god Amun look on. Others show the royal couple engaging in rituals. Note her diaphanous skirts and their assortment of intricate crowns, which are exquisite.

Temple of Queen Nefertari

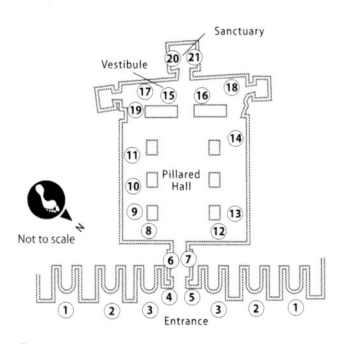

○ Murals & statues
1 Ramses II with Princes Meryatum & Meryre
2 Queen Nefertari shown as Hathor with Princesses Merytamun & Henwati
3 Ramses II with Princes Amunhikhopshef & Rahrirwemenef
4 Lintel where King offers wine to Amun-Re
5 King offers incense to Horus
6 King offers flowers to Hathor
7 Nefertari offers flowers to Isis
8 Ramses II smites Nubian prisoner before Amun-Re
9 Ramses II receives necklace from Hathor
10 Ramses II crowned by Horus & Seth
11 Nefertari offers flowers & musical instrument to Anukis
12 Ramses II smites Libyan prisoner before Horus
13 Ramses II with offerings
14 Nefertari before Hathor of Dendera
15 Nefertari between Hathor & Isis
16 Ramses II & Nefertari give flowers to Tawere
17 Ramses II offers wine to Horus & Anu
18 Ramses II offers wine to Re-Harakhte & Queen offers flowers to Khnum
19 Nefertari's cartouche between vultures
20 Nefertari offers incense to Mut & Hathor
21 Ramses II worships deified image of himself & Nefertari

Three corridors lead from the rear of the hall into the **Vestibule**, the central one passing directly into the **Sanctuary**. The back walls of the Vestibule portray reliefs of Ramses and Nefertari offering wine and flowers to Khnum and Re-Harakhte on the right and to Horus and Amun on the left. Vultures protect the Queen's cartouche on the door above the sanctuary, which is dominated by the figure of Hathor in the form of a cow watching over Ramses. On the left wall, Nefertari can be seen offering incense to Mut and Hathor while on the opposite side Ramses worships the deified images of himself and Nefertari.

⊚ Lower Nubia listings

For sleeping and eating price codes and other relevant information, see pages 11-15.

⊖ Where to stay

Abu Simbel p147

€€€€ Seti Abu Simbel, T097-340 0720-2, www.setifirst.com. Call the Cairo office, T02-2736 0890-5 or T(+202) 19780 for the best price. This is the fanciest place to stay in Abu Simbel. There are all the 5-star amenities although rooms are a little jaded, but splendid views of Lake Nasser go some way to compensate as do the 2 terraced pools set in verdant gardens. Upstairs rooms are better. Breakfast not included, discounts at the discretion of the General Manager.

€€€ Eskaleh, T097-340 1288, T012-368 0521, www.eskaleh.net. Built in the style of a traditional Nubian house, with furniture fashioned from date palms, rough stone floors, domes and terracotta-coloured walls, this little guesthouse is a delight. And though the bathrooms aren't in keeping with the rustic-style building, they are modern and sparkling. The 3 larger, more expensive rooms (doubles US$90) have more space and terraces surrounded by flowers, some have mud-brick lattice windows, all have mosquito nets, a/c, and free internet for guests. The terrace at the front overlooks the lake and vegetable garden, and there are occasional Nubian music nights. Accepts major credit cards.

€ Abu Simbel Tourist Village, T097-340 0092, Homely salmon-pink rooms all have private bath, most have a/c (doubles E£150). There's a good view of Lake Nasser from the little garden and management is kind and friendly. It's a 10-min walk from the bus stop on the edge of the village, about 2 km from the temple.

€ Nobaleh Ramsis Hotel, T097-340 0106, T097-340 1118. The cheapest option in town with huge high-ceilinged rooms at E£125. Rooms are cool and comfortable but spartan, with TV, a/c and fridge. No breakfast and you might expect a higher standard of bathroom for the price and there are no views. 2 km from the temples, but close to the bus stop, and big discounts negotiable if you call ahead. With prior warning, the manager Yassin may be able to arrange a boat to take you out on the lake.

Camping

Sometimes the **Abu Simbel Village** and the **Nefertari Abu Simbel** permit camping on their grounds, but call ahead to be sure.

Cruises

€€€€ MS Eugenie, bookings through **Belle Epoque Travel,** 17 Sharia Tunis, New Maadi, Cairo, T02-2516 9653, www.eugenie.com.eg. Constructed in 1993 in the style of a Mississippi paddle steamer, 52 a/c cabins with balcony, 2 suites, pre-Revolution decor, 2 bars, 2 large saloons, 2 sundecks, pool, jaccuzi, health club, excellent food and no enforced entertainment. Memorable features include a private sunset tour of Abu Simbel followed by a candlelit dinner on board for which the temples are specially lit.

⊘ Restaurants

Abu Simbel p147

Despite Abu Simbel's position in the middle of the desert and the fact most supplies come from Aswan, there is no problem getting a good meal.

Good *felafel* is served in the market, from a stall down the street between **Restaurant Ganoub El-Wadi** and **Wadi El-Nil** café. Wadi El-Nil café is a good spot to people watch under a tree as you sip a tea. Best of all, the correct prices are laminated onto each tabletop.

You can get an alcoholic drink at the **Eskaleh**, **Seti Abu Simbel** and **Nefertari** hotels, albeit an expensive one.

€€ Eskaleh, call ahead to enjoy an excellent 3-course dinner either on the terrace outside or in the lovely dining room among the decorative basketware, woven mats and Nubian artefacts. Vegetables and salads grown in the garden, beer and wine are available (expensive), meals are around E£75 per person.

€€ Fahd, upstairs from **Ganoub El-Wadi**, serves basic stewed veg, meat, rice and salad. Ask the price first, as it is very much negotiable (E£15 or above, depending if you eat meat) and veggies should be wary of scraps of meat in the potato stews.

€ Ganoub El-Wadi, offers simply served fish, freshly plucked from the lake. No need to quibble about prices.

€ Il Rahman, this is where tour bus drivers go to eat while their passengers visit the temples. A herby, crispy fish fillet with rice will cost you a mere E£20. Delicious fresh rice pudding from the fridge is E£2. On the opposite side of the road from the other restaurants, keep them to your left and walk towards the temples. Il Rahman is just down the road back to Aswan on the left opposite a now defunct fountain.

€ Koshari El-Arabi, serves generous portions of decent koshari.

What to do

Abu Simbel *p147*

Boat trips

If there are quite a few of you, hire a boat to visit some of the many mesmerizing islands, see part of Lake Nasser's 8000-km stretch of shore and of course view the temple from the water. You could even see crocodiles sunbathing, water monitors and golden jackals. Yassin at the **Nobaleh Ramsis Hotel**, T097-340 0106, can arrange a boat for a half day holding up to 20 people for E£500; he needs at least 24 hrs' advance warning in order to get permission from the authorities. For information on *felucca* trips, see page 115.

Cruise boats on Lake Nasser

Since the construction of the High Dam the upper part of the Nile has been effectively cut off to navigation from the lower reaches. The only solution to getting a good vessel on the lake was to set up a shipyard and build one designed for these deeper waters. The most relaxing way to tour Lower Nubian antiquities is aboard one of the elegant cruise boats. Pampered by the luxurious surroundings, high-calibre guides and excellent service, tourists can sit back and appreciate the sheer vastness of desert and lake, a sharp contrast to the lush scenery and teeming villages of the Nile Valley. Few more tranquil places exist. The boat's passengers have the monuments almost to themselves. Cruises usually last 3 nights/4 days or 4 nights/5 days starting either in Aswan or Abu Simbel. Some boats have 7-day itineraries going from Aswan to Abu Simbel and back again.

Other cruise boats on Lake Nasser with 5-star rating are: *Kasr Ibrim*, also owned by **Belle Epoque**, www.kasribrim.com.eg, see page 153, 65 rooms of an equally excellent standard but this time with 1930s art deco styling. *MS Nubian Sea* has 50 cabins and suites, and serves excellent food; *MS Prince Abbas*, owned by Movenpick hotels, www.moevenpick-hotels.com, and fully refitted to a high spec, 65 standard cabins, 18 junior suites and 4 royal suites.

See also **Lake Nasser Adventure** (see page 155) who run cruises in very small boats, which are quite unique.

Fishing

For fishermen and birdwatchers, there are a few companies that specialize in nature and adventure safaris on Lake Nasser. Fishing is particularly good here, considered big-game fishing, as the damming of the river has created the perfect environment for Nile perch to grow to immense proportions, see box, page 143. Nights are spent under the stars, camping in one of the inlets or aboard a mother ship, and days are spent on a small boat under a searing sun wrestling with the beasts beneath.

The African Angler, T097-230 9748, www.african-angler.net, are a good company to go with. They have highly trained local staff and boats specifically designed for fishing on Lake Nasser. Check their website for the latest prices.

Lake Nasser Adventure, www.lakenasser adventure.com, offer fishing trips sleeping in small boats for 1-3 people, which means complete freedom from any schedule, or via fast boats from a central mother ship. They also organize unique desert cruises, visiting not only temples but allowing time for desert treks and swimming on 2 boats sleeping up to 14. For complete luxury, the new *Nubiana* takes a max of 8 people on either fishing or desert adventures. 15% discounts between Jun and Sep.

Organized trips

Travel agencies and hotels in Aswan all run daily trips to Abu Simbel. Most reputable agencies generally transport their passengers in an a/c coach and may include a tour guide. They can also book day trips via plane.

For people on a budget, hotels offer 2 basic trips incorporating Abu Simbel (the short, E£60-70 and the long, E£70-80). The short trip picks you up from your hotel at 0330-0400 in the morning, transports you to the **temple** and gets you back by 1300. The long trip stops at the **High Dam**, **Unfinished Obelisk**, and **Philae Temple** on the way back and finishes around 1530. It's tempting to stick it all in 1 day, but the long trip feels very long. Price usually only includes transport in a minivan – some with and some without a/c. If visiting in summer, it is worth the extra few pounds to ensure you have a/c. Admission fees not included.

Both tours usually join the convoy that departs at 0400 in the morning and arrives at the temples around 0800. You only have about an hour to look around before being bussed back to Aswan or on to the next stop on your tour, which can be frustrating. Bring at least some of the food and water you'll need for the morning as prices at Abu Simbel are staggeringly high and remember there are no toilet stops between Aswan and Abu Simbel.

⊖ Transport

Abu Simbel *p147*

Bus

Buses leave Abu Simbel from outside **Wadi El-Nil Café** for **Aswan** at 0600, 1300 and sometimes 1600, E£25, 4 hrs.

Microbuses leave when full costing E£16 and these are marginally quicker. Ask people hanging around Wadi El-Nil to point you in the right direction, you might have to wait a while and scout for passengers.

❶ Directory

Abu Simbel *p147*
Medical services Pharmacy: By the turning to the **Seti Hotel**, and in the village opposite the *souk*.

Contents

158 Basic Egyptian Arabic for travellers

161 Glossary

164 Index

Footnotes

Basic Egyptian Arabic for travellers

It is impossible to indicate precisely in the Latin script how Arabic should be pronounced so we have opted for a very simplified transliteration that will give the user a sporting chance of uttering something that can be understood by an Egyptian.

Greetings and farewells
Hello	*ahlan wasahlan/ assalamu aleikum*
Goodbye	*ma'a el salama*
How are you?	*Izayak?* (m); *Izayik?* (f)
Fine	*kwayis* (m) *kwayissa* (f)
See you tomorrow	*Ashoofak bokra* (m) *Ashoofik bokra* (f)
Thank God	*il hamdullil'allah*

Basics
Excuse me	*law samaht*
Can you help me?	*Mumkin tisa'idny?* (m) *Mumkin tisa'ideeny* (f)
Do you speak English?	*Bitikalim ingleezy?* (m) *Bitikalimy ingleezy?* (f)
I don't speak Arabic	*Ma bakalimsh 'araby*
Do you have a problem?	*Fee mushkilla?*
Good	*kweyyis*
Bad	*mish kweyyis, wahish*
I/you	*ana/inta* (m); *inty* (f)
He/she	*howwa/heyya*
Yes	*aiwa/na'am*
No	*ia'a*
No problem	*mafeesh mushkilla*
Please	*min fadlak* (m) *min fadlik* (f)
Thank you	*shukran*
You're welcome	*'afwan*
God willing	*Insha'allah*
What?	*Eih?*
Where?	*Fein?*
Where's the bathroom	*Fein el hamam?*
Who?	*Meen?*
Why?	*Leih?*
How?	*Izay?*
How much?	*Bikam?*

Numbers
0	*sifr*
1	*wahad*
2	*etneen*
3	*talaata*
4	*arba*
5	*khamsa*
6	*sitta*
7	*saba'a*
8	*tamenia*
9	*tissa*
10	*ashra*
11	*hidashar*
12	*itnashar*
13	*talatashar*
14	*arbatashar*
15	*khamstashar*
16	*sittashar*
17	*sabatashar*
18	*tamantashar*
19	*tissatashar*
20	*'ayshreen*
30	*talaateen*
40	*arba'een*
50	*khamseen*
60	*sitteen*
70	*saba'een*
80	*tmaneen*
90	*tissa'een*
100	*mia*
200	*miteen*
300	*tolto mia*
1000	*alf*

Dates and time
Morning	*el sobh*
Afternoon	*ba'd el dohr*
Evening	*masa'*
Hour	*sa'a*

Day	*yom*
Night	*bil leil*
Month	*shahr*
Year	*sana*
Early	*badry*
Late	*mit'akhar*
Today	*inaharda*
Tomorrow	*bokra*
Yesterday	*imbarah*
Everyday	*kol yom*
What time is it?	*E'sa'a kam?*
When?	*Imta?*

Days of week

Monday	*el itnein*
Tuesday	*el talaat*
Wednesday	*el arba'*
Thursday	*el khamees*
Friday	*el goma'*
Saturday	*el sapt*
Sunday	*el had*

Travel and transport

Airport	*el matar*
Plane	*tayara*
Boat	*markib*
Ferry	*'abara*
Bus	*otobees*
Bus station	*mahatit otobees*
Bus stop	*maw'if otobees*
Car	*'arabiya*
Petrol	*benzeen*
Tyre	*'agala*
Train	*atr*
Train station	*mahatit atr*
Carriage	*karetta; calesh*
Camel	*gamal*
Donkey	*homar*
Horse	*hosan*
Ticket office	*maktab e'tazakir*
Tourist office	*makta e'siyaha*
I want to go…	*a'yiz arooh* (m)
	a'yiza arooh (f)
Does this go to…	*da beerooh*
City	*madeena*
Village	*kareeya*

Street	*shari'*
Map	*khareeta*
Passport	*gawaz safar*
Police	*bolice*

Directions

Where is the…	*fein el …*
How many kilometres is …	*kem kilometers el …*
Left	*shimal*
Right	*yimeen*
After	*ba'ad*
Before	*'abl*
Straight	*doghry; ala tool*
Near	*gamb*
Far	*bi'eed*
Slow down	*bishweish*
Speed up	*bisora'*
There	*hinak*
Here is fine	*hina kwayis*

Money and shopping

25 piasters/a quarter pound	*robe' gineih*
Bank	*benk*
Bookstore	*maktaba*
Carpet	*sigada*
Cheap	*rikhees*
Do you accept visa?	*Mumkin visa?*
Do you have…	*'andak …* (m); *andik …* (f)
Exchange	*sirafa*
Expensive	*ghaly*
Gold	*dahab*
Half a pound	*nos gineih*
How many?	*kem?*
How much?	*bikem?*
Jewellery	*seegha*
Market	*souk*
Newspaper in English	*gareeda ingleeziya*
One pound	*gineih*
Silver	*fada*
That's too much	*kiteer awy*
Where can I buy…	*fin ashtiry…*

Food and drink

Beer	*beera*
Bread	*'aysh*
Chicken	*firakh*

Coffee	*'ahwa*
Coffee shop	*'Ahwa*
Dessert	*helw*
Drink	*ishrab*
Eggs	*beid*
Fava beans	*fu'ul*
Felafel	*ta'ameyya*
Fish	*samak*
Food	*akul*
Fruit	*fak ha*
I would like...	*a'yiz* (m); *a'yza* (f)
Juice	*'aseer*
Meat	*lahma*
Milk	*laban*
Pepper	*filfil*
Restaurant	*mata'am*
Rice	*roz*
Salad	*salata*
Salt	*malh*
Soup	*shorba*
Sugar	*sucar*
The check please	*el hisab law samaht* (m) *samahty* (f)
Tea	*shay*
Tip	*baksheesh*
Vegetables	*khodar*
Vegetarian	*nabaty*
Water	*maya*
Water pipe	*shisha/sheesha*
Wine	*nibeet*

Accommodation

Air conditioning	*takeef*
Can I see a room?	*Mumkin ashoof owda?*
Fan	*marwaha*
Hotel	*fondoq*
How much is a room?	*Bikam el owda?*
Is breakfast included?	*Fi iftar?*
Is there a bathroom?	*Fi hamam?*
Room	*oda*
Shower	*doush*

Health

Aspirin	*aspireen*
Diarrhea	*is hal*
Doctor	*dok-tor*
Fever	*sokhoniya*
Hospital	*mostashfa*
I feel sick	*ana 'ayan* (m) *ana 'ayanna* (f)
I have a headache	*'andy sod'a*
I have a stomache ache	*'andy maghas*
I'm allergic to	*'andy hasasiya*
Medicine	*dawa*
Pharmacy	*saydaliya*

Useful words

Church	*kineesa*
Clean	*nadeef*
Cold	*bard*
Desert	*sahara*
Dirty	*wisikh*
Hot	*har*
Less	*a'al*
More	*aktar*
Mosque	*gami'*
Mountain	*gabal*
Museum	*el mathaf*
River	*nahr*
Sandstorm	*khamaseen*
Sea	*bahr*
Summer	*seif*
Valley	*wadi*
Winter	*shita*

Dodging touts

You'll get hassled less and respected more if you learn a bit of Arabic.

no thank you!	*La'a shocrun*
I told you no!	*U'ltilak la'a*
I don't want; I'm not interested	*Mish ay-yez* (m) *mish ay-zza* (f)
enough	*Bess*
finished, that's it	*Khalas*
'when the apricots bloom' (ie 'in your dreams')!	*F'il mish mish*

Glossary

A
Abbasids Muslim Dynasty ruled from Baghdad 750-1258
Agora Market/meeting place
Aïd/Eïd Festival
Aïn Spring
Almohads Islamic Empire in North Africa 1130-1269
Amir Mamluk military officer
Amulet Object with magical power of protection
Ankh Symbol of life
Apis bull A sacred bull worshipped as the living image of Ptah
Arabesque Geometric pattern with flowers and foliage used in Islamic designs

B
Bab City gate
Bahri North/northern
Baladiyah Municipality
Baksheesh Money as alms, tip or bribe
Baraka Blessing
Barbary Name of North Africa 16th-19th centuries
Basha See Pasha
Basilica Imposing Roman building, with aisles, later used for worship
Bazaar Market
Bedouin Nomadic desert Arab
Beni Sons of (tribe)
Berber Indigenous tribe of North Africa
Bey Governor (Ottoman)
Borj Fort
Burnous Man's cloak with hood – tradional wear

C
Caid Official
Calèche Horse-drawn carriage
Canopic jars Four jars used to store the internal organs of the mummified deceased
Capital Top section of a column
Caravanserai Lodgings for travellers and animals around a courtyard
Cartouche Oval ring containing a king's name in hieroglyphics
Chechia Man's small red felt hat
Chotts Low-lying salt lakes
Colossus Gigantic statue

D
Dar House
Darj w ktaf Carved geometric motif of intersecting arcs with super-imposed rectangles
Deglet Nur High quality translucent date
Delu Water-lifting device at head of well
Dey Commander (of janissaries)
Dikka Raised platform in mosque for Koramic readings
Djemma Main or Friday mosque
Djin Spirit
Dólmenes Prehistoric cave
Dour Village settlement

E
Eïd See Aïd
Eïn See Aïn
Erg Sand dune desert

F
Faqirs Muslim who has taken a vow of poverty
Fatimids Muslim dynasty AD 909-1171 claiming descent from Mohammed's daughter Fatimah
Fatwa Islamic district
Fellaheen Peasants
Felucca Sailing boat on Nile
Fondouk/Funduq Lodgings for goods and animals around a courtyard
Forum Central open space in Roman town
Fuul Fava beans

G
Gallabiyya Outer garment with sleeves and a hood – often striped
Garrigue Poor quality Mediterranean scrubland
Gymnasium Roman school for mind and body

H

Haikal Altar area
Hallal Meat from animals killed in accordance with Islamic law
Hamada Stone desert
Hammam Bath house
Harem Women's quarters
Harira Soup
Hypogeum The part of the building below ground, underground chamber

I

Iconostasis Wooden screen supporting icons
Imam Muslim religious leader

J

Jabal See Jebel
Jami' Mosque
Janissaries Elite Ottoman soldiery
Jarapas Rough cloth made with rags
Jebel Mountain
Jihad Holy war by Muslims against non-believers

K

Ka Spirit
Khedivate The realm of Mohammed Ali and his successors
Kilim Woven carpet
Kif Hashish
Kissaria Covered market
Koubba Dome on tomb of holy man
Kufic Earliest style of Arabic script
Kuttab Korami school for young boys or orphans

L

Lintel Piece of stone over a doorway
Liwan Vaulted arcade
Loculus Small compartment or cell, recess

M

Mahboub Coins worn as jewellery
Malekite Section of Sunni Islam
Malqaf Wind vent
Maquis Mediterranean scrubland – often aromatic
Marabout Muslim holy man/his tomb
Maristan Hospital
Mashrabiyya Wooden screen
Mastaba Tomb
Mausoleum Large tomb building
Medresa School usually attached to a mosque
Médina Old walled town, residential quarter
Mellah Jewish quarter of old town
Menzel House
Mihrab Recess in wall of mosque indicating direction of Mecca
Minaret Tower of mosque from which the muezzin calls the faithful to prayer
Minbar Pulpit in a mosque
Mosque Muslim place of worship
Moulid Religious festival – Prophet's birthday
Moussem Religious gathering
Muezzin Priest who calls the faithful to prayer
Mullah Muslim religious teacher
Murabtin Dependent tribe

N

Necropolis Cemetery
Noas Shrine or chapel
Nome District or province

O

Oasis Watered desert gardens
Obelisk Tapering monolithic shaft of stone with pyramidal apex
Ostraca Inscribed rock flakes and potsherds
Ottoman Muslim Empire based in Turkey 13th-20th centuries
Ouled Tribe
Outrepassé Horse-shoe shaped arch

P

Papyrus (papyri) Papers used by Ancient Egyptians
Pasha Governor
Phoenicians Important trading nation based in eastern Mediterranean from 1100 BC
Pilaster Square column partly built into, partly projecting from, the wall

Pisé Sun-baked clay used for building
Piste Unsurfaced road
Pylon Gateway of Egyptian temple
Pyramidion A small pyramid shaped cap stone for the apex of a pyramid

Q
Qarafah Graveyard
Qibla Mosque wall in direction of Mecca

R
Rabbi Head of Jewish community
Ramadan Muslim month of fasting
Reg Rock desert
Ribat Fortified monastery
Riwaq Arcaded aisle

S
Sabil Public water fountain
Sabkha Dry salt lake
Saggia Water canal
Sahel Coast/coastal plain
Sahn Courtyard
Salat Worship
Saqiya Water wheel
Sarcophagus Decorated stone coffin
Sebkha See Sabkha
Semi-columnar Flat on one side and rounded on the other
Serais Lodging for men and animals
Serir Sand desert
Shadoof Water lifting device
Shahada Profession of faith
Shawabti Statuette buried with deceased, designed to work in the hereafter for its owner
Shergui Hot, dry desert wind
Sidi Saint
Souk Traditional market

Stalactite An ornamental arrangement of multi-tiered niches, like a honeycomb, found in domes and portals
Stele Inscribed pillar used as gravestone
Suani Small, walled irrigated traditional garden
Sufi Muslim mystic
Sunni Orthodox Muslims

T
Tagine/tajine Meat stew
Taifa Sub-tribe
Tariqa Brotherhood/Order
Thòlos Round building, dome, cupola
Triclinium A room with benches on three sides
Troglodyte Underground/cave dweller

U
Uraeus Rearing cobra symbol, sign of kingship

V
Vandals Ruling empire in North Africa 429-534 AD
Vizier Governor

W
Wadi Water course, usually dry
Waqf Endowed land
Wikala Merchants' hostel
Wilaya/wilayat Governorate/district

Z
Zaouia/zawia/zawiya Shrine/Sennusi centre
Zellij Geometrical mosaic pattern made from pieces of glazed tiles
Zeriba House of straw/grass

Index

A
Abu el-Haggag 35, 38
Abu Simbel 147
   listings 153
   temples 149
Abydos 93, 94
   listings 100
accommodation 11
accommodation price codes 13
Aga Khan Mausoleum 123
Agilkia island 126
air travel 6, 8
airport information 7
Akhmim 93
alcohol 14, 18
Al-Kab 107
Aswan 117
   activities 137
   background 118
   directory 139
   entertainment 137
   hotels 132
   restaurants 135
   shopping 137
   tourist information 118
   transport 117, 138
Aswan Dams 126, 127

B
baksheesh 25
bargaining 17
Beit El-Wali 142
bicycles 8
Bigah island 128
boat travel 8
Book of Am-Duat 66
Book of Caverns 66
Book of Gates 66
Book of the Dead 64, 66
Books of the Heavens 66
Botanical Gardens 122
brick-making 95
Burckhardt, JL 148
bus travel 9

C
camel market, Daraw 113
camels 113
camping 12
car hire 9
Carter, Howard 73, 74
cobras 146
coffee 14
Colossi of Memnon 64
crocodiles 144
cultural events 16
currency exchange 23

D
Daraw 113
Deir El-Bahri 73
Deir El-Medina 83
Dendara 97
Dra'a Abul Naga 81
dress code 19
drink 14
driving 9

E
eating price codes 13
Edfu 107
   listings 114
El-Asasif 79
electricity 22
Elephantine Island 121
El-Khokha 80
embassies 22
emergencies 22
Esna 106
   listings 113
etiquette in mosques 20

F
feluccas 8, 56, 115
festivals 16
fishing 143
food 12
fuul 12

164 • Footnotes Index

G
Gardens, Botanical 122

H
hallal 18
Hathor Temple 85
health 22
hitchhiking 10
holidays 15
Horus 107
hotels 11
　　price codes 13

I
immigration 26

K
Kalabsha 140
Karnak Temple Complex 40
　　Northern Enclosure 46
　　Open Air Museum 46
　　Southern Enclosure 45
　　Temple of Amun 42
Kiosk of Kertassi 142
Kitchener's Island 122
Kom Ombo 110
　　listings 114

L
Lake Nasser 126
　　fishing 143
Lake Nasser Temples 140
Litany of Re 66
Lower Nubia 140
Luxor 31
　　activities 54
　　background 32
　　bars and clubs 52
　　climate 32
　　directory 59
　　festivals 53
　　hotels 47
　　restaurants 50
　　shopping 53
　　tour operators 56
　　tourist information 31
　　transport 31, 58

Luxor Museum 38
Luxor Temple 34

M
malaria 22
Mausoleums, Agha Khan 123
Medinat Habu 86
Memnon 61
Mo'alla Cemetery 105
Monasteries
　　Red 93
　　St Simeon 125
　　St Theodore 87
　　White 92
money 23
Mosques of Abu el-Haggag 35, 38
motorcycles 8
mummification 39
Museums
　　Aswan 121
　　Mummification 39
　　Nubia 118
　　Open Air, Karnak Temple Complex 46

N
Necropolis of the Nobles 123
　　Aswan 123
Nile cruises 8
Nilometer 121
Nubian language 151
Nubian villages 121, 126

O
opening hours 24

P
papyrus 16
Philae temples 126
photography 21
police 22
public holidays 16

Q
Qasr Ibrim 147
Qena 97
　　listings 101
Qurnat Murai 82

Footnotes Index • 165

R

ramadan 15
Ramesseum 85
Ramesseum, The 85
Ramses The Great 83
restaurant price codes 13
restricted areas 7
Roberts, David 131
Rock Temple of Al-Derr 146

S

safety 25
Sarenput I 124
service taxis 10
shawarma 12
shopping 16
Silsila 109
Silwa 110
sleeping 11
    price codes 13
Sohag 92
    listings 100
Soheel Island 131
souk 119

T

taxis 10
temples
    Al-Derr 146
    Amada 145
    Amun 42
    Beit El-Wali 142
    Dakka 144
    Edfu 107
    Hathor 85, 97
    Hatshepsut 73
    Horus 107
    Isis 128
    Kalabsha 140
    Karnak 40
    Khnum 106, 121
    Khonsu 45
    Maharakka 145
    Mandulis 140
    Montu 46
    Mortuary Temple of Ramses III 86
    Mut 45
    Opet 45
    Philae 126
    Ptah 46
    Queen Nefertari 152
    Ramses II 149
    Seti I 94
    Wadi El-Seboua 143
textiles 16
Theban Death Rites 64
Theban Necropolis 60
tomb
    Amenhoptep (Huy) 82
    Amenhotep II 70
    Anch-hor 79
    Ankhtifi 105
    Ay 73
    Dra'a Abul Naga 81
    Harkhuf 124
    Horemheb 71
    Inherkhau 84
    Khaemhet 77
    Kheruef 79
    Mekhu 123
    Mena 78
    Meneptah 68
    Nakht 77
    Neferrompet 80
    Nefersekhru 80
    Pabasa 80
    Pennout 147
    Pepiakht 124
    Peshedu 84
    Prince Amun-Hir-Khopshef 82
    Prince Khaemwesey 82
    Prince Mentuherkhepshef 67
    Queen Titi 82
    Ramoza 76
    Ramses I 69
    Ramses III 69
    Ramses IX 68
    Ramses VI 68
    Rekhmire 78
    Roy 81
    Sarenput I 124
    Sarenput II 124
    Sennedjem 83
    Sennofer 78
    Sethnakht 70
    Seti I 72
    Seti II 70
    Shuroy 81
    Siptah 69
    Sobekhotep 106
    Tawosret 70
    Tutankhamen 71
    Tuthmosis III 69
    Tuthmosis IV 67

166 • Footnotes Index

    Userhat 77
    Ramses IV 67
    Ramses VII 67
Tombs of the Nobles 76
tourist information 26
tourist offices 26
train travel 8
transport 6, 7
Tutankhamen 71

V
vaccinations 22
Valley of the Kings 65
Valley of the Queens 81

vegetarianism 13
visas 26

W
Wadi El-Seboua 143
water 14
weight and measures 27
west bank 60, 123
    listings 87
West Soheel 131

Y
youth hostels 11

Titles available in the Footprint *Focus* range

Latin America	UK RRP	US RRP
Bahia & Salvador	£7.99	$11.95
Buenos Aires & Pampas	£7.99	$11.95
Costa Rica	£8.99	$12.95
Cuzco, La Paz & Lake Titicaca	£8.99	$12.95
El Salvador	£5.99	$8.95
Guadalajara & Pacific Coast	£6.99	$9.95
Guatemala	£8.99	$12.95
Guyana, Guyane & Suriname	£5.99	$8.95
Havana	£6.99	$9.95
Honduras	£7.99	$11.95
Nicaragua	£7.99	$11.95
Paraguay	£5.99	$8.95
Quito & Galápagos Islands	£7.99	$11.95
Recife & Northeast Brazil	£7.99	$11.95
Rio de Janeiro	£8.99	$12.95
São Paulo	£5.99	$8.95
Uruguay	£6.99	$9.95
Venezuela	£8.99	$12.95
Yucatán Peninsula	£6.99	$9.95

Asia	UK RRP	US RRP
Angkor Wat	£5.99	$8.95
Bali & Lombok	£8.99	$12.95
Chennai & Tamil Nadu	£8.99	$12.95
Chiang Mai & Northern Thailand	£7.99	$11.95
Goa	£6.99	$9.95
Hanoi & Northern Vietnam	£8.99	$12.95
Ho Chi Minh City & Mekong Delta	£7.99	$11.95
Java	£7.99	$11.95
Kerala	£7.99	$11.95
Kolkata & West Bengal	£5.99	$8.95
Mumbai & Gujarat	£8.99	$12.95

Africa	UK RRP	US RRP
Beirut	£6.99	$9.95
Damascus	£5.99	$8.95
Durban & KwaZulu Natal	£8.99	$12.95
Fès & Northern Morocco	£8.99	$12.95
Jerusalem	£8.99	$12.95
Johannesburg & Kruger National Park	£7.99	$11.95
Kenya's beaches	£8.99	$12.95
Kilimanjaro & Northern Tanzania	£8.99	$12.95
Zanzibar & Pemba	£7.99	$11.95

Europe	UK RRP	US RRP
Bilbao & Basque Region	£6.99	$9.95
Granada & Sierra Nevada	£6.99	$9.95
Málaga	£5.99	$8.95
Orkney & Shetland Islands	£5.99	$8.95
Skye & Outer Hebrides	£6.99	$9.95

North America	UK RRP	US RRP
Vancouver & Rockies	£8.99	$12.95

Australasia	UK RRP	US RRP
Brisbane & Queensland	£8.99	$12.95
Perth	£7.99	$11.95

For the latest books, e-books and smart phone app releases, and a wealth of travel information, visit us at: www.footprinttravelguides.com.

footprinttravelguides.com

Join us on facebook for the latest travel news, product releases, offers and amazing competitions: www.facebook.com/footprintbooks.com.